Party Leadership in the States

Party Leadership
in the States

Robert J. Huckshorn

University of
Massachusetts Press
1976

Copyright © 1976 by
The University of Massachusetts Press
All rights reserved
Library of Congress Catalog Card Number 75-32487
ISBN 0-87023-201-0
Printed in the United States of America
Designed by Mary Mendell
Library of Congress Cataloging in Publication Data
Huckshorn, Robert Jack, 1928–
Party leadership in the states.
Includes bibliographical references and index.
1. Political parties—United States—States. I. Title.
JK2276.H8   329'.0211'0973   75-32487
ISBN 0-87023-201-0

To the women in my life . . .
Carolyn, Kevin, Kristin, and Dana

Contents

Preface

The state party chairmanship tradition-
ally has been viewed as an unimportant office occupied by faceless men
serving at the will of powerful elected officials. Those anointed with the
office were seldom recognized beyond the narrow confines of the party
elite group which elected them. It was generally assumed that the state
chairman performed one of two functions—he was the governor's liaison
with the party or, if the party was out of power, he was a focal point for
a miscellany of local party groups more interested in maintaining their
independent integrity than in cooperating to strengthen the state party.
Nowhere was the decentralized nature of the American party system
more apparent.

Fifteen years ago it was common for state chairmen to operate from
their homes or places of business. There were few headquarters or other
support services available for party building. There were few contacts be-

tween state and national party leaders. If a particular state chairman did emerge from obscurity, it was usually because he was permitted to remain in office long enough to build a successful record in electoral politics.

My original interest in the state chairmen as political officers was stimulated by personal involvement with a number of them in the early 1960s. I came to know my first group of chairmen during a year as National Center for Education in Politics (NCEP) Faculty Fellow at the Republican National Committee in 1962–63. During the ensuing year, when I served as associate director of the NCEP, wide travel brought me into close contact with numerous chairmen and other state and local party officials.

A generous grant from the National Science Foundation in 1969 enabled me to undertake a wide-ranging study of state party organizations with particular emphasis on the role of the state chairmen. During the next two and one-half years I interviewed eighty incumbent state chairmen and women and over a hundred additional national, state, and local party leaders. These included three United States senators, eight congressmen, six governors, two former governors, six former state chairmen, twenty Republican and sixteen Democratic national committeemen and women, four incumbent or former national party chairmen, and numerous staff persons and other political leaders.

The principal interviews were carried out between July 1969 and April 1972. Fifteen respondents were reinterviewed in early 1974. Care was exercised to balance the interviews according to population, geographic location, type of party system, and party affiliation. Forty-one of the chairmen's interviews were with Republicans, and thirty-nine were with Democrats. Approximately one-half were conducted in the respondent's home or place of employment, including, for those who were full time, the state headquarters. The other half were conducted during national and regional meetings of the Republican and Democratic National Committees, the Association of State Democratic Chairmen, the Republican State Chairman's Association, meetings of the McGovern-Fraser and O'Hara Commissions of the Democratic party and the Delegate and Organization (DO) Committee of the Republican National Committee. During the period covered by the interviews, chairmen were observed in action in over two dozen national, regional, and state party conferences, including several closed executive meetings of the various governing bodies. Furthermore, approximately one-third of the state party headquarters were visited and observed for periods of up to two days.

My personal experiences in national and state politics and with interviewing political leaders have convinced me that successful completion of the data collection phase of a project of this type requires personal interviews rather than the use of mailed questionnaires. As this study went forward, I became more and more certain that the personal interview was the most productive approach. Numerous party chairmen informed me that they accumulated as many as ten to fifteen mailed questionnaires at a time and, in many cases, made no attempt to complete them. Some simply discarded the questionnaires while others relied upon staff assistants to complete them. One chairman showed me an accumulation of eleven questionnaires ranging in length from one to thirty-four pages and submitted by graduate students, faculty members, and interest groups as well as partisan and nonpartisan political organizations. He had no intention of completing any of them although he expressed a willingness to grant me two hours of his time for interview purposes. The incidence of this was so common that I became increasingly convinced that personal interviews with officials who practice politics as a *vocation* are essential to this kind of data gathering. These individuals are more likely to have in their employ staff people who can assume burdens such as questionnaire completion. Needless to say, that often defeats the purpose of the study since in many cases the questions are designed to elicit the chairman's personal responses, attitudes, or opinions.

On the other hand, I have also noted that an official who practices politics as an *avocation* (such as a national committeeman or woman), who does not spend much time at it, has no staff, and is more inclined to treat politics as a hobby will normally complete his or her own questionnaires. These individuals not only have more time but normally have fewer regular assigned party and political duties, and they appreciate being asked their opinions. I do think there is an important place in research for the mailed questionnaire, but not when dealing with high-ranking, full-time, busy political elites. Such respondents are much more likely to have resources available to avoid personal involvement with questionnaire completion. It might also be noted that personal interviews provide wide opportunities for the collection of anecdotal and other individual observations which, even in anonymity, help to communicate the excitement and the human dimensions of politics.

Professor Bernard C. Hennessy has noted:

The gaps in the descriptive literature on American political parties are nowhere more obviously exposed than in the fact that no general treatment of the state party chairman has ever been attempted despite the admitted

importance of the office. About the members, duties, procedures, and importance of state party executive committees we know even less.[1]

This book is an attempt to fill in some of the gaps noted by Hennessy.
Those who reviewed the proposed project generally agreed that a structured interview would elicit most of the desired information. Questions
were developed from the sparse literature, from some unpublished manu-
scripts furnished by friends and colleagues, and from discussions with
practicing politicians. Four pilot interviews were conducted with selected
state chairmen before the questionnaire was cast into final form. The
questionnaire was designed to gather data and elicit responses that might
help to answer questions such as these: How did the office of state chairman originate? Who are the chairmen, and how did they get their positions? Where do they go in politics after their service as state chairmen?
How do they define their roles? Why do some emerge as "real" leaders,
while others have few party responsibilities and exercise little control?
What are their relationships with other party leaders both vertically and
horizontally? How do they fit into the national party structure? What are
their roles in the traditional aspects of party activities—finance, recruitment, patronage, campaign strategy, issue formulation, and public relations? How do they view their responsibilities to their local party units?
Is the chairmanship a stepping-stone or a dead end? Are there differences
between the chairmen of the minority and majority parties? Has the potential of the office been realized? I do not claim to have furnished the
definitive answers to all of these questions. These chapters do, however,
furnish the only comprehensive discussion of them to date.

The book is organized into ten chapters. The first sets the stage for
those to come with a brief history of the relevant aspects of state party
development and the emergence of the office of party chairman. Also included is an analysis of the impact of law and party rules on the powers
exercised by the party leaders.

The social characteristics and career developments of the chairmen are
discussed in chapter 2, and, due to the considerable impact of relatively
short average tenure, the causes of premature resignation or removal
from office are considered in chapter 3. Chapter 4 describes types of
party chairmen by role. The next two chapters explore the political roles
of the chairmen, both in the older and more traditional functions of politics and the newer and more modern aspects. The first of these, chapter
5, considers the chairman's role in recruitment, patronage, campaigning,
and the development of issues. The second, chapter 6, discusses the

so-called new politics—public opinion polls, modern fund-raising techniques, automatic data processing, and the increasing demands on the chairman in his role as party spokesman.

Chapters 7, 8, and 9 consider the various organizational roles of the chairman. The first of these three chapters considers lateral relationships between party chairmen in different states including discussion of the organization and function of the associations of state chairmen organized within both political parties. Chapter 8 considers the charman's role with the National Committee and the National Convention, and chapter 9 looks inward to his role in his own state and local party. Included in the latter are headquarters management, relationships with local party organizations, and association with state officeholders and elected officials. Chapter 10 summarizes the study and draws some conclusions about where the state parties and their chairmen are at the present time and where they are likely to be going in the next few years.

The cooperation exhibited by the state chairmen and other party officials was almost universal. Many sat patiently for long interviews during busy days and crowded schedules. They usually sought to furnish me with thoughtful responses and, I am confident, honest appraisals of their various roles as they viewed them. Many of them followed up by voluntarily mailing additional documents and materials to further explain their responses.

On two occasions the leadership of the Association of State Democratic Chairmen invited me to discuss the study in general terms with the members of that organization. Those in Republican leadership positions were equally magnanimous with their support and exhibited a continuing interest in the progress of the project.

The original grant proposal envisioned a two-year study during which all interviewing and analysis would be accomplished. At the end of the second year, however, only sixty interviews had been completed, and they were not well balanced between the parties. The difficulties in arranging and conducting interviews proved to be greater than anticipated. It became apparent that it was less expensive in both time and money to conduct interviews at conventions and conferences where chairmen and party leaders congregate. The ease with which interviews were attained was offset, however, by the difficulties caused by the press of official business. Some interviews had to be concluded in two or three sittings. Interviews were conducted at meetings in Miami Beach, Fort Lauderdale, Las Vegas, Salt Lake City, Des Moines, Omaha, Chicago, Colorado Springs, New York City, New Orleans, Atlanta, Cambridge, and Washington,

D.C. One-third of the interviews were obtained in Washington, D.C., since both parties have held more of their national meetings in that city in recent years in order to avoid the expense of transporting staff and supplies to distant places. Furthermore, holding conferences in the capital insures greater participation by members of Congress and, for the in-party, people from the White House. One group of four interviews was conducted while fortuitously snowed in at the Saint Louis Airport with a group of Republican state chairmen on their way, as was I, to a party meeting in Des Moines.

In addition to those interviews conducted at party meetings, which in several instances included visits to state headquarters, many trips were made to individual states for on-site interviews and headquarters inspections. These included Olympia, Washington; Phoenix, Arizona; Boise, Idaho; Denver, Colorado; Hartford and New Britain, Connecticut; Columbus, Ohio; Harrisburg, Pennsylvania; Alexandria, Virginia; Los Angeles, California; and Fort Lauderdale, West Palm Beach, and Talla-hassee, Florida. These visits proved to be invaluable as sources of interview and file data, although the advantages were somewhat offset by the considerably greater per-interview costs.

In January 1974, the Institute of Politics, John F. Kennedy School of Government, Harvard University, sponsored a Bi-Partisan Conference of State Party Chairmen. Twenty-four current and former state chairmen, twelve from each party, were invited to be participants in the conference held at the Harvard Faculty Club. Approximately twenty other chairmen and vice-chairmen attended as observers. A team of six discussion leaders served to facilitate and focus conference discussions and dialogue among participants. Of the twenty-four participants, I had previously interviewed fifteen; in addition, I had interviewed four of the observers. The conference, which addressed many aspects of the state chairman's role, did not reach a specific set of conclusions or recommendations, but it did help to focus the attention of the participants on mutual problems and to provide a forum for a valuable exchange of information. It also provided an opportunity for me to reinterview a number of chairmen and women, thus furnishing a more extended perspective on their own terms of service.

Many political scientists were consulted and asked for advice on the conduct of the project. I particularly appreciate the time and effort they put into helping me to clarify certain points and resolve particular problems. In putting together the brief history of the state chairmanship, I encountered unexpected difficulties which were mostly resolved by the staff of the Library of Congress and through telephone calls to some of the nation's leading political historians.

One unanticipated source of information proved to be most helpful. At the suggestion of John S. Saloma III and Frederick H. Sontag, I subscribed for one and one-half years to a national clipping service and received all news clippings dealing with state party affairs from every major daily paper in the nation. Although I was occasionally inundated with newsprint, the careful filing of these clippings provided an invaluable source of primary information and account for some of the notes referencing newspapers in exotic places.

Throughout the book I have used the term "chairman" in its more traditional sense to include both men and women. I considered substituting alternate terminology such as "chairperson" but concluded that, while possibly more accurate, it was also awkward and confusing. Furthermore, virtually every female party leader who was asked preferred to be called "chairman" or "chairwoman." In those cases where a female party leader is identified as such, I have used the term "chairwoman" throughout.

As is often the case, the final result was a book considerably different from the one I started out to write. Even though I had had considerable experience with state chairmen and national party leaders in both parties prior to undertaking the study, I was often surprised at the gaps in our knowledge of the state party systems. Some information that I thought would be readily available simply was not. Other explorations, however, produced a far greater lode than I could ever mine.

Finally, this project could not have been carried out without the assistance and cooperation of a great many people who gave unhesitatingly of their time and knowledge. Especially valuable was the assistance of Josephine Good and Barbara Earp of the Convention Office of the Republican National Committee and of Sheila Hixson, assistant to the secretary, Democratic National Committee. They opened their files, sat for long interviews, mailed materials, opened doors, and helped in countless other ways. R. Spencer Oliver and Graham (Rusty) Matthews of the Association of Democratic State Chairmen furnished invaluable assistance. The first three chairmen of that organization, John Mitchell of Nebraska, Severin Beliveau of Maine, and Robert Vance of Alabama, were unstinting in their efforts to be of assistance. Former National Chairman Ray C. Bliss, Republican of Ohio, and the late John Bailey, Democrat of Connecticut, provided insights about state politics that only a national chairman who had also served as state chairman could have. The heart of this book was obviously the interviews with state chairmen, and I am most grateful to all of them. Some, however, like Democrats Caroline Wilkins and Jon Moyle and Republican C. Montgomery (Gummie) Johnson, went out of their way to such a great extent that they deserve special acknowledgment.

The early versions of the manuscript were typed by Myrtle Cassel while the later ones were prepared by Diane Burgess. A number of Florida Atlantic University students contributed significantly to the project, including David M. Davis, Robert E. Jednak, Kathleen Dul, Barbara Johnson, Joan Wilson, and Debi Athos. Finally, I wish to express special thanks to my colleague Everett Cataldo, Florida Atlantic University, and to Cornelius P. Cotter, University of Wisconsin-Milwaukee, and Bernard C. Hennessy, California State College at Hayward, for reading all or parts of the manuscript. Their helpful suggestions and insightful critiques cast light on initial errors and strengthened the final product. Obviously, none of those who gave so generously of their time is responsible for any errors, omissions, or misjudgments of mine.

Robert J. Huckshorn
Boca Raton, Florida

Party Leadership in the States

1 The State Party Chairman: Growth, Origins, and Legal Authority

"Laws governing the party?" Professor, there are no laws!
A western state chairman

The state parties are the only hope for our party system. If we aren't able to pull ourselves together and make the system work, I am afraid the party as we know it won't survive.
A Republican national committeewoman

I really believe that the state parties are all that will keep the party system from going under. The national committees don't know what they are doing and don't have any power. The local parties, in my area at least, are worthless. Only in our state headquarters is there any evidence of life.
A midwestern state chairman

A sophisticated public opinion survey is not needed to reveal that most citizens know little about the political party organizations in their states. The identity, role, and function of the state party chairman are a mystery to the average man whose knowledge of elected public officials is limited but whose familiarity with lesser-known party officials is virtually nonexistent. None of this is very surprising. As David M. Olson noted, the whole concept of party is often difficult to grasp, even for the enlightened student: "The very fact that parties are an American invention may be an important reason why parties here, compared to other countries, are highly variable, elusive to find, difficult to define, and frustrating to study." [1]

The lack of visibility associated with the state party organization, and particularly with the state chairmanship, arises from several factors. The general public fails to take an active part in state government and politics. National events and Washington politics overshadow the action in Bismarck, Carson City, Boise, and Indianapolis. State party affairs are not uniformly well covered by the news media. Many of the more important activities of the party are hidden from public view. Furthermore, the party leader's constituents, those who are activists and workers, are a small, self-contained group unknown to the public at large.

Several state chairmen have noted that there is considerable confusion in the public mind about what constitutes a political party organization. Lines of authority and responsibility do not flow in the party hierarchy as they do in business, labor, military, or educational organizations. The man at the top of the party pyramid may not really be the top man. The party structure is ill defined and obscure. The people who run it often do not have a wide public identification, and the chairman's relatively short term often does not grant him the time to broaden his following.

Finally, the general lack of membership requirements in the American party system lends an ephemeral quality to party affairs. No action is required to join, to maintain membership, or to leave the party (except in closed-primary states where the act of voter registration does require a declaration of party affiliation). It is difficult for the party leader to develop loyalty among the party's followers or to command attention from the media when the membership and the leadership are both transitory. As one chairman put it, "It is hard to lead the troops when you don't know who they are."

These elusive qualities of state parties have deep historic roots. The party system was an invention which emerged from the post-Revolutionary need to accommodate political growth. The origin of the state party chairmanship is lost in the haze of history. One cannot pinpoint when the state chairmanship, or indeed the state party system, materialized.

In time, the native American love for organizational purity and for legal description led to the party's structure, activities, and responsibilities being defined through written law. Some states provided detailed and specific law to govern the parties. Others passed legislation outlining the general nature of the party system but left it to the parties themselves to provide more detailed by-laws.

In this chapter I wish to accomplish three purposes: first, to present my argument that state party organizations today show signs of increasing maturity and self-renewal which may ultimately form the basis for a new and stronger party system. If the system of American politics is at an impasse, as some have suggested, then a new start must be made. It is my contention that there is emerging new evidence to suggest that such an organizational renewal may be under way—the impetus coming from some elements of imaginative state party leadership across the nation.

Second, the chapter reviews the historic development of the American party system and specifically the state chairmanship. Political historians and political scientists agree that many of the problems besetting the party system have historical antecedents extending back to George Washington, and a brief review serves to bring the emergence of the system into focus. Finally, the chapter provides an analysis of party law and, to the extent possible, its impact on the powers and responsibilities of party leadership.

The American Party System: New Growth in the States

That the founding fathers did not anticipate the development of parties is attested to by their failure to provide even a rudimentary structure for them. The same men who contrived an intricate interlocking structure of federal and state governments feared the creation of a party structure through which the limited electorate of their day could channel its factional choices. As a result of this fear, the state parties grew as separate and distinct entities. Seldom did they become organized as pyramidal hierarchies with the lower levels responsible to the higher. Seldom was authority concentrated in a single individual or statewide office. Seldom did the membership maintain a sustained interest in party affairs. Finally, there was seldom any attempt to enforce even rudimentary party responsibility.

One of the sharpest critics of American parties, James MacGregor Burns, described them as "mere jousting grounds for embattled politicians; at worst they simply do not exist, as in the case of the Republicans in the rural South, the Democrats in the rural Midwest." [2] V. O. Key, Jr., noted in 1956:

The most apparent, and perhaps the fundamental, incapacity of state parties lies in the frequency with which the leadership corps is fractionalized and lacking in both capacity and organization for action. Some state party organizations, to be sure, have an evident vitality as well as a fairly high degree of coherence. Yet, a more common situation is the almost complete absence of a functioning statewide organization.[3]

Now, twenty years later, the state parties are not the political eunuchs they once were. Some of them, to be sure, continue to suffer from organizational weaknesses associated with the proliferation of candidates engendered by the long ballot, a lack of volunteer workers, financial anemia, widespread member apathy, and occasional local bossism. The greater number, however, show more vital signs today than they have throughout their long history.

This assertion is supported by convincing evidence. As always, in dealing with 100 separate entities, one must indulge in considerable generalization. The signs of revival outlined in this book may be considered trivial by some of the more demanding advocates of responsible parties. Meaningful signs of party responsibility are as scarce today as they have ever been. Nevertheless, party responsibility cannot develop in the absence of a strong organizational substructure. Protected by tradition and lethargic from lack of use, the basic mechanisms of party government remain intact. The past twenty years, however, have recorded the emergence of a new vitality in state parties. This has not come about as a result of public demand, nor has it resulted from national party efforts. It has, in fact, been an "inside" job. A new and different breed of state party leader, bolstered by a simultaneous growth of new political techniques, has sought to challenge tradition and initiate those changes necessary to provide new strength to the system. The changes have not been uniform. There are still state party organizations that remain buried in the past. But the growth cycle is there, and widespread change is apparent.

There are several reasons why state party organizations have embarked upon this strengthening process. First, the number of states in which rival parties contest with each other in competitive two-party systems has increased. Noncompetitive party systems in the South, the Northeast, and the Midwest have all experienced rapidly developing opposition parties. The resultant competition between contending organizations, the prospects of actually winning elections, and the demand from those who have won have all joined to force revitalization. In many states of the Old South, for instance, no state headquarters for the dominant Democratic party existed prior to the growth of Republicanism. An active party organization was not necessary to success, and the highly personalized and factionalized political groups that dominated southern politics for so many years were loathe to encourage more formal organization.

Second, the period of escalating population growth in the United States coincided with the rapid postwar development of modern campaign techniques and apparatus. As described in chapter 6, the science of public opinion polling, organized fund raising, and automatic data processing all brought escalating demands for organizational continuity and long-range planning. These demands, in turn, brought calls for permanent headquarters with paid state chairmen and/or executive directors to provide necessary continuity.

A third reason for the improved power position of state parties, according to many state chairmen, is their recent inclusion as voting members of the national committees. This move represented the first time that an elected state party official, with assigned duties and responsibilities, was brought into active national participation. National committeemen and women were occasionally important within their state parties, but they often viewed their role as an avocation. The chairman, on the other hand, is much more likely to see politics as a full-time vocational enterprise.

Finally, the development of the state chairmen's national associations has provided an impetus to act. The chairmen, in regular meetings, have provided themselves with a mechanism for the exchange of ideas and the development of strategy. They have also responded by attempting to keep their own parties competitive with their neighbors'. Innovation has often bred innovation.

It must again be emphasized that these signs of growth and these new departures have not been universal. There remain state organizations with little ambition and few successes. There are still states dominated by a single party which neither needs nor wants a stronger organizational structure than now exists. There are numerous states where the state party leaders serve as little more than errand boys for an incumbent governor. But there are fewer than there used to be, and the collective attitude toward strengthening the party is improved.

Most political scientists and journalists who have advocated strong responsible parties have devoted themselves almost exclusively to national institutions. Their concerns have been with the relationship between the president and Congress, the need for philosophical realignment of the electorate, the procedural democratization of the House and Senate, and improving the nominating process. The aim of the reformers may be true, but they may be firing at the wrong target. National party reform and responsibility cannot be accomplished without a strengthened state and local foundation. Efforts to bring about greater party responsibility at the national level might be wasted without attending to the state organizations. The president so dominates his national party that it cannot function without his personal solicitation and participation. The party out of power is so devoted to survival that it often cannot function at all. The congressional parties, representing, as they do, collective parochial interests, are so grounded in internal tradition that change, at best, will be evolutionary. Both congressional parties are primarily responsive to presidential initiatives. In short, national politics is presidential politics. As such, it may represent the poorest choice of target for bringing about greater party responsibility.

The burden of presidential dominance is not so great at the state and local levels. State party organizations, more closely tied to state constitutional offices, may be more amenable to change. They have more offices to fill and more opportunities to win. To repeat, it is unlikely that responsible national parties will be possible without strong state parties. The movement to that end is already under way. Those seeking more responsible parties might well concentrate some of their attention on the party foundations rather than focusing all their attention on the national superstructure.

That the American political parties find themselves in this predicament is a product of their origin and growth. They emerged because of a need for formal channels of electoral response, and they got their start in post-Revolutionary America.

Post-Revolutionary Development of Political Parties

In his Farewell Address, George Washington warned the people against the "baneful effects of the spirit of party." The admonition was clear evidence of party division which had emerged well before the end of his second term. Washington's disappointment over the rapid growth of party factionalism did not allay the development of political parties, nor did it constrain his two favorite cabinet members from assuming opposing leadership roles in their formation.

Alexander Hamilton, the secretary of the treasury, was the recognized leader of the faction calling itself Federalist. Generally men of substantial social status and wealth, the Federalists represented the officeholders and the early aristocratic voting public. In growing opposition was a coalition of small farmers, small property owners, and local political leaders principally native to the southern and middle Atlantic states whose allegiance was to Secretary of State Thomas Jefferson and his friend and fellow Virginian, James Madison. Hamilton and the Federalists advocated a government based on strong executive leadership, centralization of power, and economic policies benefiting business and commercial interests. Jefferson's Republicans favored decentralization of power, strong legislative leadership, and an economy favoring workers, farmers, and small shopkeepers.

Party growth prior to 1800 was slow and uneven. Party factions developed quickly in some areas and spread rapidly to adjoining states. In other places division into partisan groups developed slowly or not at all. Some states emerged into the nineteenth century with partisan conflict in full bloom and party organizations of nearly equal strength. In others the parties were unevenly matched, with a dominant party facing little or no opposition. As is true today, particular economic, social, and historical circumstances accounted for the shape of the party division and the precise course of party organizational development.

Jefferson left the cabinet in 1793 to work at developing state and local party organizations. He became a candidate for president in 1796 but was defeated in the electoral college by only three votes by Vice-President John Adams. Jefferson came back in 1800 to be elected president and to watch as the Federalists, who had seldom bothered to organize party machinery in the localities, disappeared into history. By 1816 the Federalists had ceased to exist entirely. From this experience, the first crucial lesson of party life was learned—party organizations cannot be successful without an effective grass-roots political organization at every local election level. Some of the younger Federalists belatedly realized this and attempted to organize locally. The rapidity with which local organizations sprang into existence is demonstrated by the fact that in 1792 there were almost no noticeable organizations in any of the fourteen states that comprised the Union, but by the end of the first Jefferson administration in 1804, Republican local organizations had emerged in every state. In some states they were followed by competing Federalist organizations. Republicans, however, consistently led the way in the creation of state and local organizations.[4]

The campaign of 1800 was the catalyst for developing widespread party organizations in the states. Historians have long believed that the Republican party organization was forged by Jefferson and his followers from a coalition of existing state and local factions. Claude Bowers, a leading historian of the era, described Jefferson as surveying the field and finding "in almost every state local parties, some long in existence," prompting him to ponder, "Why not consolidate these local parties into one great national organization, and broaden the issue to include the problems of both State and Nation?"[5] Political scientist-historian Wilfred E. Binkley states: "Like all our major political parties, this earlier one to organize constituted a loose federation of local parties. . . . Jefferson set out to negotiate the necessary connections and understanding among them."[6]

Noble E. Cunningham suggests the need to revise this appraisal of the beginnings of political party organizations. He notes that the mass of evidence does not support this earlier theory and suggests instead that parties developed out of continuing divisions within Congress and the administration. Party growth, he holds, was clearly a product of national political forces—not local. Divisions grew within Congress and quickly took on partisan overtones. Certain national issues, such as the Jay Treaty, served as catalysts for political division and party organization.

Most of the early groups that developed in the states were little more than committees of correspondence. They held frequent meetings, listened to speeches, elected committee officers, and memorialized state legislatures and the Congress on the issues of the day. They did not, however, seek to elect members to office and could not accurately be called parties. It is more probable, according to Cunningham, that they were closer to what we normally think of as pressure groups.[7] They did serve to further divide the electorate, and they served as a ready channel between the citizenry and the national government. By the mid-1790s the democratic societies had disappeared, and more formal types of party units had taken their place.

Most of the state party organizations were formed in 1800 and ensuing years. Virginia Republicans were busy throughout the summer and fall of 1800 organizing votes for Jefferson. Similar efforts were under way in Maryland, New Jersey, and South Carolina. The Federalists did not sit idly by without making any organizational effort. Stephen G. Kurtz and David H. Fischer report that full-blown Federalist organizations existed in New York, Pennsylvania, and New Jersey prior to 1800. They were held together by strong leadership and maintained an active correspondence.[8] The Federalist organizations in these states, however, were exceptions to the general rule of Federalist disorganization. The real organizational effort of the period belonged to the Republicans. Generally speaking, party organization in most states was similar, consisting principally of networks of county and city committees which met, nominated candidates, agreed on the designation of electors, and directed campaigns. It is likely that the earliest state party chairmanship was an outgrowth of these state and local committees. Professor Richard McCormick notes that by the early 1800s every state had some form of state central committee, including a chairman. The most highly centralized of them were in Virginia and Massachusetts.[9]

Cunningham reports that on January 21, 1800, a meeting of legislators and interested citizens was held in the capital of Richmond for the purpose of designating Virginia's electors. At this meeting:

a "republican Ticket" of electors was agreed upon, and a committee appointed to prepare a plan of organization for conducting the campaign. In accordance with the recommendations of this committee, three subsequent meetings were held that week and the Republican party in Virginia was given definite organization.

A "General Standing Committee" of five members was established at Richmond, and Philip Norborne Nicholas was made its chairman. This committee, entrusted with the overall direction of the campaign, was to act as a central committee of correspondence.[10]

Chairman Nicholas promptly wrote to each county committee's most prominent member:

Inclosed you will receive a copy of the proceedings of ninety-three members of the legislature and a number of other respectable citizens, convened for the adoption of the means, best calculated to give support to the Republican ticket. . . . This object is to be effected, by repelling every effort which may be made by persons adverse to the republican interest, either to misrepresent the principles of the law upon this subject, or to excite prejudices against the persons who compose the republican ticket.

If anything should occur in the several counties, which in the opinion of their committees may be prejudicial to the general interest, they will communicate it to the general committee in Richmond, who will take such measures as appear to them adapted to remove the evil.

The committees in the counties will, in communicating with the general committee, address their letters to Philip Norborne Nicholas, *without annexing the word Chairman;* this is enjoined to avoid interruption of their correspondence.

The committee have only to observe further, that you are considered as chairman of the committee of your county; and it is recommended that you forthwith call a meeting of your committee, and notify to the general committee in Richmond, as early as possible, their willingness to co-operate in promoting the republican ticket.[11]

Through such means, the Jeffersonians broadened their appeal to all political and economic groups. Their growing success was matched by the declining fortunes of the Federalists. The election of Jefferson in 1800 was the first concrete manifestation of success and was followed by successive elections of Madison and Monroe. But electoral triumph brought division, and by 1820 the Republicans had split into two factions, the Democratic Republicans and the National Republicans.

During the next twenty years the conflict between the two grew, and by 1840 two separate political parties had emerged on the national scene. These parties, the Democrats and the Whigs, both possessed the economic and geographic characteristics of national parties. During this period Andrew Jackson and his followers reorganized the Democratic party to accommodate the newly admitted states and to remove suffrage restrictions. The Jacksonians inaugurated what Richard McCormick has labeled the "second American party system."

Political power shifted from the eastern seaboard to the western and southern states and from the upper and middle classes to the less well-off. Wilfred Binkley notes that it was the depression of the 1820s that provided the seedbed of the Jacksonian movement. Both the rural and urban masses perceived that the prevailing hard times were a result of their betrayal by the ruling class. The conviction grew that the common man had little to say about the government, and Jackson offered a means of changing that.[12] The inauguration of President Jackson not only shifted political power but ushered in the era of mass membership parties.

Between 1824 and 1840 parties were formed in every state and were based on state and regional reactions to various presidential candidates. It was a period when ballots grew longer as Jacksonian popular democracy created more public offices to be filled. The first national party committees were established, and the phenomenon of the party boss appeared in many large cities. Popular participation by an expanded electorate called for more elaborate political organizations. In some cases, these elaborate organizations became political machines. Platforms developed as a means of communicating ideas and issues to the voters. Possibly of more lasting importance, though, was the entrenchment of the idea of the two-party system.

Party organization itself underwent little change during the period. The legislative caucus was abandoned in most states by 1828 and was replaced by the state convention system of nomination. The parties were managed by officeholders who had strong vested interests in their success and who wanted to make them work in a more businesslike fashion. Strong party machines developed in some of the eastern states—New York, New Jersey, and Delaware. By 1840 there were two organized parties contending in every state in the presidential election. The parties of the middle states were the most highly organized, while those in the South were least organized. Growth in organization, added to the development of the convention system of nomination, brought politics to the masses. Whereas the legislative caucus had been dominated by small semisecret committees, the convention involved large numbers of party activists. This led to the development of poll committees, auxiliary units, and ongoing state central committees. In every state the parties began to elect officers to run the party between conventions. References to particular individuals as "Chairman of the State Central Committee" or "State Committee Chairman" began to appear in party documentation and news articles of the period. Some of them, like Isaac Hill of New Hampshire, were elected chairmen, while others were party organizational leaders who had simply emerged. Thurlow Weed of New York, J. M. Niles of Connecticut, John Clayton of Delaware, Amos Kendall of Kentucky, and Stephen A. Douglas of Illinois were party leaders of this type, and they had their counterparts in every state.

Thus did the American state party organizations develop. Their growth was out of phase from state to state and different plateaus were reached at different times, but the parties continued to organize throughout the nation. The creation of the first state chairmanship appears to be lost in the maze of rapidly growing party organizations. The need for leadership almost certainly emerged within the organizations themselves, and the availability of seasoned leaders in most of the states made it a simple step to convert a recognized but informal leader into a formally elected one.

The state chairmanship had assumed its present-day form by the turn of the century. From about 1890, published descriptions in various state party histories describe the position very much as it might be described today. Arthur C. Millspaugh, writing in 1917, noted that in Michigan

The nominal manager of the state campaign is the chairman of the state central committee, but during the nineties, it is said, the secretary and the head of the speakers' bureau were the actual directors of Republican campaigns. The Democratic state chairman in 1890 and 1892 informs me that prior to those years the state chairman had been a figurehead. In recent campaigns the chairman has appeared to be the real directing head of the organization, although in both parties the secretaries have been experienced and valuable assistants and have been practically in complete charge of the routine work.[13]

The relationship between the parties and the law has never been clear. With fifty separate legislatures contributing to the body of legal controls, some intricate webs have been spun. When statutory law combines with party by-laws, the result is predictably entangled. Yet the party leaders must operate within the law and, in some cases, draw their power from the law. We turn, then, to the formal aspects of legal controls governing the activities of the state party chairmen.

The Legal Basis of the Party Chairman's Authority

Even though American political parties developed without the aid of the state, they are governed by laws adopted by the state. Most states provide for the formal organizational structure of the parties and describe the powers of party officials within the context of state law. Virtually all states control election administration, including provisions for voter registration, maintenance of polling places, and requirements for candidate certification. Where these activities involve the political parties, the law usually specifies their role. State laws regarding party organizations and officers range from a few which are so minimal as to be almost nonexistent to some so detailed that many hundreds of pages are required to contain them. The laws covering primaries, caucuses, elections, and political parties of the Commonwealth of Massachusetts are published in a bound volume, 7½ by 10 inches, and containing 534 pages. South Carolina, on the other hand, repealed all laws regulating the parties in 1944 in order to give the Democrats the best possible chance of evading regulation by the federal courts after the U.S. Supreme Court outlawed the "white primary."

In those states which do not have a body of law governing party organizations, the parties themselves operate under self-imposed by-laws. These represent a wide variety of formulations ranging from a few mimeographed pages to rather extensive and detailed descriptions of party structure and the personal responsibilities of party officers. By 1972 many of these by-laws were badly outdated and in need of major revision. The two national committees, particularly the Democratic National Committee, brought about significant changes in the by-laws and election laws in many states through imposition of new guidelines for national convention delegate selection and for party democratization.

These changes ranged from minor modifications of existing party or state laws to major overhaul of the entire structure of party law. The Ohio Democrats, for instance, adopted that party's first constitution creating a state central committee and executive committee and mandating cooperation between the state and county committees.[14] The Washington Republicans adopted sweeping new rules which tightened state party control over auxiliary organizations and centralized fund raising. As stated in the *Republican Report:*

The State Central Committee on August 8, in a series of major changes in its governing rules, moved to make all fund raising in behalf of Republican causes more responsible to the legal county and state party central committees. . . .

The State party's governing group acted to bring its 2 state-wide, cooperating auxiliaries, the Washington Federation of Republican Women and the College Republican League, into active participation with the State Central Committee and the Committee's State Executive Board. . . .

Specifically, the new rules provide that "any statewide or multiple county auxiliary organization soliciting funds, or county auxiliary organization soliciting funds outside of its county, shall first consult with and obtain approval of the state central committee chairman or its finance chairman when designated for this purpose."

These changes were intended to strengthen the hand of the state chairman and to reduce internecine warfare over money raising.[15]

And, finally, the Wyoming State Democratic Convention revised the party by-laws in 1973 to conform with the election code passed by the state legislature that year. The new election code mandated that political parties make the following substantive revisions in the rules which govern them:

Change the date of the election of the County Chairman and other County Central Committee officers from March of even-numbered years to November of odd-numbered years.

Change the date of the election of the State Chairman and other State Central Committee officers from April of even-numbered years to December of odd-numbered years.

Allow more representation on County Central Committees from large precincts.

Make the 23 County Chairmen bona fide voting members of the State Central Committees.

These changes were designed to provide earlier election of party officers in order to furnish the newly elected officials with four additional months to prepare for elections and to move modestly in the direction of the one-man, one-vote principle.[16]

Reform of the rules governing the power allocation within a state party is different from those modifications designed to bring about change in the ratio of delegate groups in state or national conventions. Most of the state parties have undertaken the latter kind of reform because they were required to by their respective national committees or by national convention resolutions.

In most states the Democratic party undertook to rewrite party by-laws and/or to achieve statutory revision through legislative action. Republicans in about one-half of the states revised their party codes and sought legislative changes in organizational relationships. In at least a dozen states the two parties cooperated in the presentation of a legislative program designed to bring about party reforms desired by both.

Beyond question, reform was needed in many states. In the Republican party matters were brought to a head through a combination of demands from the anti-Goldwater segments of the party and from the Republican governors. The changes were carried out under the spur of the Delegate and Organization (DO) Committee. The Democrats, having suffered wrenching internal dissension at their 1968 national convention, responded by establishing the McGovern-Fraser Commission and the O'Hara Commission. As a result, both parties undertook the first real efforts to reform state law governing party organizations in many years. Changes were still being made in both parties in mid-1975, and the ultimate long-range results are uncertain. The election laws and party by-laws considered here were those in effect prior to the 1972 modifications.

To ascertain the legal basis of authority of the state chairman and of the political parties, it was necessary to analyze state election laws and party by-laws. Election laws were collected from all fifty states and from the eighty-nine parties with published by-laws. These served as the primary resources for a content analysis carried out by David M. Davis (see appendix).

He found that approximately 95 percent of the controlling legal provisions were contained in party by-laws, leaving only 5 percent to be extracted from the state election laws. Most of the latter concentrated on matters relating to state election administration. The states, on the whole, have adopted general legislation leaving operative party controls to the legally constituted parties.

There were over 1,100 separate items identified from both sources of law. Similar but distinctly worded provisions were eventually combined and recombined into 249 powers, which were categorized in eleven homogeneous groupings, as follows:

1. Qualifications, method of election, and terms of office for the chairman and other state party officials

2. The appointive powers of the chairman, including appointments of party officials, members of committees, and nominations to state boards and commissions

3. The power exercised by the chairman in removing party officers at both the state and local levels

4. The power of the chairman to fill vacancies in state and local party positions and vacancies among national convention delegations

5. The responsibility of the chairman to act on behalf of the state executive committee or central committee or other official party groups

6. The functions assigned to the executive (central) committee and the role of the chairman as its presiding officer

7. The responsibility of the chairman to approve or to veto local party decisions

8. The role of the chairman in state and national convention processes

9. The power of the chairman to intervene in the activities of local party conventions

10. The functions of the chairman in election administration as well as in general election campaign practices

11. The power of the chairman to vote in his capacity as presiding officer and manager of the party

Each separate general law or party by-law item which allocated power to the state chairman in each of the eighty-nine parties was placed in one of these eleven groupings. Then, through an intricate and complex system of evaluation, an "Index of Effectiveness" was arrived at, the results of which suggest the degree to which any chairman can utilize his party's by-laws as a justification for his official actions.

The results of this analysis can be summarized as follows: (1) There are very few legal qualifications for becoming a state chairman. For example, only four state parties legally require the chairman-elect to be a member of the state executive committee at the time of his election. A legal requirement that the chairman be a member of the committee as a prerequisite to election sometimes demands fancy footwork in order to clear the way for the election of a designated nominee. In 1970, Jon Moyle, the personal choice of Florida's Governor-elect Reubin Askew and Senator-elect Lawton Chiles, was unable to offer himself as a candidate for state Democratic chairman until the state committeeman from his home county resigned. This resignation cleared the way for the acting state chairwoman to appoint Moyle to the state central committee, thus making him eligible for election to the top party post.[17]

(2) Powers of appointment to party offices are both the most extensive and the most important of those granted the state chairman. The appointive powers of the chairman are often a barometer of his overall political strength. Positions to which the chairman can make appointments include those of executive director, finance chairman, standing committee chairman, members to fill vacancies on the state committee, and campaign chairman. These are all positions clearly located within the party hierarchy and responsible to the chairman. Obviously, the appointments available to any particular chairman will vary from state to state.

In some states the party chairmen are being brought into an active participatory role in the appointment process for state offices. Again, Florida may serve as an example. Under the sweeping election law revisions passed by the 1973 Florida legislature, a seven-member State Elections Commission was created to investigate and recommend disposition of alleged violations of the state's tough campaign finance laws. The commission is composed of three Democrats and three Republicans appointed by the governor from lists of fifteen names furnished by each state party chairman. The original six appointees then meet to provide the governor with a list of three nominees from which he appoints the chairman of the commission. All seven commissioners are subject to confirmation by the Senate. This represents one of the first times that the state party chairmen have been brought into the state appointment process so directly.

Until the reforms in the delegate selection process were adopted in 1971 and 1972, the state chairmen had an important role in that process in many states. Although their role in direct selection of delegates to attend the national conventions has diminished, the Democratic chairmen are still responsible for setting in motion the machinery through which the delegates are selected. Although few chairmen derive much power from state laws and party by-laws, it is clear that their appointive powers are often a barometer of the overall legal power that they possess.

(3) It might be assumed that the state chairmen derive power over their state committees from the party by-laws, but that is not often the case. In some states, to be sure, the by-laws provide the chairman with the power to preside over meetings of the executive (central) committee, to call meetings, to rule on procedural matters, and even, on occasion, to appoint members of the central committee. Most of these are normal duties assigned to any presiding officer in any organization. The fact that many state parties do not see fit to provide formal grants of power to the chairman to carry out these routine functions is a commentary on the

general lack of importance of state law and party by-laws to the functioning of the parties. Most of the chairmen interviewed noted that they did, indeed, have the power to perform such routine tasks, but it was derived from custom, not from law.

The act of voting on the state committee or related committees is not judged to be important to the chairman's successful accomplishment of his mission. However, the absence of authority to vote is deemed important by many chairmen. The power derives from the implicit threat—not the actual vote itself.

(4) The state chairman's power to appoint state convention personnel is not a measure of his overall power at the convention. Only 24 percent of the chairmen have the power to make any convention appointments, and almost all of them are at the committee level or below. The chairman's role at the convention may be an important one, indeed a dominating one, but his ability to exploit that role does not stem from formal grants of power.

(5) The state chairmen do not have much formal power of supervision and management over election campaigns. Few are provided any form of legally mandated authority to manage campaigns. In those states where a chairman serves in a campaign capacity, it is through his own initiative and not a responsibility thrust on him by the by-laws of the party.

It is clear from the interview data that most state chairmen pay little attention to formal powers provided by law. They are usually aware of those actions which are forbidden to them by state law or party by-laws, but they do not feel inhibited by the lack of a formal mandate. Most feel that the power of appointment is crucial to their success. It is the one form of internal patronage left to them, and they use it to attempt to weld the party together behind them. Most of the respondents suggested that their real power was of an informal nature and flowed either from their relationship to a sitting governor or from their position as recognized party leader of an out-party. A western Republican literally snorted when asked how much of his power derived from written law:

I don't even know what the law says. I can't imagine it saying anything that would be helpful. Our law in ——— was written by the old progressives and, for the most part, is restrictive. I think I will be better off not knowing what the law says. Ignorance of the law will be my excuse if I get into trouble.

Even so, the law governing organizations must be taken into account by some chairmen. Another westerner, a national committeewoman, stated that she had been instrumental in helping to get the current party chairman elected.

I told him that he had better take a close look at the state law as well as the by-laws of the party. I have been around a long time and he is a relative newcomer. His powers are greatly circumscribed by the party by-laws that were written about thirty years ago to bring ———— [a former state chairman] to toe. The chairman is forbidden in writing to do many of the things that a modern-day chairman must do if he is going to be effective. Some of our recent leaders have simply ignored the rules, but that always leaves them open to criticism if an antagonistic faction arises. Well, he took a close look, and he and the senator passed the word that either we rewrote the by-laws or we could look for a new chairman. Fortunately, no one wants the job, so we are currently rewriting the by-laws. I think we are simply going to repeal most of them and free the chairman's hand.

The Mystery of Control

In the catalog of concerns about the functions of political parties in modern America there must be a special page reserved for organizational problems. Party organizations, operating under an ill-defined and often dependent leadership, have risen to their present level of prominence through a series of historical accidents. Parties were not carefully conceived and well nurtured. Instead, they grew out of the personal conflicts that beset the Washington administration, and although they were issue-oriented in those early years, they became much less so in later ones. The formal structures that grew up to house them differed in every state, and the lines of responsibilities between the national and state levels of the organizations to this day remain unclear. Yet parties quickly took their places among those institutions that serve as bridges between the people and the government.

The political parties have had good times and bad. They have undergone periods of great stress and of impressive stability. They have, at times, risen above themselves to produce leaders and to support issues which transcended narrow partisan concerns. At other times they have fallen to such depths of petty politics and have been led by men of such questionable repute that they were hard pressed to survive. With this kind of history it is not surprising that a need to control them by law manifested itself. Legislatures, usually under public pressure, attempted to regulate party affairs and political structures by passing general as well as specific legislation. These efforts have almost always been subject to strenuous debate and have, on the whole, resulted in minimal state legal regulation. Legislators who gained their seats under the party's banners have been asked in turn to regulate and circumscribe the activities of the party. They have, in effect, been asked to rock the boat while they occupied the seats. At the same time the parties have not sought state regulation. The consequence is that the two political parties are among the most prominent self-governing institutions within the framework of American government. Party officers derive whatever powers they have from sources other than law.

2 Social Characteristics and Career Development

Nobody ever got anywhere in politics by
being state chairman. It is a dead end if
I ever saw one.
A western state chairman

I literally would not now be governor if it
had not been for my service as state chairman. The chairmanship enabled me to make
the kinds of statewide party contacts to give
me a base from which to run.
A midwestern governor

I know that a lot of people in politics think
the state chairmanship is a dead end and
that it represents the top of the ladder for
those who hold it, but I must say that I
know a lot of former chairmen who are
now in elective office, and one is in the
president's cabinet.
A Republican national committeeman

In 1954 Donald R. Matthews wrote
that "the social and psychological characteristics of the individual officials
acting within a political institutional framework must be considered before
an adequate understanding of politics and government is possible." [1]
Since that time the blossoming of the literature describing the social origins and career development of American political leaders has been impressive. Most such research has concerned national, state, and local
legislators.[2] Other scholars have traced the career development and personal characteristics of national committee members,[3] city councilmen,[4]
party workers,[5] and governors.[6]

Party Leadership

Among American political leaders, the state chairmen are an elite group.
They are elite because of the positions that they hold as the elected

leaders of their respective state political parties. Individually, they may be wise or they may be foolish. They may attempt to restructure their party organization or they may swim with the tide, making few changes and building on the framework that has been put together by others. Their success may be measured in terms of offices won, money raised, and images furbished. Their impact upon the party may be slight, even though the candidates of that party continue to win and hold office. In short, they represent those mysterious qualities that go into political leadership and may well reap benefits from, or blame for, events over which they have had little or no control. Henri Peyre has described leadership as one of three topics "on which no wise man should ever attempt to write." [7] Notwithstanding Peyre's warning, books continue to be written describing those qualities which allegedly contribute to "leadership."

Most of the writings on leadership make small contribution to the study of a political elite such as the state party chairman. As noted by James David Barber, "Leadership is not a fixed set of qualities possessed or even sought by all leaders everywhere. The characteristics relevant for leadership vary with the situation." [8]

Particular political cultures tend to define their own criteria of leadership. The wide variety of political organizations in the fifty states necessarily means that the party leaders in each state will emerge from a distinctive type of political cocoon. Some state chairmen will inherit an ongoing, activist, well-financed party organization carrying a party banner under which many have been and will continue to be elected. Others will assume the headship of a party more recognizable by its parts than its whole. Those states with a highly personalized political organization will define for the party leader a mediating role far different from that of his counterparts in other states. And some will inherit parties that have had few organizational successes and no electoral victories for a long period of time with little hope for reversing the trend. The chairman's role in such a party, therefore, may be perceived as that of caretaker. The quality of the leadership, however, often reflects the quality of the party.

Austin Ranney and Willmoore Kendall have noted that the word *leader* has at least three distinct meanings. It connotes either (1) a man whose *attainments,* in terms of a particular standard or set of standards and values, rank "high" when compared to the attainments of his contemporaries; (2) a man to whom persons engaged in a particular activity "defer" because of the "status" he enjoys; or (3) a man who *emits stimuli* that are "responded to integratively by the members of a group" so as to forward the performance of whatever activities are characteristic of that particular group. The authors note that these three meanings of *leader* are not mutually exclusive and that a single individual might be regarded as a leader in all three senses.[9]

Ordway Tead, a pioneer in studies of administrative leadership, has noted that there are many types and styles of leadership. The qualities required are subjective, but they include clear purposefulness, the cultivation of creative abilities of associates and subordinates, and a sense of the public interest.[10] This is perhaps as good a definition of the ideal for a party chairman as any other.

This brief discussion of leadership qualities presupposes that such qualities are among the criteria applied in the selection of party chairmen. If, in fact, that is so, the party chairmen come no closer as a group to fitting the definition than do other political elites. There is little doubt that many state organizations of elected leaders do seek the best available talent to serve as party chairman. The fact that many do not, however, cannot be denied. Some governors purposely select unimaginative and uninspired party chiefs as a means of reducing their competition for party leadership. In one state the secretary to the party automatically succeeds to the chairmanship when there is a vacancy, often providing the state committee members little opportunity to evaluate leadership potential. There are many patterns, as we shall see, and they do not all guarantee that those with the most leadership qualities will be elected to head their parties.

Personal Characteristics of State Chairmen

Two recent studies have traced the personal backgrounds and careers of state party chairmen. In the first, Robert Agranoff and Edward F. Cooke conducted a 1963 questionnaire survey of 415 chairmen (205 returned) spanning the years 1930–63.[11] The second effort was a profile of state party chairmen serving in 1966, based upon an 82 percent return from the total universe of 100 respondents. Published in 1970, "State Party Chairmen: A Profile," by Charles W. Wiggins and William L. Turk, provided a particularly useful opportunity to compare the growth of sophisticated party organizations in the states between 1966 and the 1969–72 dates of my interviews.[12] The authors also collected personal data which I have occasionally referred to for comparative purposes. All other data used in this chapter, including the tables, were developed from my interviews with state chairmen.

The state party chairman as represented in this collection of data is a white male of early middle age, who is either a Protestant or a Catholic and has a college education. That brief description does not tell us much about the types of individuals who become state chairmen. In order to understand their place in the party system, it is necessary to more closely examine the backgrounds and personal characteristics of the individuals who hold these important party positions.

Age   State party chairmen appear to be a bit younger than do other political leaders who have been subject to study. The median age of all chairmen included in this survey was 44 years, with the Republicans slightly older (46.5 years) than the Democrats (42 years).[13] These medians differ only slightly from the 1966 Wiggins and Turk findings of a Democratic median of 46 years and a Republican median of 43.[14] And the overall median age for both parties between 1930 and 1963 was found to be 44 years by Agranoff and Cooke.[15] This would suggest that there has been little change in the tendency to elect generally younger men and women to state party leadership posts in the last forty-five years.

The relatively young age at which state chairmen are elected derives from several factors. Wiggins and Turk speculate that "organizational leaders" are younger than "decision makers" (namely, political leaders elected by the voters) due to the political party's emphasis upon organization structures as opposed to governmental policy making. They note Robert Presthus' finding that "organizational leaders" in two small New York communities were eleven years younger than members of the policy-making elite.[16]

One state governor, interviewed in 1972, stated his belief that

State chairmen probably are younger than state legislators or congressmen. I think that has certainly been true in ———. I would guess that it is a product of the different constituencies. The state chairman has to impress a relatively small number of active party leaders in order to get elected. They are looking for different qualities than the voters are looking for when they elect a legislator. The party people are going to be looking at political qualifications such as experience in campaign management, fund raising, and such things. The voters are more interested in the kind of public personal impression the candidate makes and what he stands for. It probably takes longer to build up the latter kind of reputation than it does the former.

And it should not be forgotten that many chairmen are not elected at all but are merely the choice of an incumbent governor. They were probably chosen in most cases because they had successfully managed the governor's campaign.

This suggests that it is more time consuming to become a viable candidate for public office than for party office—that the process of expanding personal acquaintances, mastering the organizational hierarchy, and de-claring candidacy takes more time because the audience is the voter group rather than the party activist group. The state chairman, however, may have arrived at the organizational pinnacle in a relatively short time by managing a successful and personally rewarding campaign for some pub-lic official. Both sides of this equation support the Presthus position. In either case, the out-party chairman may be a product of his reputation with the party activists and the in-party chairman may be a product of the governor's campaign. In neither case has he necessarily had to spend as much time building that reputation as has the candidate who is pre-senting himself to the voters. He may well be elected at a younger age because he does not have to spend as much time selling himself to the public (voters as opposed to party activists), and the political ladder which he is climbing may not have as many rungs.

Sex   The overwhelming predominance of male officeholders in the United States does not need much documentation. In 1974 Ella Grasso was elected governor of Connecticut, the first female in history to be elected to gubernatorial office without being preceded by her husband. In 1975 the Ninety-fourth Congress had no female senators, and only eighteen members of the House were women. There have been sizable gains in the number of women elected to state legislative seats. In 1964 only 351 women were elected as legislators; by 1975, however, 595 women were serving although that still represented only 7.5 percent of the total state legislative seats.

The number of women who have been elected to the state chairman-ship is not much more impressive. Agranoff and Cooke were able to iden-tify only two names that appeared to be those of women from the list of 415 state chairmen between the years 1930 and 1963.[17] Wiggins and Turk found only three state chairwomen in 1966, all Republicans.[18] During the period of this study there were eight state chairwomen elected, four in each party. It should be noted that in most states chairmen and vice-chairmen are of the opposite sex; thus, most vice-chairmen are women, and they will succeed to the chairmanship in case of an in-cumbent's death or resignation. In few cases, however, do the women who succeed to the post run for it or get elected to it in the ensuing party election. Two of the chairwomen, one from each party, first succeeded to the office after the resignation of the chairman and were later elected in their own right. Ann Cramer, Democrat of Florida, succeeded to the office of state chairman in 1970 but was not elected to a full term. She came back in 1975, however, to be elected in her own right. One of the Republicans, Lorraine Orr of Nebraska, served two terms as party vice-chairwoman before running for the top post and getting elected in 1967 and reelected in 1969. She noted, however, that her election would not have been possible without the support of Nebraska's Republican governor who encouraged her election.

It is noteworthy that until recently state Republican parties have been more inclined to elect women to head the state committee than have the Democratic parties. This may be due to the long-standing competition at the national level between the Women's Division of the Republican National Committee and the National Federation of Republican Women, a semiautonomous party group. The conflict between the leadership of the two groups began in the 1950s and brought many women into party affairs at both the state and national levels.[19] Some party leaders suggest that the intense rivalry between women in the two groups may have served to enhance their interest in seeking election to important party posts.* It is also possible that the early inclusion of state chairmen as voting members of the national committee in 1952 gave Republican women a greater incentive to seek election to the top party office in their states.[20]

Race   There was only one black state chairman in office during the period covered by this study. The 1968 Democratic National Convention recognized and seated a Mississippi delegation of liberal, predominantly black "Loyalists" headed by Aaron Henry over a group of conservative, predominantly white "Regulars" led by Governor John Bell Williams. Henry was elected state chairman in 1968, and his group was recognized by the Democratic National Committee as the official Democratic party of Mississippi. Although outnumbering the Loyalists by better than two to one, the Regulars were excluded from participation in national party affairs. By mid-1975 the two factions were discussing rapprochement, and there was a reported movement toward unity. No other state party had elected a black chairman although some had placed Negroes in other key positions within their organizations.

Place of Birth and Length of Residence in State   In spite of the massive poplation shifts in the United States during this century, state chair-

---

* One high female official of the Democratic National Committee maintained in an interview with the author that the state vice-chair positions, all but one of which were held by a woman in 1970, were of such great importance in the Democratic party structure that the women were "content" in the second-level positions. Two other DNC officers, including a national chairman and another important DNC woman leader, discounted this argument. It should be noted that the reorganization and restructuring of the DNC adopted in 1972 and revised in 1974 include *both* the state chairmen and the highest ranking officer of the opposite sex as members (see below, chap. 7).

men tend to be natives of the states in which they serve. Sixty-five percent were lifetime residents of their states, with Democrats (69.2 percent) outnumbering Republicans (60.9 percent). Eighty percent had lived in the state in which they held office for twenty years or more.

These findings do not differ markedly from those concerning other political leaders. The vast majority of state legislators were born in the states which they serve, and the same pattern holds for members of Congress. Seventy-eight percent of the members of the U.S. Senate and 81 percent of the members of the House were born in the state from which they were elected to the Ninety-second Congress. Huckshorn and Spencer found that 70 percent of the nonincumbent candidates for the House in 1962 had lived in the state from which they ran for twenty-one years or longer, and 83 percent had been lifelong residents.[21]

At the other end of the spectrum, none of the chairmen had lived in their states for less than five years and only 5 percent for less than ten years. This would suggest that long residence, old family, and wide-ranging personal acquaintance are important to the selection of state chairmen just as they are in election to public office. In short, they do not differ substantially from any other group within the elite corps of United States politics. (See table 2.1.)

Most studies of the social origins of political decision makers have shown them to have been born and reared in small-town rural America.[22] Forty percent of the state chairmen, however, were born in cities with a population of 10,000 or over, with 22.5 percent being born in cities of over one-quarter million population. Republicans were more likely to

Table 2.1   Length of Residence in State

	Democrats (N39)	Republicans (N41)	Total (N80)
1–5 years	0.0%	0.0%	0.0%
6–10 years	7.7	2.4	5.0
11–15 years	5.1	4.9	5.0
16–20 years	0.0	14.6	7.5
21–30 years	10.3	7.3	8.7
Over 30 years	5.1	7.3	6.2
Life	69.2	60.9	65.0
NA/DK	2.8	2.4	2.5

NOTE: Columns do not total to 100 percent due to rounding.

come from small-town or rural origins than were Democrats, who were more likely than Republicans to come from large cities. As shown in table 2.2, approximately the same number of chairmen from both parties emerged from cities of 10,000 to 250,000 population.

The type of individuals chosen to be state chairmen today are likely to be representative of urban America. The fact that they are often lifelong residents of their states is not surprising; that has been true of political elites for many years. But the fact that many of these party managers are from urban backgrounds while the political candidates still often represent rural environments is noteworthy. Possibly the voter yearns for candidates who represent "old-fashioned" American rural virtues while party strategists know that they must rely on modern, urban-oriented party managers.

Occupation   State chairmen represent occupational groups which permit them the time to serve in their party posts. They are usually lawyers, businessmen, and increasingly, salaried party officials. As in virtually all political elites, lawyers predominate. Thirty-three percent of the chairmen in both parties claim the law as their principal means of livelihood. Almost twice as many Democrats as Republicans are lawyers, while the number of businessmen among the Republicans is about double that of the Democrats. One Democrat made his living as a farmer and another as a physician while two Republicans worked as newspapermen. Two of the chairwomen identified themselves as housewives. Two Republicans were elective state officeholders and claimed that as their regular occupation. (See table 2.3.)

A group which deserves increasing attention is composed of those who are full-time, paid state chairmen and who make their living in no other

Table 2.2   Type of Place of Birth

	Democrats (N39)	Republicans (N41)	Total (N80)
Rural farm	7.7%	9.8%	8.8%
Small town (under 10,000)	25.7	31.7	28.7
Small city (10,000–250,000)	41.0	39.0	40.0
Large city (250,000 or over)	25.6	19.5	22.5

NOTE: Columns do not total to 100 percent due to rounding.

Table 2.3   Occupation

	Democrats (N39)	Republicans (N41)	Total (N80)
Lawyer	43.6%	22.0%	32.8%
Businessman	20.5	43.9	32.1
Small business	5.1	19.5	12.3
Manufacturing	5.1	4.9	5.0
Banking	5.1		2.5
Insurance/real estate	2.6	14.6	8.6
Lumber	2.6	4.9	3.7
State chairman (full-time, paid)	20.4	14.6	17.5
Government employee	2.6	7.3	4.9
Elected official		4.9	2.5
Journalist		4.9	2.5
Housewife	2.6	2.4	2.5
Pharmacist	2.6		1.3
Retired	2.6		1.3
Farmer	2.6		1.3
Physician	2.6		1.3

NOTE: Columns do not total to 100 percent due to rounding.

way. Seventeen percent of all the state chairmen classified themselves in this way, a slight preponderance being Democrats.*

Thirty-one percent of the chairmen stated that they were paid a salary by their state committee. Two state party organizations budgeted a salary but the chairman did not accept it, either because he was independently wealthy or because the party treasury was in such poor shape as to preclude payment. The median salary was $19,200, with the Republicans receiving a median salary of $20,615 compared to the Democratic median of $17,666. An equal number of Republicans and Democrats are paid. Salaried state chairmen are a relatively new phenomenon in American politics. Only 4 percent of those who are paid indicated that the

---

* The fact that Wiggins and Turk found that 39 percent of the state chairmen "indicated that their positions were considered to be full-time" does not mean that they necessarily made their entire livelihood from that source. In both their findings and mine, these designations are difficult to sustain because of outside activities that are less readily visible to the researcher. On the whole, my assignment to "full-time" status should be more reliable due to the personal interviews used as opposed to mailed questionnaires. Efforts were made to substantiate claims of full-time professional status.

party had been paying a chairman's salary prior to 1960. Paying of salaries to the state chairman is one manifestation of party interest in improving party organizations. Many of those states that do not pay a salary do employ a paid executive director. Sixty-six percent of the state party organizations employ an executive director, with an approximate median salary of $15,000. Some chairmen have reached the conclusion that it might be better to have an unsalaried chairman with a full-time, paid executive director, but that idea has not caught hold in many places.

It should be noted that 74 percent of the chairmen receive actual expense reimbursements or a lump-sum expense account. It was noted that several of those state parties that do not pay expenses (usually because they cannot afford to) tend to select chairmen who are wealthy enough to assume the burden of their own expenses in office. In those cases, personal wealth becomes a criterion for holding the office. It might also be noted that 25 percent of the chairmen indicated that the state party also paid the expenses of the members of their respective national committees.

There is considerable controversy in both parties over whether a chairman should be paid or not. Those who believe that he should argue that it helps to professionalize the party by bringing talented people to the chairmanship in spite of their inability to pay their own way. They argue that to demand that the chairman pay his own expenses and work without salary has the effect of reducing the reservoir of talent available for the job to those who are wealthy or are in occupations that do not need the everyday attention of the holder. Generally speaking, those who oppose salaried party positions argue that the chairmanship should be a position of honor and that the person elected to it should not assume the burden unless certain of the adequacy of his own financial resources. One Republican said that he did not think a state chairman should be paid because it puts the chairman in a position of being an employee and therefore creates difficulties in the solicitation of volunteers who work for no pay. Most of the opponents of salaried chairmen maintain that the party would be better off employing an executive director to work under a part-time, unpaid chairman. Nevertheless, there is a clear trend toward paid state chairmen *and* paid executive directors. Many of those involved in politics at the state level believe this to be a move toward greater professionalization.

Religion   Having knowledge of the religious affiliation of a particular group of political leaders is useful when the leaders are elected by voter constituencies. Such data can help to determine over- and under-representation by particular creeds as well as voter discrimination against particular religious minority groups. When dealing with party leaders who are chosen by other party leaders, not usually representative as a voting electorate, religious affiliation has less meaning. Nevertheless, it may be noted that 73.2 percent of the Republican state chairmen were members of various Protestant sects, while only 51.3 percent of the Democrats were. Given the preponderance of Protestant Republicans, this is not surprising, nor is the fact that 33.3 percent of the Democratic state chairmen were Catholics while only 14.6 percent of the Republicans were. Only three chairmen were Jewish (two Republicans and one Democrat) while two Republicans were members of the Church of Jesus Christ of Latter-Day Saints (Mormons).

Education   The state chairmen as a group are quite well educated, with 76 percent holding at least one college degree. Of these, 42 percent held graduate degrees, predominately in law and business administration. At the lower end of the educational scale, only one Republican failed to complete high school and only 7.5 percent of both parties ended their education at that level. Democratic chairmen had slightly higher educational achievements than did the Republicans, with 82 percent of the former completing four years or more of college as opposed to 70 percent of the latter. The Democrats far outstripped the Republicans in graduate education with 60 percent of the former and 27 percent of the latter having earned advanced degrees. (See table 2.4.)

Table 2.4   Highest Educational Level Attained

	Democrats (N39)	Republicans (N41)	Total (N80)
Secondary school, incomplete	0.0%	2.4%	1.2%
Secondary school, complete	10.0	5.0	7.5
Post-secondary trade school, complete		4.9	2.4
College, incomplete	7.7	14.6	11.2
College, complete (4 years)	82.0	70.0	76.0
Graduate or professional school, incomplete	2.6		1.3
Graduate or professional school, complete (M.A. or equivalent)	2.6	4.9	3.7
Graduate or professional school, complete (Ph.D., M.D., LL.B., J.D., or equivalent)	56.4	21.9	39.1

NOTE: Columns do not total to 100 percent due to rounding.

Of those who attended college, 49 percent graduated from public, state-supported universities or colleges while 32.5 percent were graduates of private schools. Five percent attended both a public and a private school before graduating. Democrats graduated from private institutions (many of them Catholic-supported) in twice as many cases as did Republicans.

More chairmen of both parties held a law degree than any other above the bachelor's. Thirty-six percent of all chairmen held the law degree with Democrats outnumbering Republicans two to one. One Democrat earned a medical degree.

In the case of the state chairmanship, the type and level of degree held are more important in terms of the amount of time available for the job than in terms of preparation for the job. In the cases of both lawyers and businessmen, the key educational quality was the fact that both groups were better able to assume the burdens of the party because more time was available to them. Thus, as far as the chairmanship is concerned, the effects of education are more accurately assessed as those of occupation based on education. It might be argued that lawyers are better prepared to understand the intricacies of party law and of party input to legislators, but this would be a difficult argument to sustain with any evidence. (See table 2.5.)

Political Experience   Avery Leiserson's assertion in 1958 that the state chairmen tend not to be "political executives in their own right" is not borne out by the results of this study.[23] The state chairmen who were in office during the 1970–72 period had considerable experience in a

Table 2.5   Highest College Degree Held

	Democrats (N39)	Republicans (N41)	Total (N80)
B.A., B.S., B.S.Ed. (or equivalent bachelor's degree)	23.1%	43.9%	33.7%
M.A., M.S., M.A.T., M.P.A. (or equivalent master's degree)	5.1	4.9	5.0
LL.B., J.D. (or equivalent law degree)	51.3	21.9	36.3
Other	2.6		1.3
None	7.7	19.5	13.8
NA/DK	10.3	9.7	10.0

NOTE: Columns do not total to 100 percent due to rounding.

wide variety of political offices, both appointive and elective. These eighty state chairmen had served their parties in various capacities for a median span of 12.5 years—the Republicans for 14 years and the Democrats for 11. Less than 5 percent of them had never held any political office prior to their election as state chairman.

Almost 15 percent of state chairmen had run for and won elective political office prior to becoming party head. Nine percent held public office while occupying the position of party chairman. These ranged from seven who were state legislators to one who was governor (Marvin Mandel of Maryland) and others who were simultaneously attorney general, state treasurer, or congressman (Watkins Abbott of Virginia). Most of those who have run for public office or have served in appointive offices believed quite strongly that their experiences were immensely helpful in carrying out the duties of the chairmanship.

The state chairmen developed their interest in politics at a variety of points during their careers. Twenty-five percent became active while in high school or earlier. Twenty-two percent became active during their years in college although the Democrats outnumbered the Republicans three to one in this group. Most chairmen became active in particular campaigns, attracted either by a strong ideological attachment to one or the other parties or by a particular candidate. Forty-four percent of the chairmen could be categorized in this way, with the Republicans far more likely to have become involved due to a particular campaign (R, 63 percent; D, 23 percent). Nine Republican chairmen became involved in politics in the period from 1962 to 1964 because of their respect for Senator Barry Goldwater and his ideological beliefs. Eight became involved in 1952 or 1956 to help in the election or reelection of Dwight D. Eisenhower. Democrats were much less likely to become involved because of loyalty to an individual candidate, with only three claiming involvement due to the candidacy of Adlai Stevenson in either 1952 or 1956 and three due to the candidacy of John F. Kennedy in 1960. Democratic chairmen, on the other hand, do suggest greater involvement out of allegiance to their party's tradition and belief. It may be that Republicans are more likely to attach themselves to a strong candidate because of the perpetual minority status of their party with the voters. As one Republican notes:

I learned very early in my first venture into county politics that being a Republican was not going to get me very far. I tried to work for the party, but there was not much of a party to work for then. So I bided my time until 1956 and volunteered to head the Eisenhower campaign in the county.

We carried the county for Ike, and that helped to focus some attention on me and gave me my start.

A presidential contest was only one of many stimuli that first caused the chairmen to become active in politics. Eighteen percent of the Democrats and 10 percent of the Republicans developed their interest through their parents' involvement. Twelve percent in each party became interested through active participation in Young Democrats or Young Republicans. Ten percent of each party became involved through support of a political candidate other than presidential, although 15 percent of the Republicans and 3 percent of the Democrats attributed at least a part of their initial interest to a presidential contest. Here again, the greater number of Republicans suggests the realization on the part of these young party activists that the chances for success in the Republican party of the 1950s and 1960s lay with the presidential races rather than more hopeless contests at the state and local levels. This was particularly true in the South. A scattering of chairmen gave other reasons for their early involvement ranging from becoming a candidate themselves to concern over state or national policies, local "good government" campaigns, and campaign management.

Sixty-three percent of the chairmen had held three or more positions in politics prior to becoming chairman. As noted in table 2.6, these first positions cut across the entire spectrum of elected and appointed public and party offices.

Obviously, most of these individuals held several additional positions at later dates in their political careers. All of these data suggest that the state chairmen today are not merely "window dressing" campaign managers who are rewarded with an empty appointment to the party chairmanship. They have considerable political background and have engaged in many party activities throughout the hierarchical levels of their parties. Many of them have been candidates themselves, although not always successful, and almost all of them used the contacts built up within the structure of their parties in their quest for the state chairmanship. Even those who were chosen for the position by the governor, and merely ratified by the party committee, have reached the pinnacle of organizational politics by climbing an ill-defined career ladder. Their success was due to a thorough grounding in state and local politics to a far greater extent than has previously been believed. Most of them worked their way to the top, and even though some were appointed by an elected party leader, their prior experiences in practical politics certainly cannot be dismissed.

Furthermore, the chairmen were involved in more than just political party positions. Twenty-eight percent of the Democrats and 22 percent of the Republicans during the 1970–72 period had run for and been elected to public office. In addition, three Democrats and one Republican had held appointive office or were in an appointed office while serving as chairman, including a former assistant secretary of the U.S. Department of the Interior and several members of a variety of state commissions. Three chairmen in each party had run for and been defeated for elective

Table 2.6   First Position in Politics Prior to Selection as State Chairman

	Democrats (N39)	Republicans (N41)	Total (N80)
YD-YR officer (college, local, state)	17.8%	14.6%	16.3%
Precinct leader (ward captain, chairman)	20.5	22.0	21.3
City party leader (other than chairman)		4.9	2.5
County chairman	7.7	9.8	8.9
County party leader (other than chairman)	2.6	4.9	3.8
Congressional district party leader	2.6		1.3
State party chairman	5.1		2.5
State party executive committeeman	5.1	4.9	5.0
State party leader (other than chairman, finance chairman, state committees)	2.6	2.4	2.5
Campaign manager for candidate (or assistant manager)	5.1	14.6	10.0
Elected city official	10.3	4.9	7.5
Elected county official	2.6	2.4	2.5
Elected state official (other than legislator)	2.6	2.4	2.5
State legislator	5.1	2.4	3.5
Appointed city official	2.6	2.4	2.5
Appointed county official	2.6		1.3
Appointed state official			1.3
Appointed national official		2.4	1.2
No previous political office	5.1	4.9	5.0

office, including two who had run for governor and one for Congress. Thus, the experience of state chairmen transcended the management side of politics.

The State Chairmanship as a Stepping-stone

The state party chairmanship serves as a stepping-stone to elective office in a surprisingly large number of states. It is not the political dead end that it is perceived by some to be—for example, one western Democrat, who said, "Neither my predecessor nor myself has pursued public office, and after glancing at the track record of my earlier predecessors I am not very encouraged." A Republican, too, noted that "the state chairmanship in _____ is a dead end. Every chairman who has run for office has been defeated." Yet the evidence suggests that those who served as state chairmen in the decade between 1962 and 1974 did remarkably well in pursuit of elective public office.

There were 516 state chairmen between 1962 and 1974, 270 Republicans and 246 Democrats.* In some states a particular party might have had only a single chairman during the entire ten years. John Bailey of Connecticut, for instance, spanned the entire period and remained in office until his death in 1975. Some parties, at the other extreme, changed chairmen often. The Republicans of Tennessee had nine chairmen in ten years while the Democratic party of New Mexico had eight during the same period.

* The names of the state chairmen during this period were collected from the offices of Jo Good, National Convention Coordinator, Republican National Committee, and of Sheila Hixson, Assistant to the Secretary, Democratic National Committee. The Republican lists extend back to 1952, while the Democratic lists were available only after 1962. For convenience and comparability, therefore, this analysis was based upon the period from 1962 to 1974 inclusive. The lists of chairmen with the indicated dates of their service were typed in parallel columns on a sheet designated for each state. The incumbent chairman was then asked by letter to make any corrections and to indicate which of the chairmen for his or the opposition party had run for office, which office, and to describe the election outcome. Of the 100 requests sent, all but fourteen responded. Telephone calls were initiated to party leaders in those fourteen states. The compilation used in this section, therefore, is as complete as possible and has been verified by one or more political leaders in each state. Short-term temporary chairmen and extended vacancies were not included in the compilation.

The analysis of the data was performed by three students: Rita Hamm, Joan Wilson, and Barbara Johnson. A separate analysis was performed on the Republican lists back to 1952 and showed no difference in the mean average length of service from the 1962–74 period.

In several states no chairman of either party had attempted to run for higher office during the decade studied, but in Delaware every one of the four Republican chairmen not only ran for high political office but won. Nebraska sent three state chairmen to the U.S. House of Representatives, and Idaho had three Democratic chairmen who unsuccessfully ran for governor. Hawaii, North Carolina, and Wisconsin had two each who ran for governor and lost.

During the 1962–72 period, 33 percent (144 of 435) of all the state chairmen were candidates for political office after serving as chairman. More Republicans (39.0 percent) than Democrats (32.5 percent) were candidates, although the success ratio was approximately the same. Republicans won in 22.4 percent of the elections and Democrats in 20.0 percent.

As noted in table 2.7, the offices successfully sought by chairmen were often high ones. Four Republicans became United States senators and five became governors of their states.[24] No Democratic chairmen were elected to the Senate, but five were elected to gubernatorial office. Thirteen Republicans and six Democrats ran for but failed to win a seat in the Senate, and eight Republicans and seven Democrats were unsuccessful in their bids for the state governorship. Of the sixteen chairmen who won election to the U.S. House of Representatives, ten were Republicans and six were Democrats. An additional six Republicans and five Democrats ran for the House but lost.*

Two neighboring New England state parties provided an interesting variation to the stepping-stone pattern in 1973 and 1975 respectively. In 1973 the Vermont Democratic party elected former Governor Philip Hoff state chairman. Hoff's election was brought about without the support of the incumbent governor. And in early 1975 the New Hampshire Republicans elected former United States Senator Norris Cotton in spite of the support of another candidate by Governor Meldrim Thomson.

The political office most commonly sought by former chairmen is membership in the state legislature. Thirty-five chairmen ran for state legislative office during the ten-year period and thirty of them won. Nineteen Republican chairmen won, while only eleven Democrats were suc-

---

* The trend continued in the 1974 elections. Ten present and former state chairmen ran for governor of their respective states although only one of them was victorious. Two incumbent chairmen ran unsuccessfully for the U.S. Senate; and two former and two incumbent chairmen ran for the House of Representatives. In this group of candidates Democrats outnumbered Republicans two to one, possibly a by-product of the political climate generated by Watergate.

cessful. Most of the thirty were elected to the state Senate rather than the lower house.

It is clear that the state chairmanship is not a political dead end. The chairmen not only run for office but run successfully for high office. A surprising number run for statewide offices such as U.S. senator and governor. One senator who had served previously as chairman of his party for three years stated:

It was clear to me from the beginning that the chairmanship had a great deal of potential as a launching pad. I had an opportunity to develop party contacts and make friendships throughout the state, and I had the resources of the headquarters, meager though they were, to consolidate my position. One year I made twenty fund-raising speeches in various counties, and I visited every county in the state. I organized two state conventions, over which I presided. I appointed several party groups or committees which pleased a lot of people. Most important, however, every two or three months I put out a newsletter which was primarily a report on my activities in behalf of the party. By the time I had decided to run for sure, I was one of the best-known party leaders in the state.

Although there is little systematic evidence available, chairmen have also been appointed to high administrative and policy-making offices directly from the state chairmanship. Republican C. A. Brimmer, Jr., was appointed Wyoming attorney general in 1971 by Governor Stanley Hathaway, a former Republican state chairman himself. Republican William Steger of Texas was appointed to a federal district judgeship in 1970 by President Nixon. The president also appointed, at about the same time, Missouri Republican Chairman Elmer Smith as head of the Saint Louis regional office of the Department of Housing and Urban Development.

Table 2.7   Offices Sought by State Chairmen between 1962 and 1972

Result	Senator		U.S. Rep.		Governor		Attorney General		Treasurer	
	D	R	D	R	D	R	D	R	D	R
Elected	0	4	6	10	5	5	2	3	1	1
Defeated	6	13	5	6	7	8	0	2	0	1
Total	6	17	11	16	12	13	2	5	1	2

Howard Hausman, Republican chairman of Connecticut, was appointed to the State Public Utilities Commission by Governor Meskill.

Among the Democrats, the major appointment was that of Georgia Chairman David Gambrell to the United States Senate to replace the late Richard Russell. Gambrell had been chosen for the chairmanship by Governor Jimmy Carter, who also appointed him to the Senate. Gambrell was defeated for renomination two years later and ran unsuccessfully for the Democratic gubernatorial nomination in 1974. Even though Democrats have held more elective positions during the period studied than have Republicans and have had more opportunities to make appointments of party chairmen to state offices, the Gambrell appointment was the only one reported in the Democratic party.

It might be hypothesized that minority chairmen in one-party or modified one-party states would constitute the largest group of those running for office. Conventional wisdom has held that the chances for success for state chairmen were small, suggesting that these party officers would run primarily as ticket fillers in hopeless contests. However, these data suggest that just the opposite is true. As shown in table 2.8, of the forty-five successful candidates (1962–72) for governor, U.S. senator, U.S. representative, and other elected state constitutional offices, forty, or nearly 90 percent, were from two-party or weak two-party states as defined by David G. Pfeiffer.[25] There were no candidates for office in either party in modified one-party Republican and one-party Republican states and only five in modified one-party Democratic and one-party Democratic states.

Of those who ran for these same four offices but lost, the same pattern prevailed. Of the fifty-four candidates who ran, forty-six (85 percent) ran in two-party or weak two-party states, while only nine (15 percent) were

Lt. Governor		Auditor		State Judge		State Senator		State Rep.	
D	R	D	R	D	R	D	R	D	R
6	0	2	0	2	3	5	12	6	7
4	2	2	1	0	2	2	1	1	1
10	2	4	1	2	5	7	13	7	8

on the ballot in modified one-party or one-party states, and all but one of them were Democratic. Of the total of ninety-nine who ran for high office, eighty-six (87 percent) were from weak two-party or two-party states. It might be hypothesized, therefore, that the state chairmen see the party headship as a viable stepping-stone to elective office. These chairmen are not serving as ticket fillers but are principally party officers in competitive two-party states and apparently view the chairmanship as a true launching pad where they can build upon their statewide party contacts and name identification in their quest for higher office.

One Republican governor, who had served for three years as state chairman just prior to announcing for office, stated:

I had not intended to run for office when I accepted the job as chairman. To tell the truth, other chairmen in ——— had not fared too well at the polls. But as the time came to think about a candidate for governor, I was faced with two facts that I felt were important enough to warrant seriously considering running myself. First, the only candidate to announce was a nice guy who would be a total flop as a candidate, and secondly, I was asked to run

Table 2.8   High-Office Seekers Classified by Party Competition type, 1962–72

Office	One-Party Democrat	Modified One-Party Democrat	Weak Two-Party Democrat
Elected			
Governor	0	0	1
U.S. senator	0	1	2
U.S. representative	1	2	0
State constitutional officer	1	0	2
Totals	2	3	5
Defeated			
Governor	0	3	3
U.S. senator	0	0	2
U.S. representative	3	1	1
State constitutional officer	1	0	0
Total	4	4	6
Grand total	6	7	11

NOTE: Party competition system developed by David G. Pfeiffer, "The Measurement of Inter-party Competition and Systemic Stability" *American Political Science Review* 61 (June 1967):457–67.

by a group of state legislators who were concerned about the top of the ticket. I really began to think about it then and, quite frankly, got the bug. I decided to put out some trial balloons and generally received a favorable reaction—I might say, in fact, a highly favorable reaction. My friends noted that I had been a good state chairman, was rather widely known in the party throughout the state, and had no major weaknesses. I decided in February to make the race.

This was typical of the thinking that often went into the decisions to run. Collectively, the chairmen had been selected as party leaders, suggesting that they were personally impressive (1) to the party officers or (2) to a governor who had selected them for ratification. They had been in office for an average of two and one-half years, which had given them an opportunity to travel widely and to broaden their acquaintanceship throughout the party structure. Some, but not all, had impressive successes in electing candidates to office during their tenure and basked in the glow of a successful chairmanship. A few had consolidated their positions with the limited party patronage available. And, finally, they were

Two-Party	Weak Two-Party Republican	Modified One-Party Republican	One-Party Republican
2	1	0	0
7	0	0	0
8	5	0	0
12	0	0	0
29	6	0	0
9	0	0	0
14	0	0	0
8	1	0	0
8	0	0	0
39	1	0	0
68	7	0	0

likely to know the sources of money in the party so that their major financing was often assured prior to their announcement.

There is little with which to compare this record of candidacy. The fact is, however, that almost one-fourth of all the chairmen who served between 1962 and 1972 were able to win their party's nomination, and forty-five of them were successful in winning election to the top elected positions in their states.

The Characteristics of Party Leaders

It is reasonably easy to describe the social and career characteristics of state chairmen. On the whole, they do not differ markedly from other groups of political leaders. They are generally white, moderately young, successful, and well educated. Just as is the case with state legislators, some are full time and some are part time. There is nothing startlingly different about the ways in which they became active in politics, although at this particular stage in their careers they have opted for "administrative" political office as opposed to "policy-oriented" elective office. A significant portion go on to run for (and often win) elective office once their service as chairman is completed. It is the area of leadership responsibilities that poses the greatest problem in determining their impact on state party organizations and the political system.

As noted earlier, Ranney and Kendall distinguish three distinct connotations for the term *leader:* (1) personal attainments compared to some unidentified set of values and standards against which measurement can be made; (2) status deference as measured by the respect of colleagues or contemporaries; and (3) performance stimuli as determined by the ability to meet the responsibilities of the positions.[26] That these three criteria for "effective leadership" are not mutually exclusive attests to the obvious. Despite general lack of standards, it is apparent in working with the state chairmen that those who can be described as true leaders generally meet all three criteria.

It is dangerous to designate by name certain chairmen as *real* or *effective* party leaders because they *seem* to fit these descriptive criteria. There are too many intangibles, and the values applied to them are far from definitive. Nevertheless, numerous chairmen clearly do serve as true leaders of their respective parties. Some meet the requirements of leadership because they work with a governor or leading party figure who wants them to *lead* and who lends the prestige of his elective office to their efforts. It would be folly to attempt to unravel the many strands that go toward explaining those types of relationships. Some chairmen are placed in a position with vast opportunities to exercise *true* leadership because of the nature of their party in relationship to the opposition party. These are sometimes accidents of political history. In short, it is impossible to determine why one chairman emerges as a "leader" and another as a "holder of the office." In considering those who could be described as possessing traits of "leadership," it is clear (in a subjective sense) that they do possess qualities of "clear purposefulness," the ability to stimulate "the creative abilities of associates and subordinates," and "a sense of public interest." [27]

Nevertheless, even those who possess the requisite leadership traits are often unable to make their mark on the state party. Change flows from time, and many of those elected to state party office do not remain in power sufficiently long to make an impact. One of the principal problems facing state party organizations is the brevity of many party leaders' terms in office.

3 Length of Service: The Problem of Tenure

As you know, the average state chairman
has been in office for one year.
A western state chairman

Something must be done to increase the
length of time the chairmen are in office. It
is now only eighteen months on the average
in the Republican party, and I understand
the Democrats are even worse.
A midwestern state chairman

I am having to resign next week in order to
tend to my business. I have been in office
for a year and a half and even that, I understand, is considered to be a long time.
A western state chairman

State party organizations, if they are to
prosper, must overcome some challenging problems. One of them arises
from the remarkably short tenure enjoyed by state party chairmen. The
rapid turnover of chairmen in many states has been deleterious to the development of stronger parties. To bring about stronger party organizations,
a number of components are essential. First, the party leaders should
be of an energetic temperament determined to bring about change. The
degree to which this determination is present often depends upon the
attitudes of the governor, especially in those states where the chairman
serves as his agent. Gubernatorial support, or tacit concurrence, is usually necessary in those parties if the chairmen is to mount a successful
building campaign. Chairmen elected independently, whether of the party
in or out of power, may have a better chance of success since they are
not as likely to be responsible to an elected public leader.

45

Secondly, the flow of money must be assured. With few exceptions those organizations which have been successful in improving grass-roots and headquarters operations have had an assured regular income flow. This kind of financial insurance is important if the chairman is to be allowed the freedom to concentrate on organizational rather than budgetary matters.

Within the context of this discussion, the third component is the most important. The chairman, and his aides, must have sufficient time to plan and to carry out the objectives which they have set for themselves. This, unfortunately, is the shoal upon which many organizational efforts founder. As has been widely noted, the tenure of the average state chairman is considerably truncated. Indeed, the short tenure of party chairmen may be the most serious detriment to building an effective party organization.

Length of Service of State Chairmen

During the thirteen-year period between January 1962 and December 1974, there were 516 state chairmen in both parties. The Republicans had 270 chairmen while the Democrats had 246. In order to determine the average length of service for these individuals, each chairman's term was converted into months in order to arrive at a mean average. When the average for all 270 Republicans is computed for the twelve-year period, it shows a mean average tenure of two years, nine months. The average Democratic term was slightly longer at three years, one month. During the period under consideration, however, several chairmen in both parties served extraordinarily long terms which had the effect of skewing the mean. Republicans Harry Rosenzweig (Arizona 1965–75), Victor Smith (Illinois 1960–73), and Clarke Reed (Mississippi 1966–75) all served for at least ten years during the period covered by this analysis. As has been noted before, John Bailey, Connecticut Democratic chairman from 1946 to 1975, was in office during the entire period, and James Ronan (Illinois 1952–73) and James Peeler (Tennessee 1961–73) served for at least ten years during that period. When these six exceptionally lengthy terms are excluded from the calculation, the mean average drops to two years, seven months in both parties.

Furthermore, 60 percent of the Republican chairmen in office in mid-1975 began their terms after June 1973, and twenty of them were elected in the first six months of 1975. This sort of rapid change has led to a widespread belief in both parties that the turnover of state chairmen is even greater than it really is. But some of those with the greatest seniority in their positions have been in office a sufficiently long time to produce the average two years, seven months tenure over the more extended period of time.

Chairmen do not leave office because they are forced to by law. Only three state parties forbid the chairman to succeed himself after his first term. The remaining party by-laws either permit reelection or remain silent.[1] One of those states where regular rotation is required is California. The by-laws of both parties in that state forbid immediate reelection to the post beyond the initial two-year term. One Democratic chairman, Charles Manatt, served one term from 1971 to 1973 and was elected for another two-year term in 1975.

In the Republican party there is seldom ever a contest for state chairman, since the vice-chairman almost always succeeds to the post. The real conflict, therefore, is over the vice-chairmanship, which is the customary stepping stone to party control two years hence. The 1971 election described by the *Sacramento Bee* is typical:

Dennis Carpenter is expected to be succeeded by Putnam Livermore of San Francisco at tomorrow's [Republican] committee election. Livermore is uncontested for the post.

Bitter rivalry has developed, however, in the race for the vice-chairmanship. Gordon C. Luce, 45, San Diego savings and loan company president; and Clifford R. Anderson, Jr., 42, Pasadena attorney, are the candidates.[2]

Luce went on to win election as vice-chairman and was elevated to the chairmanship two years later, just as Carpenter had been elected vice-chairman two years before assuming the chairmanship. Some contend that there are distinct advantages to the nonsuccession rule. It does provide fresh leadership on a regular basis, and it enables the prospective chairman to serve an apprenticeship as vice-chairman before assuming the higher office. Critics point out, however, that the disadvantages often carry more weight. For instance, it is not uncommon in the California Republican party to elect a moderate to one office while selecting a conservative for the other, even though the ideologies of the two top officers sometimes prevent them from working effectively together. Furthermore, as one long-time GOP figure noted during an interview: "A couple of times over the years we have elected a vice-chairman who proved to be a poor choice. We always ended up electing him as chairman two years later even though we knew there were better men available. No one wants to violate the tradition."

This lament applies equally to both parties in California. In recent years both the Democrats and Republicans have been forced to discontinue the services of strong and effective party chairmen who were willing to continue serving but were forced aside by the nonsuccession rule. The consequences, however, are probably no more dire than in other states which legally permit the chairman to succeed himself. In many of them, natural attrition effectively limits the term to approximately two years regardless of greater legal flexibility. Nevertheless, many party leaders believe that a nonsuccession rule is unnecessarily self-limiting and that a talented chairman should be permitted the option of remaining in office if he should choose to continue his service.

The abbreviated tenure of state chairmen is primarily a product of resignation. When a chairman resigns prematurely (or voluntarily relinquishes the office), it is often difficult to determine the real factors which contributed to that decision. Resignations occur for a wide variety of reasons. Some popular chairmen terminate their service at the height of their prestige. Their departure is usually noted with genuine regret. Others have been participants in long intraparty controversies, and their leaving is openly greeted with expressions of relief. In either event public explanations are often at variance with actual facts.

From the beginning of 1969 through 1972 there were 108 resignations, excluding those who were automatically retired by term limitations. Of that number it was possible to determine the factors which brought about 82 (76 percent) of the resignations. The remaining 24 percent left office without making a public statement or furnishing any reason for their determination to step down.

Two sources of information were available to help explain the reasons for voluntary retirements. First, all respondents were asked to comment on the rapid turnover in the office, both in their own states and across the nation. Most of them had noted the high rate of turnover of chairmen, and the judgments which emerged were both impressionistic and informative. Responses ranged from simple explanations—for example, "he resigned to run for office"—to long discursive explorations of intraparty squabbling which ultimately led to the chairman's departure.

A second important source of information was provided by a substantial collection of news clippings covering every major daily newspaper in the nation and extending over a period of one and one-half years. Most news stories included statements from the outgoing chairman as to his reasons for leaving. Many papers published analytical background pieces, usually written by political editors and professing to offer the "inside" version of the change in party command.

Voluntary retirement, as used here, means that it was initiated by the incumbent chairman on his own volition, the decision to resign being an individual one based on personal motives. Political pressures, so far as it could be determined, were not responsible for these retirements. As shown in table 3.1, voluntary resignations occurred for a variety of reasons. Some incumbents resigned in order to run for or be appointed to public office. Others left office to serve as campaign managers for major office seekers. Most were forced out by unanticipated personal and/or financial problems.

Involuntary resignations were initiated by others. They often culminated a factional fight in which the incumbent's side lost. Also included as resigning involuntarily were a few chairmen who sought reelection but were defeated. Some of these defeats could be attributed to party factionalism, but others resulted from a party judgment that the incumbent was not competent to continue in office. They were involuntary in the sense that the chairman sought to remain in power but without success.

Throughout the interview phase of this study, a persistent theme recurred. The topic of the most widespread concern in party circles was the shortness of the average state chairman's term. Governors, national committee personnel, and the chairmen themselves, all expressed concern over the effects of limited tenure on state party affairs. Their concerns

Table 3.1   Voluntary or Involuntary Resignation or Retirement of State Chairmen, 1969–72, (N82)

	Democrats	Republicans	Total
Voluntary resignation or retirement			
Personal or financial problems	8	8	16
Appointment to public office	5	10	15
Decision to run for public office	4	8	12
Campaign management	4	2	6
Other	6	8	14
Total	27	36	63
Involuntary resignation, retirement, or contested defeat	9	10	19
Total	36	46	82

were not with great issues such as building responsible parties. They were more elementary than that. Their interest was in continuity and in achieving immediate goals. The problem of premature resignation was perceived to be of such great moment that it need be addressed in some detail.

Voluntary Resignation or Retirement:
Personal and Financial Problems

As is true of any person holding a new position of responsibility, the state chairman must use his initial months in office for "learning." Under the best of circumstances a new chairman must broaden his range of acquaintances, determine which of his colleagues are reliable and competent, plan his programs, and seek by whatever means are available to unravel the tough and knotty problems of party politics. If he is an agent of the governor he must do all of these things while providing partisan back-up support. Those who are elected independently, whether from the in- or out-party, will often have even greater responsibilities based on their greater autonomy. An activist chairman needs time to communicate the excitement of his mission. But time is one of the elements not allotted to him in generous amounts. The brief term enjoyed by the average chairman does not provide sufficient opportunity for him to stamp the political party with his personal imprimatur.

Sixteen resignations of the eighty-two accounted for were forced by personal circumstances. Generally speaking, there were four causes cited for voluntary retirement or resignation: (1) an unexpectedly costly expenditure of time away from the means of livelihood; (2) financial burdens imposed by party necessities on personal resources; (3) frustrations associated with attempts to mold the party to one's own program planning; and (4) deteriorating family life. Resignation usually followed a personal assessment of the alternatives open to the chairman.

Although some chairmen are full time and are paid, most assume their party responsibilities on a part-time basis. The only thread of commonality noted among these sixteen was that two-thirds of them were part time and unpaid. In spite of that tradition, they often discovered that their full time was required as operating head of the party. The personal consequences were often disastrous.

One Republican chairman from a western state was interviewed on the day he resigned. His lament was a familiar one:

It takes so much more time than most men who take the job expect. It takes a very wealthy man or a man with absolutely nothing to do to be able to spend the time and the money necessary to do a good job. Once the man gets the job, he finds out how time consuming it is and has to get out or have his business or profession ruined. When the profits of my ——— company began to slide, I knew I had to get back to take care of it.

Another cited the losses to his law firm caused by his absences. The partners in the firm, after two years, asked him to resign from the firm or from the party chairmanship. For obvious reasons he chose to retain his law partnership and relinquish the unpaid position of chairman.

Several chairmen resigned because of substantial drains on their personal financial resources. In every case these were well-to-do individuals who were well aware of the general expectation that they would contribute to keeping the party afloat. One Republican noted that he spent $60,000 of his own money during his first four years in office. In spite of considerable wealth, the burden finally became too great and he tendered his resignation. Another Republican paid the salary of the secretary to the party amounting to $10,000 a year. After two years he concluded that the honor wasn't worth the sacrifice. A Democrat who resigned after one year in office did so because:

I spent $6,000 of my own money just to keep the party going during the past year, and the damage to my business because of my frequent absences is incalculable. I never dreamed the costs would be so high. Not only that, no one really sympathized with me. It was almost like they picked me because they knew I had the money to carry on the party.

Some newly elected chairmen enter office with few ideas and no plans. It is their intent to serve as caretakers of an ongoing organization. Others, however, campaign for the post, or are selected for it, because they hope to develop innovative organizational programs which will "get the party moving again." They were sometimes disappointed. Some parties are led by established cadres who do not want to change the status quo. They respond to prodding by the chairman by rejecting his proposed changes or ignoring them. This ultimately leads to a level of frustration which results in his resignation.

Wiley Wasden, elected Republican chairman of Georgia in mid-1969, resigned in January 1971 after the state executive committee voted eleven to seven to defeat a reorganization plan he had sponsored. Wasden's plan

called for the hiring of a Washington consultant for two years to help
reorganize the state party and to raise funds. The executive committee
reportedly attempted to reach a compromise on a one-year contract to
be approved by the state central committee, but Wasden considered the
matter a vote of no-confidence and resigned.[3]

A Democratic chairman resigned after fifteen months in office charg-
ing that he was unable to accomplish his major goal of putting the party
on a pay-as-you-go basis:

> I wanted to put together a permanent means of financing the party
> through small contributions. Unfortunately, all my plans were contingent on
> approval of the state committee. The national committeeman didn't want to
> approve the plan because he was convinced that it would undercut the influ-
> ence of labor in the party. He felt that a successful contributors' plan would
> make the candidates less dependent on labor, and he believes that the union
> people are the backbone of the party.... He persuaded the committee to
> turn down my plan and I had no alternative but to resign. I had staked every-
> thing on having enough money to operate with and being out from under the
> yoke of the union bosses, and that just wasn't to be.... This is a very frus-
> trating job.

The frustration is not always based on a reluctance to act. Three
chairmen noted during interviews that their honeymoon with the governor who selected them did not last out their full term. In fact, two of
them were not on speaking terms with the governor although they
headed the party which elected him. Political events or policy disagreements had eroded their support and had caused the previously close relationship to deteriorate. Internal controversies of this kind are often carried on inside the party and are not widely noted, although occasionally
a clash will be fought in the newspapers and other public forums. In each
of these three cases the incumbent chairman decided to ride out the controversy to the end of his term. In other such instances, however, the
chairman resigns quietly, offering no explanation for his action.

Finally, a few chairmen resigned because of deteriorating family life.
Long hours, financial sacrifice, and public controversy take their toll.
One chairman was threatened with divorce, and others were simply unable to adjust to constant separation from wives and children. Resignation offered the only alternative to family suffering.

Voluntary Resignation: Seeking Public Office and Managing Campaigns

Between 1969 and 1972 almost half the chairmen who resigned did so in order to run for or be appointed to public office. As was noted in chapter 2, the chairmanship is an important stepping-stone to higher office. From 1962 to 1974, 36 percent of the chairmen ran for office after serving in their party position. The three years included in this analysis of the cause of resignation found twenty-seven chairmen resigning to run for or be appointed to higher public office. Twice as many Republicans as Democrats ran for office, probably because the first term of the Nixon presidency provided the extra incentive for them to move into the electoral arena. The offices sought included governor, U.S. senator, lieutenant governor, and, at the lower echelon, county executive officer.*

Appointments made at the state level included the state public utilities commission and secretary of transportation. Those at the national level included several subcabinet posts and some federal judgeships. Republicans were the beneficiaries since their party controlled the White House.

Six chairmen of the eighty-two resigned to become campaign managers for others. One, John Burns of New York, resigned to assume a management position in the 1972 Lindsay-for-President campaign, while the other five joined state campaigns for governor or senator. Fourteen resignations were attributed to a variety of other causes. These ranged from general frustration with the job of chairman to personal legal difficulties which, in a few instances, resulted in convictions for felonies and misdemeanors.

Most chairmen enter office with a conviction of capability. They feel that they are fully prepared to meet the challenges of the job. Most of those who resigned voluntarily could have completed uninterrupted terms. But, unlike any other political office, the state chairman is expected to lead although limited in available time and funds. The rapid turnover caused by a taxing resignation rate and the fact that most of the chairmanships are unpaid puts the state party leader in a class by himself. Resignations from public office are relatively rare; once elected, officials

* In 1974 alone at least fifteen state chairmen or former chairmen ran for high office. Ten Democrats and five Republicans ran for either governor or member of Congress. One, John Burton, Democrat of California, was elected to the House of Representatives to fill an unexpired term. The development of the state chairmanship as a stepping-stone to elected office continues.

serve out their terms. Unpaid public offices are even rarer; the availability of salary and expense money is an important factor in decisions to run. The state chairman, however, is expected to serve as banker, coach, referee, psychiatrist, manager, father-confessor, and executioner, often without pay and sometimes at his own expense. Many conclude that resignation or retirement is an attractive alternative.

Paid vs. Unpaid Party Chairmen: A Continuing Controversy

If lengthening the chairman's time in office is essential to effective party operations, it behooves us to consider those matters which stimulate premature resignation. As we have seen, an important factor in restricting the terms served is the personal cost involved. Most chairmen are unpaid. Even those who receive a salary, however, often face a severe personal financial drain. The question of paid vs. unpaid chairmen is the subject of considerable controversy within the political parties. The debate has gained momentum in recent years as more parties have moved to pay their chairman.

The number of parties moving to a system of paid chairmen has increased rapidly since 1961. In that year only eight Republican and five Democratic parties paid their chairmen. By 1974 this number had grown to fourteen Republican and thirteen Democratic party organizations or 34 percent of the total.[4] The number of paid chairmen in the Republican party had almost doubled in that ten-year period, while those in the Democratic party had nearly tripled (table 3.2). Only one state party had formally ceased to pay its chairman after having done so previously.

Annual salaries ranged from $8,000 to $35,000 in the Republican party and from $10,000 to $30,000 in the Democratic. The mean salary for the Republicans in 1974 was $19,142; for the Democrats, $17,769. The movement to salaried state chairmen has been attributed to the

Table 3.2 Comparison of Paid State Chairmen by Party, 1961–73

	1961		1973*	
	N	%	N	%
Republicans	8	16	14	34
Democrats	5	10	13	33

* These figures include four parties which provide a salary but had been unable to pay the stipend because of a perilous financial situation.

greater professionalization of party politics, much of which occurred during the decade of the sixties. As one long-time Republican chairman explained the phenomenon:

You must realize that the early 1960s were a period of political ferment in both parties. Kennedy was in the White House, and people were impressed with the personal organization that put him there. Yet the Republicans controlled many of the larger states with an incredible number of nationally known governors such as Rockefeller, Reagan, Scranton, Volpe, Smylie, Rhodes, Love, and others. Many of those governors were proponents of professional politics. They believed in and used polls, computers, and mass advertising. They bought as many of the accouterments of modern campaigning as they could afford. Because of that . . . it was necessary to have a party chairman who could devote long hours and full time to the job. The old system of part-time politics no longer seemed to be so attractive in many states.

In spite of the substantial movement to paid chairmen, the subject remains a matter of considerable controversy within the party systems. Opponents argue that service as the party chairman should be a citizen's responsibility. They argue that the party should spend its money on practical politics: campaign materials, opinion polls, and improved staffing. Some contend that paying the chairman causes difficulties in fund raising. As one put it: "How can you go to people in the party and ask for money to run your campaigns if they know that it is going into someone's pocket? We appeal to our party workers to donate their time and money, and then we turn around and pay the chairman for his time."

In 1971, Francis Esposito, Democratic chairman of Vermont, argued against inaugurating the practice of paying the state chairman. If the post were a paid one, he said, "the job would then be nothing more than a political plum. Whoever was chairman would be looking to his job and he would cater to those who picked up the freight. . . . He would create more friction between factions of the party. He would promote the people who pay his salary." [5]

A Minnesota Republican active in several gubernatorial campaigns advocated returning to the system of part-time, unpaid chairmen. State Senator Paul Overgaard, in an interview with a local newspaper, suggested that a chairman could do a better job of providing leadership if he didn't have the post on a full-time basis. He proposed that the party select an unpaid, part-time chairman but move to hire a full-time, paid executive secretary who would be responsible for the day-to-day mechanical operations of the state party office. "It is difficult for a full-time paid chairman to speak up and provide leadership," he added, "because such a chairman is in effect an employee." [6]

On the other hand, those advocating the move to full-time, paid party leadership contend that the greater technical needs of party management require the selection of men and women of high caliber who understand the modern professional techniques necessary to modern party politics. One of them noted that

It is really hard to watch us spend thousands of dollars every year to do the kind of job we want to do in polling, data processing, and improved fund raising when you pick some county chairman to lead you and he doesn't know a poll from a warthog. Paid chairmen are a good investment because you have a broader pool from which to select your talent and because you are much more likely to get a guy who understands professional management.

The argument for a "citizen" chairman is invalid, the proponents argue, because it restricts the choice of chairman to those who are wealthy and who can afford the time away from their means of livelihood. This, in turn, is often responsible for the rapid turnover in chairmen who discover that they are needed to prevent a decline in their own personal fortunes. One proponent of salaried chairmen noted that "unpaid chairmen are often more beholden to outside interests and are subject to greater pressures from powerful people who like to dabble in party politics." If true, some parties exacerbate the problem by even failing to reimburse party leaders for out-of-pocket expenses.

Twenty-five percent of the state political parties do not pay the chairman's personal expenses. Sometimes the effect is to make the cost of holding office so great that the pool of available talent is narrowed to those who are wealthy or who simultaneously hold a state patronage position. Furthermore, the cost of serving has increased with the recent development of the state chairmen's associations and the addition of the chairmen to full membership in the national committees. These groups ordinarily meet at least twice each year, and most of the chairmen attend and take part. They are expected to attend regional party meetings as well. Travel expenses are considerable, and routine day-to-day expenses add to the burden. Expense budgets range from $2,000 to $10,000 annually and are reimbursed upon presentation of receipts.

Most parties, seeking greater professionalism, have employed an executive director to manage the headquarters and assist the chairman in his political and administrative chores. This began on a large scale somewhat earlier than the move to paid chairmen. By 1973, 66 percent of the parties (R, 78 percent; D, 54 percent) employed a full-time director. Characteristically they averaged forty years of age and more than half were college graduates. Salaries normally fell within a range of $10,000 to $15,000, although a few made less than $10,000 and one made $29,000.

Executive directors/secretaries were recruited from a wide variety of backgrounds. Most of them had been employees of other political organizations or were practicing journalists (both print and electronic), but a substantial number were from the world of business. Students were also popular choices, particularly those with experience in practical politics.

Of those executive directors in office in 1973, one-half had served less than one year. Only 9 percent had served for five or more years. Four party chairmen had been elected to office directly from positions as their party's executive director.* Of those who had served for less than one year, approximately one-half were the first to hold the position of executive director in their party. That suggests that there is indeed a trend toward permanent, full-time, paid managers to maintain headquarters and serve as aides to the elected chairmen regardless of whether he is full or part time or paid or unpaid.

Clearly, state party staffing is becoming more professionalized. Not only are more chairmen paid salaries than ever before, but more parties are experimenting with the employment of full-time assistants for them. A few of these men are little more than personal secretaries to the chairman, but most occupy central positions in the organization and some serve as alter egos to their chairmen. According to a survey of state headquarters carried out by the Republican National Committee in 1969, over half had also employed full- or part-time finance directors and public relations aides, adding further emphasis to the picture of increasing professionalism emerging in state political organizations.[7]

Through these efforts, the parties have attempted to make the leadership more attractive in order to broaden the base of potential candidates. The overall effect of these professional enhancements is impossible to measure. However, it seems likely that the out-parties particularly have been able to appeal to a broader group of potential chairmen than would have been possible had there been no salary, expenses, or administrative assistance. Of those who acknowledged that the availability of salary was

---

* A number of major officeholders in the United States previously served as their state party's executive director. One of the best known is Senator George McGovern who was executive secretary of the South Dakota Democratic party in the early 1950s.

a factor in their decision to accept office, all were serving in parties which were out of power.

Debate over the payment of salaries has largely been between those who support greater "professionalism" and those who view party leadership as a civic duty. Subjectively, it would appear that the emoluments offered have attracted individuals to office who might not otherwise have agreed to serve.

Involuntary Resignation

Involuntary resignation or retirement is usually a manifestation of intra-party politics and external political events at high levels. For definitional purposes these retirements include: (1) those who resign under fire in midterm; (2) those who reluctantly decide not to seek reelection because of widespread intraparty opposition; and (3) those who seek reelection but are defeated by a nonincumbent.

Approximately one-fourth of the resignations during the 1969–74 period were involuntary ones (table 3.1). One of the recognized stakes in the political game is control over the party chairmanship. But bruising party battles, election losses, ideological conflicts, and loss of a gubernatorial sponsor can create situations which make an incumbent's continuance in office untenable. Such resignations are almost always a sign of considerable internal party turmoil. Sometimes the incumbent chairman is at the vortex of the conflict. Others, however, are the innocent victims of forces beyond their control. In any event, resignation offers them the only way they can gracefully exit.

It is not uncommon for a chairman who has presided over the party at the time of a major election defeat to be forced out of office. It goes without saying that some candidates must lose. If the losses are normal and expected, the party leadership usually survives unscathed. Clarke Reed, the Republican chairman of Mississippi, has presided over a nascent party that has enjoyed few victories, but he has remained in office since 1966. If, on the other hand, defeats are widespread and come as a surprise, the chairman may become a victim, rightly or wrongly, of the leadership group's search for a scapegoat.

Immediately after the 1970 loss of both congressional seats and the governorship, the Republican chairman of South Dakota, Charles Howard, was under considerable fire from within his party. Many blamed Howard for the losses, saying that he was "not forceful enough" during the campaign. Howard withstood the pressure for several months before leaving office. He acknowledged that he "considered resigning immediately after the elections" but did not because "the party was in a state of shock." [8]

The defeat of an incumbent governor will often trigger events which ultimately lead to the resignation of the chairman who served him as a political agent. A New England Democrat described his political demise in this way:

> The governor picked me two years ago, and it was widely known that I was his man. I did much of his political dirty work and I managed his campaign for reelection. He was overconfident, refused to listen, and ran a low-key campaign. He lost badly and I lost with him. Without his support there was no way they would reelect me, so after assessing the votes, I declined to run again.

Dan Lynch, elected Colorado Democratic chairman in 1969, lost his bid for reelection in 1971 as a result of the charges of an opposition faction that he had not administered the party well and had been an absentee chairman. Although Lynch served full time and was paid a salary of $15,000 per year, during his term he became a popular speaker and panelist at national and regional party meetings discussing an innovative fund-raising program he had devised. His opponents acknowledged that his fund-raising efforts were successful but charged that the party's headquarters operation was burning up most of the newly generated contributions and had accumulated a $20,000 deficit. Although Lynch ran for reelection he was unable to overcome his critics and was defeated.

Ideological rifts occasionally are responsible for a chairman's resignation. The most widely noted of these in the late 1960s was that of Ody Fish, widely respected chairman of the Wisconsin Republicans. At the time of his unexpected departure he was serving as chairman of the National Conference of State Party Chairmen. His resignation was believed to be a result of ideological infighting. The *Washington Post* reported that the resignation of Fish "was widely regarded as a rupture between liberals and conservatives in the [Wisconsin] party ranks." Fish, who had been reelected without opposition only five months earlier, was quoted as saying only that "he was weary from his party duties." [9] Wisconsin Republicans, however, described a widening gap in party ranks caused by the successful efforts of conservative Republican legislators to curb moderate Republican Governor Warren P. Knowles' proposed spending programs. Fish was a close personal friend and political ally of Knowles.

Finally, from 1969 to 1974 two state chairmen, one Republican and one Democrat, resigned after being indicted. One pleaded guilty to negligent homicide involving a fatal automobile accident, and the other pleaded guilty to charges of bribery and extortion after admitting that, while an officer of the state, he demanded and received a $20,000 payment from a construction company seeking a state contract. Another Republican resigned after an arrest for speeding, but he was already under fire because of numerous controversies surrounding his business firm. Another Democrat resigned after a number of controversial stock deals came to light resulting in fifteen persons being indicted. The chairman himself was not indicted on felony charges but was named a defendant in a civil damage suit brought by stockholders of an enterprise in which he was alleged to have been involved.

These were unfortunate and isolated events. Most resignations result from more mundane internal political events. Let us look more closely at two representative examples of involuntary departures from leadership positions.

Factional Democratic Politics in Kentucky

In June 1971, Shelby Kinkead resigned as Democratic state chairman of Kentucky after having served only six months. He was replaced by J. R. Miller, who had been his predecessor, having served as chairman from 1967 to April 1971. The story behind this switch from one man to another and back is illustrative of the events which lead to involuntary resignations.

Malcolm E. Jewell and Everett W. Cunningham note that Kentucky meets two of the criteria of bifactionalism as used by V. O. Key, Jr., in *Southern Politics*.[10] Most of the vote in Democratic primaries is usually divided between two candidates, and the winning proportion is seldom more than 50 percent. Kentucky comes closer to meeting both of these criteria than any other state included in Key's work.[11] There appears to by some disagreement between scholars who have dissected Kentucky politics as to what constitutes the party factions. Jewell and Cunningham maintain that "the factional conflict is not between classes or regions or between urban and rural voters. . . . The difference between the factions often seems to be simply a difference between those in power and those who are seeking power."[12] John Fenton, however, argues that "the basic division within the Democratic party in Kentucky is between the rural folk and the Eastern Kentucky urban and Bourbon people."[13]

The nature of the factions is of little concern here, but the recognition of them as semipermanent determinants in Kentucky politics is, since their existence helps to explain the repeated changes in Democratic state chairmen. There were six changes in the chairmanship between 1961 and 1971, if J. R. Miller is counted twice, providing an average tenure of one year, six months, considerably below the national average. Kentucky Democratic factionalism has been largely a result of clashes between two prominent party leaders since the mid-1940s—A. B. (Happy) Chandler and Earle Clements. The political descendants of these two were the active participants in the 1971 conflict.

In 1959 Lieutenant Governor Harry Waterfield, running with Chandler's support, lost his bid for governor to Bert Combs of the Clements faction. Combs selected Edward Breathett as his candidate for governor in 1963, and Breathett defeated Chandler in his bid for a third nonconsecutive term.* After Breathett's four years in office, Democratic hegemony temporarily ended in 1967 when his candidate for governor lost to Republican Louie Nunn. At the same time Democrat Wendell Ford, Combs' former administrative assistant, was elected lieutenant governor. By 1971, Combs and Ford had emerged as the two major rivals for the Democratic nomination for governor and, of course, as the two factional leaders.

As the highest ranking elected Democrat in the state in 1967, Lieutenant Governor Ford asked his campaign manager, J. R. Miller, to become state chairman. Miller was described by the *Louisville Courier Journal* as "one of the most powerful men in the Commonwealth of Kentucky . . . who instinctively knows how to propel a candidate to victory . . . what issues to stress . . . where to seek campaign funds" [14] He is a leading citizen of Owensboro, Kentucky, and is manager of an electric cooperative. He has been a key man behind the scenes of Kentucky politics for many years. He was active in the campaign to elect U.S. Senator Virgil Chapman almost thirty years ago and has put together a string of electoral successes since that time. During Ford's service as lieutenant governor, Miller occupied the state chairman's office until his 1971 resignation to manage Ford's campaign for governor. Miller and Ford were distressed when Miller was succeeded by Shelby Kinkead, an insurance executive and supporter of the Combs-Breathett faction. At that time

* Kentucky governors, other state constitutional officers, and some legislators are elected a year before the presidential election, while county officials and other legislators are elected a year after the presidential elections. This full calendar of elections results in almost constant campaigning for one office or another.

the state Democratic Central Committee was controlled by the Combs-Breathett group.

After a bitter primary Combs was defeated and Ford nominated, leaving the party chairmanship in the hands of Kinkead, now something of a lame duck without a political supporter as the Democratic gubernatorial nominee. Within one month Ford made it clear that he wanted Kinkead's resignation. According to Kinkead, as reported in the *Louisville Courier Journal,*

Ford told [me] May 27 that Ford was giving consideration to closing the Democratic Party headquarters in Frankfort. I stated that in my opinion it would be a serious mistake and that he, as victorious nominee for governor, together with the other nominees, could make full use of the headquarters and should participate in financing the operation. . . .

He [Ford] would make no commitment about finances and he suggested that I give consideration to resigning, as he expressed it, "in the interest of party unity."

In an attempt to leave no stone unturned to continue the operation of party headquarters, I called a meeting of the executive finance committee on Tuesday, June 8. . . . I was informed, in effect, at that meeting that no consideration would be given to financing the headquarters until I vacated the chairmanship. Certain members of the executive finance committee then called upon Mr. Ford and I was informed after their meeting that he was inflexible in his determination that I resign as chairman, going so far as to indicate he would seek a confrontation with me before the entire state Democratic Central Executive Committee.

I believe such a confrontation at a later date would be injurious to our Democratic Party, and, in light of this and the fact that no financial support for party headquarters would be forthcoming from the Ford campaign group if I remained in office, it was obvious that my effectiveness as chairman would be greatly diminished.

No matter how much I might question Mr. Ford's opinion as to the unifying effect my resignation might have on the [Democratic] Party, Mr. Ford is the nominee for governor, and, as such, has certain prerogatives, including the prerogative of making a mistake.

Many of my friends in the Democratic Party, both on the state central committee and outside the committee, urged me to retain the chairmanship. A canvass of committee membership indicated to me that I could have received sufficient votes to have remained in office, but in view of the foregoing and the fact that I would not want possible punitive action taken against those who would stand up for me, I made my decision to resign.[15]

On June 19, 1971, the Democratic State Central Committee elected J. R. Miller state chairman by unanimous vote. Miller again assumed the duties of the state chairmanship—but this time as a political agent of a Democratic governor.

This exchange of office between Kinkead and Miller illustrates a number of important factors which help to bring the position of state chairman into focus. Miller clearly personifies the role of Political Agent to the governor (to be described in chapter 4), a position he gained by serving as campaign manager. His return to power came about after Kinkead was forced out of office by the circumstances of electoral politics. Yet a factionalized state central committee, recognizing the strength of a newly elected governor and his desire to have a trusted colleague in control of the party machinery, voted unanimously for Miller's return to office. The relationship between the governor and the chairman is necessarily close. The governorship is the major political prize in Kentucky, and the winner is both the party and factional leader for four years. He is the recognized legislative leader and plays a major role in organizing the state convention and selecting the delegates to the national convention. The governor controls a considerable amount of contract and personnel patronage, which gives him leverage with local politicians. His need for a trusted political operative to control the party for him is manifest.

The chairman, on the other hand, is dependent upon the goodwill and the trust of the governor. He can never permanently bridge the fissures in the party, but he should be able to temporarily paper them over. He can only do that through the exercise of surrogate power derived from the governor. The Democratic state chairman of Kentucky, like numerous others in her sister states, blends power garnered in his own right with power generated directly through the governor's office. Democrats have usually been able to win the governorship in spite of the factional fights that they seem to enjoy so much. At some future date growing Republicanism, however, may force the Democrats to unify themselves if they are to successfully compete. When that time comes they may need a different kind of state chairman. A series of Republican governors might force the Democrats into a more competitive posture and would open the possibility that a more independent party chairman might emerge.

Effects of a Gubernatorial Defeat in Florida

The loss of a governorship is a severe blow to a political party. It immediately thrusts the party organization into a defensive posture and removes many of the perquisites of party power, such as patronage. The 1970 defeat of Florida Republican Governor Claude Kirk set in motion a party conflict which publicly centered around control of the state chairmanship but was in actual fact a competition for control of the party.

On January 9, 1971, the final scene in the political drama of G. Harrold Carswell was played out at the Florida Republican Executive Committee meeting in Orlando. On that day the Republican state chairmanship was captured by the supporters of former U.S. representative and Senate candidate William Cramer. The new state chairman, L. E. (Tommy) Thomas, Panama City automobile dealer, defeated incumbent Chairman "Duke" Crittenden of Orlando, who had the support of the factional alliance controlled by Senator Edward Gurney and former Governor Claude Kirk, Jr.

The factional fight developed out of the abortive attempt by Gurney and Kirk to nominate Carswell as the GOP senatorial candidate over Cramer, who was credited with virtually founding the Republican party in the state. Kirk had long been jealous of Cramer's power, and Gurney did not want to see a junior senator elected who might overshadow him in prestige.[16] Only a few days after the Senate refused to confirm Carswell's appointment to the Supreme Court, Gurney and Kirk persuaded him to file for the Senate nomination. Cramer, who had been urged to run by President Nixon, was infuriated, and even though he defeated Carswell by a two-to-one margin, he did not forgive Gurney and Kirk. After Cramer lost the Senate seat to Democrat Lawton Chiles, he went into private practice but retained influence with his followers and control over his position as a member of the Republican National Committee.

The 1971 meeting to elect a state chairman was the first formal confrontation between the two factions since the election. The behind-the-scenes intraparty struggle had, however, been going on for months. Duke Crittenden had been named party chairman in 1969 after the resignation of William Murfin who accepted a federal appointment from newly elected President Nixon. Crittenden's first year in office was relatively uneventful, but as the campaign for governor and senator warmed up in 1970 he became increasingly enmeshed in controversy between rival Republican candidates for both offices.

Accusations of favoritism by Kirk opponents broke into the open in midsummer when reports began circulating that Crittenden favored Kirk and was actively working for his renomination in spite of the fact that two other prominent Republicans were running in the primary. Although Crittenden denied the allegation, the criticism continued.

The chairmen of three major counties challenged a party headquarters poll of party officials as to how they would vote in the primaries for governor and senator. They told the press that the poll would be divisive and might be used against the anti-Kirk people and called upon Crittenden to explain his sponsorship of the poll.

In mid-September, Republican gubernatorial candidate Jack Eckerd distributed a half million campaign tabloids describing the Florida Republican party as bankrupt because "millions of dollars have been drained from party funds by the Governor in less than four years . . . ," a charge Crittenden dismissed as "a lie." [17] He responded that the state organization had never been in better financial condition and called on Eckerd to quit attacking the party. The effect of the episode, however, was to further convince many Republicans that Crittenden was an agent of Kirk and was aiding in his renomination campaign.

After Kirk's overwhelming defeat by Reubin Askew and Cramer's loss to Lawton Chiles, pressure mounted to purge the party of Kirk supporters—chiefly State Chairman Crittenden. One of the most prominent leaders of the anti-Crittenden move said, "The State Chairman must be tough and articulate enough to command the headlines with 'attack, attack and more attack' on the new Democratic administration. He should be a sort of Republican Governor in exile." [18]

These were the preliminaries to the January 9 Republican Executive Committee meeting where the Kirk-Gurney forces faced their opponents —the Cramer faction. In early December, Tommy Thomas challenged Crittenden and promised, if elected, to reunite the party, move party headquarters to Tallahassee, the capital, and open district headquarters around the state.[19]

When the committee meeting opened in Orlando the outcome was in doubt. Both candidates had the support of major Republican figures and appeared to have about equal support from the 134 delegates (two from each county). Thomas' supporters believed that their candidate was ahead but were fearful that last minute circuit court judicial appointments and other "midnight" appointments by Kirk would erode Thomas' support.

The first crucial vote was not on the candidates but was a move by the Thomas forces to get approval for a secret ballot on the election of chairman. Traditionally the chairman had been elected by roll-call vote—a tradition the Crittenden people hoped to maintain. The challengers, however, believed they would pick up support from waverers if the vote were a secret one. When Crittenden put the question of the secret vote, he ruled the voice vote as "nay." However, a demand for a roll call on the issue decisively reversed the chairman's call by a recorded vote of 80–40.[20] The secret vote on election of a chairman was then held, and Thomas unseated Crittenden 68–54. Senator Gurney immediately made a move toward unifying the two factions as did the outgoing and newly elected chairmen. Thomas announced that he was moving party headquarters from Orlando to Tallahassee, invited Gurney to address the luncheon meeting of the executive committee, and disclosed that he and Crittenden had agreed privately in advance that they would combine forces for party harmony regardless of the outcome.[21]

Thomas was in a position to assume the role of Independent Out-Party leader as described in the next chapter. He was elected over the active opposition of the leading incumbent Republican officeholder, Gurney, but his principal support came from a faction controlled by a nonincumbent and recently defeated party leader, Cramer. Duke Crittenden's loss of the state chairmanship on a vote of the executive committee was a good example of a contested defeat. Intraparty conflicts of this nature are often decided quietly in party councils. At times, however, the factional division is so great, and control of the party of such moment, that the action must be played out in public.*

The Impact of Chairman Turnover on State Parties

John S. Saloma and Frederick Sontag have noted that "a high rate of turnover in state party leaders means a loss of continuity in state parties but it also means that new groups can advance their own representatives and objectives rapidly, even to the point of taking over existing state party organizations." [22]

The two premises contained in this statement are true. There is certainly a significant loss of continuity in a state party system which changes

* Four years later, in January 1975, Thomas was defeated in a close election by William Taylor. The Gurney-Cramer controversy had been lost in the mists of Watergate and the indictment and retirement of Senator Gurney. Taylor, reportedly at the urging of Congressman Lou Frey of Orlando, ran on a platform calling for strengthening the party organization, establishing a system of field representatives, and bringing in new blood. Thomas was blamed by some for the Republican defeat in the 1974 elections.

chairmen on the average of once every two and one-half years. Furthermore, each change of chairman means that new individuals with different bases of support move into the political arena. The degree to which this is true varies from state to state; some organizations are so closed that the infusion of new blood is deliberately discouraged. Others, however, have shown a propensity for change, including support for an effective leadership cadre over a long period of time.

The chances for improved operations in a state organization are enhanced by the selection of active, intelligent, and imaginative state chairmen. Without assisting them with good party workers, adequate finances, and necessary power, however, even the best of choices will be unable to rescue a moribund party from the doldrums. That remains a problem to be addressed later.

Admittedly, the condition of the political parties at the state level is so varied as to defy generalization. Furthermore, there is no adequate means of measuring party effectiveness. Election victories may be a way to measure electoral success, but they do not provide a yardstick for organizational effectiveness. The poorest of organizations in a one-party state can manufacture election victories without difficulty. The truly effective party organization must be measured by the ease with which money is raised, the seriousness with which issues are presented, the care with which candidates are screened, and the energy devoted to the dispatch of voters to the polls. None of these attributes can be accomplished in many states until a more stable party leadership evolves. That kind of leadership cannot evolve unless party leaders are provided with the resources necessary to allow their continuance in office for a period of time which will permit them to accomplish their goals. The problem of short tenure was described succinctly by a western Republican leader who noted that the biographical handbook on national committee members was sewn and bound while that for the state chairman was loose-leaf.

As is shown in the next chapter, there is currently a wide variation in the type of state chairmanship that exists in the various state parties. Reinvigoration of the political party structures below the national level will depend upon a sure understanding of the power relationships which now exist.

4 Types of Party Leadership

I only do what I am told. If the governor
wants something done, then I do it. If he
doesn't want it done, I don't. It's as simple
as that. He is the boss.
A western state chairman

I have a good deal of independence. I really
work for the executive committee since we
do not have a governor. In fact, we don't
have much of anything in the way of elected
offices. People don't blame me for that,
though, since they all know what the
situation is.
A southern Republican state chairman

He [the state chairman] doesn't ask the
governor what he should do. He tells him
what he is going to do. He has hand-picked
two governors and got them nominated and
elected. They know how they got there.
An eastern national committeewoman

A former governor of a western state
remarked during an interview four years after his defeat:

In my opinion the state chairmanship is an anachronism and a holdover
from earlier days when party organization was more important and when
party leaders, such as the state chairman, had more grease in the form of
patronage and jobs to keep the party machinery moving effectively. During
my years as governor the state chairman has always been my hand-picked
man. I have had three of them. The first, Mr. ———, was my campaign
manager and was the most effective because I trusted him and used him. The
next two, ——— and ———, were chosen because they would be ineffective, and I wanted to be my own state chairman and have total control of the
party organization in my office. To accomplish this, I built an infrastructure
in the governor's office, along with some selected political supporters from

69

outside. These three or four staff men and political friends carried out my political chores for me. I truly believe that a strong governor must exercise control of his party and cannot leave that control to an individual elected by the county chairmen or the state committee, both made up of inactive amateurs in more cases than not.

Other party leaders in the state confirmed the governor's assessment of his state chairmen and the relationship which he maintained with them. One of the state chairmen also confirmed it but pointed out that the governor's subsequent defeat was, in his opinion, largely due to his reliance on close personal political operatives who were as removed from the organizational structure of the party as was the governor himself. It may be common practice for a governor to use the office of state chairman for personal benefit, but the relationship is usually more complex than that. Unlike the dichotomous in-party, out-party roles of the national chairmen, determined largely by the overwhelming presence of the presidential office, the state chairmen tend to be trichotomous. In this chapter we shall explore the variety of relationships which exist between the chairmen and other party and elected officials in the diverse systems which exist in the fifty states.

No effort has been expended by political scientists toward classifying state chairmanships, although considerable work has been done on party system classification. Party classification schemes have always been difficult because they encounter inherent problems of comparison according to economic, social, and historical variations. Differences among the states produce a series of varied party systems, and scholars have known too little about state election laws, organizational structures, political personnel, and the process of change to make meaningful comparisons.[1]

Role Classification

Role is a set of expectations for a person in a particular position. These expectations may change on the part of the political actor and on the part of those who react to him. The passage of time brings changes in attitudes, goals, and relationships. A new chairman must learn what his role is but may choose not to confine himself to the traditional pattern of expectations. Role learning is a process of political socialization, but as the party leader becomes more familiar and comfortable with his role, subtle changes in performance often take place. Thus, at any given time the role conception may differ when the actors remain the same.

Role classification relies extensively on in-depth interviews. In order to collect sufficient data for a classification scheme, this survey included four open-ended questions, to be answered by each of the eighty chairmen and chairwomen interviewed. They were:

I am interested in determining how you were selected to be state chairman. I realize that there is a formal election procedure, and I do want to know what it is. However, I also have been told by party officers that there is an informal selection procedure through which chairmen are chosen. Would you tell me just how your selection and appointment or election came about?

Would you describe for me your philosophy of party leadership? That is, do you view the party chairmanship as an office through which you can mold the party in some fashion; or do you believe that a chairman should follow the lead of some elected leader or the state committee?

How do you visualize the role of the state chairman in our party system? That is, do you see him as a mediator between party factions; a policy maker; a builder of party organization; spokesman for the governor or other elected party leader; a link between the national and local party organizations?

Please describe for me your relationship with the state committee; the governor; the county party chairmen; the state legislators of your party.

Sixty-nine of the eighty party systems presented a fairly consistent pattern of the role relationships between the party leaders, elected officials, and party organizations. The exceptions were parties which had just elected a governor for the first time in many years, thus providing the chairman with a new role as in-party leader. In a few instances, internal stability had been shattered by the election of a particularly dynamic and activist chairman whose appearance on the scene created tumultuous

Table 4.1   State Party Chairmen Classified by Role

	Democrats		Republicans		Total	
	N	%	N	%	N	%
Political Agent	13	33.3	13	31.7	26	32.5
In-Party Independent	11	28.2	13	31.7	24	30.0
Out-Party Independent	15	38.5	15	36.6	30	37.5
Total	39	100.0	41	100.0	80	100.0

change in a relatively short time. The classification difficulties were overcome by additional interviewing tempered by an element of subjectivity.

Three distinct types of role situation emerged from this analysis: the *Political Agent* who serves as the partisan arm of an incumbent governor; the *In-Party Independent* who exercises power in his own right and maintains his position regardless of who holds the governorship; and the *Out-Party Independent* who serves without an elected public leader and is recognized as *the* party leader. (See table 4.1.)*

In-Party and Out-Party Chairmen

The literature on national parties has viewed the role of the national chairman on an in-party/out-party power dimension. Control of the presidency has been the crucial determinant. Cotter and Hennessy devote an entire chapter to the role differences between the in-party and out-party national chairmen. They note that "How the national chairmen play their roles will be determined, in large part, by the presence or absence of a political superior in the White House." [2]

For the in-party there is no ambiguity of leadership, and the chairman does as he is told. The out-party leader, on the other hand, gains recognition by virtue of his position but may not exercise control simply by virtue of possessing the chairmanship. Even though he is the national chairman he may have to contend with competing leaders on Capitol Hill, the defeated presidential candidate, or important officeholders in major states. He, nevertheless, occupies a leadership vacuum with the possibility of becoming the "real" party leader.

Virtually nothing has been written regarding the in- and out-party

---

* It will no doubt be noted that I have not furnished a list of specific assignments of chairmen by name to the three categories. This was a conscious omission decided upon for two reasons: First, a number of respondents furnished me with extended and very frank interviews based upon my promise not to "embarrass" them by statements of direct attribution, some of which might alter their political relationships within their own party or state. A published list of types of chairmen, with a complete description of the criteria used for assignment to particular categories, might well do that, and I am constrained to avoid such compromising particulars. Secondly, in a few cases (not over four or five) changes occurred within the political fabric of particular states during the course of the interview period which, in effect, might have brought about a reclassification from one category to another. Party systems in the states today are quite fluid, and a few changes of this kind should be expected as personalities and party control of public offices change. Furthermore, lateral reclassification of this type would not significantly change the percentage results as chairmanships are moved from one category to another. Nor does this have any effect on the efficacy of the classification scheme itself.

variations in the state chairman's role. It is probable that most writers have assumed a direct parallel with the pattern of power that prevails in the national committees. That is, the in-party chairman is the governor's choice for the job, is ratified by the state committee, and serves the party indistinguishably from serving the governor. The out-party chairman, on the other hand, perhaps would exercise more real leadership in his party, serving as organizational supervisor, policy maker, campaign manager, fund raiser, and opposition spokesman. These assumptions would be natural ones. They would not, however, be entirely accurate.

In-party/out-party status is of considerable importance to establishing the role of the state chairman, but it is not necessarily the deciding factor in that determination. In many states the governor is not considered to be the head of the political party. Even when in power, the Democratic party of Illinois has more often than not been under the domination of Mayor Richard Daley of Chicago. The late U.S. Senator Harry Byrd of Virginia dominated the Democratic party of that state for decades despite the party's control of the gubernatorial office.

Some governors operate personal organizations which bypass the state party structure presided over by the state chairman. Others must work with a chairman who is elected independently of the governor's influence and operates as a free agent. In one-party factional states, governors control their own faction but leave the state chairman to preside over the coordination of other factions which are controlled by political competitors. In a few cases a particular chairman, building upon different foundations, has been able to exercise long-term control over the party organization while serving several governors. A case in point is that of Connecticut's long-time Democratic state chairman, the late John Bailey.

Bailey was first selected as state chairman in 1946 after managing the nomination of Wilbert Snow as the candidate for governor over a better-known candidate, Chester Bowles. Having painfully witnessed Bailey's political muscle and organizational ability firsthand, Bowles asked for his support in his second bid for the governorship in 1948. Bailey, who had remained in office as chairman after the defeat of Snow, agreed and undertook to manage Bowles' successful bid for the statehouse.

After losing his bid for a second term in 1950, Bowles temporarily dropped from the Connecticut scene, and Bailey undertook to groom Congressman Abraham Ribicoff as his candidate for governor. Ribicoff was elected in 1954 and reelected in 1958. Bowles' bid for a U.S. Senate nomination in 1958 was short-lived when John Bailey, with the support of Ribicoff, quietly threw his support to Thomas Dodd, thus assuring his nomination in the Democratic convention. Dodd went on to win the Senate seat, thus further strengthening Bailey's control over the party.

John Dempsey was the third Connecticut governor whose election was managed by Bailey. Dempsey served for ten years and announced, much to Bailey's surprise in 1970, that he would not be available for a third term. A little-known candidate was selected by the Democrats, and the office of governor was lost to the Republicans for the first time in sixteen years. With that loss Bailey became an out-party chairman. In 1974 Bailey again succeeded in securing the Democratic nomination for his personal choice, Representative Ella Grasso, who was successful in her bid for the governorship.

During his quarter-century as state chairman, Bailey survived defeat and party infighting among nationally known political leaders. He established himself in the mid-1950s as the most powerful Democrat in the state, and his support was considered essential to nomination and election. In the course of one of several long interviews, Bailey said, "My relationship with the Democratic governors of Connecticut is based on the fact that I hand-picked them and got them elected." His claim, though perhaps exaggerated, was not far off the mark. Bailey was also a legislative leader and served as a crucial communications link between his governors and the party apparatus. As former Governor Chester Bowles described the relationship:

Because John Bailey acted as an effective communications link between the party and my office, I was able to convince most of them [the party leaders] that what I was striving to do was not only good government but also good politics.

Bailey had organized my campaign for the nomination with skill and I had come to rely on his advice on tactics and timing. He was interested not only in politics as such but also in the art of government. He had an unsurpassed knowledge of the legislative process, worked hard at his trade, and personally read every bill that came out of committee. I not only strongly supported his election to the chairmanship of the State Democratic Committee; I consulted with him on almost all matters related to my operation.[3]

In many states the type of state chairman chosen is heavily dependent upon the wishes of the governor. Some governors want a chairman who will serve as their political lightning rod. One governor noted:

I was elected in a hot factional fight and barely squeezed through. My first chairman was picked largely to take the heat off me. He did his best but survived less than two years. At that point, I decided that I had to lead the fight myself, and I selected a different kind of chairman with a different mission the second time around.

Some governors recognize the importance of the party chairman to the success of their legislative programs and select a person who can build and supervise a strong party organization as a vehicle for control and direction of the legislature. One such chairman described himself as the "deputy governor for political affairs." The decline in one-party states has brought with it a growth in the number of competitive minority legislative parties, and some governors have had to deal with an active legislative opposition for the first time in their state's history. Without precedents to work from, they have often used the state chairman as a means of accomplishing that purpose. Some have become, in fact, legislative lobbyists for their governors' programs. A midwestern chairman reported:

I am the first chairman to serve under a Democratic governor in many years. I was the governor's finance chairman and I know where the bodies are buried. That gives me added leverage with the legislators. We don't believe we can get reelected unless we establish a strong legislative program. I spend almost all my time lobbying the program and raising money.

The governor's leadership depends not only on the existence of a strong party organization but also on his ability to control it; one does not necessarily automatically follow the other. Much depends on the caliber of man in the state party chairmanship.

Among the weakest chairmen in the nation are those of the dominant party in noncompetitive states, particularly in the South. If candidates in a one-party factional state can be elected to high office without regard to party organization, they are more likely to show their allegiance to the personal supporters who helped to elect them. Several of the Republican state chairmen in southern states controlled by Democratic governors are more active and more visible than are their Democratic counterparts. And in Alabama, the Democratic chairman, Robert Vance, maintained a position of power in the face of opposition from the governor only by building a separate organization alongside that of George Wallace.

As noted earlier, in Mississippi there are two state Democratic party groups, one recognized as official by the Democratic National Committee and led by Aaron Henry, a black party activist, and the other composed of the old pre-1964 southern Democratic party. Needless to say, there has been little interaction between the Democratic governors of the state and the Henry forces.

The state party systems are constantly changing. The rise of Republicanism in the South, increased competition by Democrats in traditionally Republican states, shifting voter allegiances (including formal changes of party registration), the widespread growth in the number of independent voters, and widespread reelection difficulties for incumbent officeholders have all combined to bring important shifts in party competition within the various states.

Some chairmen have been successful in developing considerable concentrations of power in the office by virtue of personal style and individual initiative. That is understandable in an in-party with a governor who wishes to stamp his own brand on his party and carefully selects a chairman to help him wield the branding iron. It is more mysterious and more difficult to explain in an out-party, with minimal organizational machinery, few rewards, little enthusiasm, and a history of defeats. Yet, there are numerous examples of particular chairmen turning a party around in that fashion.

Certain Republican state organizations in the mid-1960s flowered under nationally known, usually colorful, issue-oriented or ideologically committed governors. Nelson A. Rockefeller of New York, Ronald Reagan of California, William Scranton of Pennsylvania, Daniel Evans of Washington, James Rhodes of Ohio, John Love of Colorado, Robert E. Smylie of Idaho, Winthrop Rockefeller of Arkansas, Robert Ray of Iowa, George Romney of Michigan, and John Chaffee of Rhode Island all fit this mold to some extent. In most instances they were supported by one or more colorful and innovative state chairmen. Men such as Craig Truax, Jean Tool, C. Montgomery Johnson, Ray Bliss, and Caspar Weinberger were not widely known to the general public but helped to define new standards of effectiveness for party leadership. Even in those states where little chance existed of capturing major offices, dynamic young state chairmen such as John Grenier of Alabama, Searle Penney of Connecticut, and the late David Scull of Maryland assumed control, sometimes only briefly, over the political destinies of their states.

The implicit, if not the explicit, assumption underlying party classification schemes is that parties may be categorized by some established criteria. Classification by level of competition is one of the most widely used of these schemes. It is relatively easily accomplished through analysis of voting behavior and electoral success. Classification by party structure or organizational effectiveness is more difficult because of the lack of accepted criteria as well as the great diversity of the party systems. The interlocking relationships woven by legal responsibilities, minority-majority status leadership, personality, political environment, and the impact of the gubernatorial office make it difficult to unravel the strands essential to arriving at any acceptable classification. It is easy to categorize parties as "in" or "out." That determination is based solely on possession of the governorship. There is an implication, however, that all in-party chairmen behave in the same way, as do all out-party leaders. This is, of course, demonstrably untrue. Furthermore, some chairmen naturally fit within more than one class. Those initially selected as a Political Agent may, in time, become powers in their own right.

Since there are no logical or accepted criteria by which party organizational effectiveness might be measured, it is necessary to rely upon the perceptions of those involved in order to arrive at a classifications system. Consequently, as noted earlier, the roles of the party chairmen as used here have been derived from extensive interviews which lead to this trichotomous classification scheme.

The Political Agent

The Political Agent serves as the partisan arm of an incumbent governor or, in a few cases, some other elected official who, by virtue of his position and in lieu of the governorship, is able to exercise party control. The Political Agent has organizational responsibilities and serves as manager for the party. He serves, in effect, as the governor's deputy for political affairs. He seldom exercises real control over the party apparatus, usually deferring to the governor whom he serves. In many states an incumbent governor is the recognized leader and spokesman for his political party. He has attained this position by virtue of his successful campaign for the gubernatorial office and, by winning, has assumed the burden of party leadership. This may not mean that he has a large personal following in the party but only that he currently holds a position of power and of recognized leadership potential. His party leadership role may rank well down in the list of responsibilities that have come to him by virtue of his election. He himself may not rate the political role highly. A governor who has defeated an organizational favorite in the primary election or one presiding over a severely factionalized party may be the party leader in name only. Yet he may seek to lead and to unite in order to bring order to the party and to exercise whatever party discipline is available to him in dealing with the legislature.

This fact was noted by Coleman Ransone, a leading student of state government and politics, when he stated that

It is primarily because we do not really have party government at the state level that the governor must continue to play the role of politician even after his election. . . . The idea of disciplined parties in the legislature who work with the governor to execute a party program is largely a none-too-effective myth at the state level. The governor is elected in an atmosphere of factional politics and he continues to operate in that atmosphere in his dealings with the legislature, with his department heads, and with the other members of the executive branch.[4]

In those states where party discipline and unity are not very evident, the governor may wish to pull the contending factions together in order to accomplish his policy goals. In those states where more highly disciplined parties are the rule, the governor may want to exercise a more continuous control over party affairs in order to remain in personal command of his political forces. Furthermore, there is some evidence to suggest that the people are looking to governors for leadership more often than in the past. As a result, the governor may feel that it is imperative that he attempt to serve as political leader simply because his party constituents expect it of him.

Nevertheless, in most states the exercise of party leadership by governors has been difficult and sometimes impossible. The decentralization of party power permits county and local leaders to hold their positions regardless of who occupies the governor's chair. These leaders, of course, owe the governor nothing, leaving him with limited means to impose party discipline. State legislators, with whom the governor must work if he is to get his programs adopted, are elected separately, in limited constituencies, and often at different times. Divided party control often forces the chief executive to bargain with factions in his own and the opposition party within the legislative and executive branches. Finally, the use of the constitutional powers he commands, such as the item veto, may create more enemies than friends. Combined with the growth of state civil service systems, which undercut much of the patronage power, these negative factors have carved out party leadership roles which are often more than the governor can effectively assume. In actual fact, however, the governor will be looked to by his followers as the elected leader of his party, and this may provide the stimulus to build a party record.

The office of governor is important, and in some cases omnipotent, in state politics because it is the office, and not the party, which is provided for in the constitution. The result is that the office serves as the major raison d'être for the party itself, and the value that the party places on control of the office may well be tied to the perceived role of the governor in the party's future.

With all of these considerations in mind it is hardly surprising that some governors feel the need for an agent to serve them in their dealings with the party organization. As one governor noted:

I got elected largely in spite of the party organization. I am the first governor to represent the ———— party in many years, and I won the office without much party help. Nevertheless, my first year in office has convinced me that I must either take over the party and make it my own or reconcile myself to the fact that I will not be able to carry out my campaign promises. In order for me to function effectively I must be able to make the ————s in the legislature see the light and go along with me. Otherwise, my political career is going to be short, and the effectiveness of the party in this state will be destroyed.

Another, more fortunate governor in a midwestern state described his relationship with the party in this way:

I have been the recognized leader of the party for some years. I was approached by a group of the more powerful county leaders and asked to run. I checked with the legislative leadership of the party and received their support. I had strong party support from both of the major factions in the party and I won rather decisively. I have tried to treat everyone fairly and not to play favorites. I have sorted out those party leaders who are most reliable and who appear to have control of their people. I work with them closely and have had pretty good cooperation from them. Those who appear to me to be weak or who are not enthusiastic about my governorship have either been replaced or have been coddled. The result has been a honeymoon of nearly two years' duration. I believe that just about everyone will tell you that I am the party leader.

Both of these governors are served by state chairmen who have assumed the role of Political Agent. The chairmen were both hand-picked by their governors and in each case had served as campaign manager. They are trusted advisors who maintain a close relationship based on long years of personal loyalty, political stewardship, friendship, faith, and trust. Neither chairman appears to be offended when the governor and/or his personal staff reject his advice, but in both cases that seldom appears to happen. Chairmen serving these two governors have carved out for themselves an important role as political lightning rod. One of the chairmen described his role in this way:

I protect his flanks and try to divert partisan flak. I devote myself to the Man and do whatever appears to be in his best interest. I really believe that the governor's success guarantees the party's success and have no difficulty in my own mind reconciling my position as party leader with my role as the governor's man. These two aspects of the job are inseparable, it seems to me.

The other offered this explanation of his relationship with the chief executive:

I am the governor's agent in the party; he maintains his control of the party through me; that doesn't mean that I am a puppet; he listens to me; he takes my advice often, but sometimes we disagree on things and he then makes up his mind on the basis of what he personally wants to do. I have daily contact with the governor, mostly on party matters. I help with the party officials throughout the state. If he needs someone called in the party in some county, I call them. We clear positions for appointment. I represent him at places when he can't be in two places at once. So that, in general, he either calls me or I call him, I would say, once a day. By the same token, I don't have veto power over anything. I can make suggestions and I can tell him what I think about things, but he has on occasion simply ignored me and gone on.

The state chairman as Political Agent occupies a peculiar role. At times he is purposely overshadowed by the governor, operates quietly behind the scenes, and is self-effacing to the point of political obscurity. At other times he is in the forefront of the political battle, taking the brunt of the partisan slings and arrows and serving as a target to deflect attention from the governor when that appears to be politically advisable.

Twenty-six state chairmen (32.5 percent), thirteen in each party, can be identified as Political Agents. These men and women see themselves differently than do other state chairmen. In fact, even though the term *Political Agent* is a typical example of academic jargon, a surprising number of respondents described their roles using those very words:

I am the governor's agent. I am a top appointed official in the party, and I see that as meaning that I am a representative of the governor as the elected top official in the party.

The role of the state chairman is a mixed bag. It involves almost equal parts of organization, campaigning, mediation, public relations, advancing for the governor, being advocate of the governor, being a whipping boy. I feel, from watching it at close hand for five years, that it's essential that the state chairman be the governor's agent, serve the governor in whatever way he can.

I consider myself to be [the governor's] agent in charge of running the Republican party and particularly in charge of rebuilding it. The relationship is extremely close. I am the governor's man but I'm not his puppet.

Although not always the case, the assignment of an agent's role to the chairman is often signaled by the way in which his candidacy is announced and his election is carried out. In those parties where it is customary for the governor to choose the chairman-designee, the media often provide easily recognized clues. Thus, in April 1970, the *New York Times* reported that the New Jersey Republican state chairman was "the personal choice of Governor William T. Cahill." [5] And the "strong hand of Governor John J. Gilligan was in evidence Sunday as the Ohio Democratic Party executive committee named [the Democratic] state chairman." [6] At the time of Nebraska Republican Chairwoman Lorraine Orr's resignation in 1971, the *Lincoln Star* described her as former Governor Norbert Tiemann's "handpicked [choice] for the leadership post upon his election in 1966, and he also led the drive for her selection to a second term in 1969." [7] A final example is the *Miami Herald's* report in 1970 that "Jon Moyle, the handpicked nominee of Governor-elect Reubin Askew and U.S. Senator-elect Lawton Chiles, will be the new chairman of the Florida Democratic Party." [8]

The duties of the Political Agent are varied. Although they differ from party to party, they normally include patronage matters and serving as party spokesman, legislative liaison, and political strategist. One summed up his role this way:

I meet three times a week with the governor on appointments. I make suggestions; he makes suggestions; and we agree on a list of acceptable nominees to present to the patronage committee which I head. All party matters are discussed between us. We work closely on legislative affairs, deciding those which I will handle and those which will be taken care of by himself. We even confer on statements that either of us are scheduled to make.

In patronage matters the chairman usually serves as the acknowledged link between the party and the governor. He is almost always a member of the patronage committee and usually is the chairman of it. One of his principal roles is to prevent any job-related development from embarrassing the governor. Most chairmen consider patronage problems to be an undesirable but necessary part of their job. It does represent, after all, one of the few remaining bastions of party influence. Consequently, most Political Agents are involved in every step in the patronage process, from screening of applicants to the final selection process.

Many governors prefer to speak for themselves, and especially when their pronouncement will be well received. In controversial matters, however, the chairman, as Political Agent, may be called upon as spokesman to draw partisan fire away from the chief executive. Normally, these occasions do not involve matters of state but concern matters of politics. Several chairmen noted, however, that they often serve as the floater of trial balloons for their respective governors.

Legislative liaison represents a major role for most of these chairmen. If the governor wishes to force action on the part of his legislative party, without at the same time alienating key legislators, he may call upon the chairman to handle such delicate matters for him. For the most part the chairman's role as legislative spokesman for the governor is widely recognized and respected. A dozen state chairmen served concurrently as members of the state legislature, permitting them wide latitude in carrying out this phase of their duties. One Republican noted:

I have been in the Assembly far longer than I have been state chairman. I guess everybody there knows me as the governor's arm-twister and reward-giver. It is just taken for granted that I speak for the guy and that what I say in party matters counts. Ordinarily I can scrounge some votes for him on policy matters too.

Some chairmen consider themselves lobbyists for the party (governor's) program. Thus, a midwestern Democratic chairman stated:

I'm in constant contact with the governor. I am his agent to the party and the legislature. During the session I am primarily a lobbyist. The governor makes all policy statements and develops all policy without my help. I simply try to carry it out through the legislature. We have such strong majorities in the legislature that I usually am able to get our entire platform, which is really the governor's platform, adopted.

Other chairmen who serve as agents meet daily or weekly with the chief executive to plan party strategy and to determine what action to take in delicate political matters. Most acknowledged that the governor sometimes does not follow their advice, but when important political decisions are made the agent-chairman is usually a major participant in the decision-making process. Such decisions usually concern party matters, such as fund raising, party reform, organizational problems, and the governor's speaking schedule. The relationship between the two is normally very close, as suggested by the following comments:

The governor is my best friend. I was his choice for state chairman, and the executive committee backed him on this. I was elected unanimously and have been reelected unanimously. I think a state chairman where the party has the governorship has to act in this way.

I'm on the phone with the governor or see him in person every day. You have to understand that [the governor] and I have spent many nights getting drunk together, and we simply think alike, act alike, and do everything together. We have for years. He wouldn't think of making a major policy pronouncement without clearing with me; and whether I agree or not, he at least clears so that I can prepare my responses to the party people which will support him whether I agree with him or not. On state issues I always give in to the governor. On national political issues and on party issues he gives in to me most of the time. I tell him what he thinks, and he decides what he's going to do.

I keep the governor fully informed. I talk to him about twice a day, mainly on state patronage. The governor in ——— cannot succeed himself, so that he needs to make his record in a short four years and is almost a lame duck before he takes office. This governor has for the first time in any party turned patronage over to the state party headquarters completely. We handle all patronage. He appoints who we tell him to appoint. He makes no checks on his own. He simply makes the appointments that we clear for him to the county organizations.

I did a lot of work for the governor, lobbied for him, tried to make peace between the Speaker and the Senate president, and I also testified on easing the laws on registration—all these things I was asked to do by the governor and all of them I undertook. I was with him almost every day on some matter or other.

Three chairmen described themselves as agents of officeholders other than the governor. In each case the chairman's party did not control the governorship but did control another major elective office. One Democratic chairman acknowledged that he served at the pleasure of a big-city mayor and was the mayor's formal contact with the party hierarchy. He conceded that the mayor's power in the state party was so dominant as to preclude an effective role for the chairman. Nevertheless, he identified himself as a Political Agent since he holds office at the pleasure of the mayor and does his bidding in state political affairs.

Two chairmen stated that their allegiance was to a United States senator. In each case the senator was the only major statewide officeholder from the party, and in each state the senator's personal organization served, to a large extent, as the state party organization. Because of geographic distance, both chairmen described their role as that of a senator's local representative to his own party organization. In neither case were the chairmen making any attempt to organize the party more broadly, nor were they devoting any energy to the election of other officeholders.

The governor's attitude toward the political party normally determines whether or not he is to be served by a chairman as Political Agent. Some governors wish to maintain control of the party because they view it as a crucial vehicle for political leadership. In the short run the party leadership can be helpful in bringing the governor's program to fruition. In the long run he may see his political future inextricably tied to that of the party. In either case it is important that he have a trusted surrogate formally in charge of party affairs.

The Political Agent need not be a lackey or a puppet. Some of them are among the most effective and successful state chairmen currently operating within the political system. The parameters within which they operate are drawn by the governor. If he wants to keep the reins of party control taut he may arrange the election of a chairman who will do his bidding. Some chairmen are permitted no discretionary power at all. They are truly the governor's man. They do what they are told and undertake nothing on their own. At times their principal statehouse contact is not the governor at all but is a senior staff aide. It might be said that they administer the political party *for* the governor.

Other chairmen, also operating as Political Agents, enjoy an entirely different relationship with their chief executive. They, in fact, administer the party *with* the governor. They are encouraged to engage in forthright in-house discussion of party problems and plans, and their opinions are valued. They are loyal to the governor but they are not subservient to him. They are supported in efforts to build the party in general—not just in the governor's image. One of them described the relationship in this way:

The governor and I grew up together. We attended school together and we entered politics together. I managed his first campaign and we lost. When he decided to go again I was one of those encouraging him. He asked me to manage his campaign again and I did. Election night, after it became clear that we had won, he asked me what I wanted and I told him I wanted to take over the party. . . . He stage-managed the resignation of the old chairman and my election by the executive committee.

I have been engaged in building the party ever since. I have his complete support and I don't do anything without his agreement. He has not been afraid to say no. But most of the time we fight it out, and I have been able to convince him that what I want to do is right. He asked me to take over patronage and I did. It's a pain in the ass but he can't have every Tom, Dick, and Harry pounding on his door demanding jobs. We pretty much isolated him from that.

He asked me to work out some kind of ongoing fund-raising scheme so that we wouldn't be so dependent on big money, and we are just completing a new sustaining program to do just that.

We have a good relationship built over a long time. He needs someone he trusts to run the party for him and I am the guy.

Political Agents come in many varieties. Some are integral members of the governor's team; they serve without being subservient. Others do as they are told and are permitted little flexibility. The key to identifying the Political Agent is understanding his relationship with the governor.

The In-Party Independent Chairman

The In-Party Independent Chairman is one who serves a party which controls the governorship but who was elected without the active support of the incumbent governor, defeated the governor's choice for the chairmanship, or occupies a place of party power in his own right. He usually has a fixed term which antedates the governor's. Some chairmen have been in office for long periods of time and have seen several governors elected during their tenure. In a few instances the governor's support has been important at the time of the chairman's election, but, once elected, the In-Party Independent serves independently of the governor.

Twenty-four chairmen (30 percent) are classified as In-Party Independents. (See table 4.1.) Thirteen are Republicans and eleven are Democrats. They represent states in various geographical areas of the country and with a variety of party systems. In four states both chairmen are classified as In-Party Independents. One midwestern state has a long tradition of political independence, and past efforts by governors to inter- fere in the selection of the party chairman have been counterproductive. As that state's In-Party Independent Chairman describes the situation:

You probably know that the leadership of both parties in ———— is sep- arate from the governorship. Although we are in power now, the same is true when they are in power. There was one instance in the early 1960s when Governor ————, even before he was inaugurated, announced his choice for state chairman, and when the committee met, the man got only two votes. Our state committees, in both the Republican and Democratic parties, are very independent—to the point of being jackass stubborn.

Four of the twenty-four In-Party Independents served in southern par- ties, three of them in traditional one-party Democratic states. Yet, even with the governorship guaranteed, they operate independently, either because of traditional party factionalism or because the official organiza- tion is normally separated from the governor's personal organization. One party in the South, long noted for personal factionalized politics, has enjoyed a tradition of independent party chairmen (and state central committees) since the late 1940s. Although the chairman of that par- ticular party was not interviewed, his Republican counterpart said that the Democrats had decided years ago that the safest way to free the party organization from fratricidal political machinations was to maintain its absolute independence.

An example of a southern In-Party Independent is Robert Vance, Democratic chairman of Alabama. Vance, elected to a four-year term in 1966, was reelected in 1970 with the support of Governor Albert Brewer, having defeated the candidate of the Dixiecrat elements of the party. An editorial in the *Alabama Journal* put it this way:

[Vance] created a new party which has at least a chance to function as an authentic political party, one which can meet the Republicans in honest competition.
  Control of the state party governing body will shift from the rural, county- courthouse politicians to the representatives of the urban areas of Alabama.
  Negroes will be brought into active participation in a party which has not had a black on the state committee during this century. . . .
  The state party moves closer in philosophical kinship to the National Democratic Party. The new "statement of principles"—the first such docu-

ment ever formally adopted by the Democratic Party of Alabama—is quite compatible with national Democratic policy.[9]

Vance was again reelected in 1974. In 1970 George C. Wallace was again elected to serve as governor of Alabama, and he too was reelected in 1974. The Alabama Democratic party is clearly an example of the state chairman as an independent within the in-party.

Most In-Party Independents function effectively without active support from the governor. In effect, they do not need each other. Vance and Wallace march to different drummers. One considers himself the leader of the "Democratic party" in Alabama, while the other is the leader of a loyal personal following. There is, no doubt, considerable overlap between the two groups. Wallace's efforts to achieve the American Independent or Democratic presidential nominations since the mid-1960s have kept him preoccupied with personal goals and with his own national following. Vance, who believes that the Alabama Democrats must have a voice in national Democratic councils, has concentrated on party building in both organizational and ideological terms. In 1973 he was elected as chairman of the Association of State Democratic Chairmen but in 1975 was defeated for reelection to that office by Donald Fowler, chairman of the South Carolina Democratic party.

Party factionalism in some states is so widespread that efforts by an incumbent governor to impose his brand on the party are unhesitatingly rebuffed. In 1971 the politically obscure mayor of a Dallas suburb, Roy Orr, was elected state chairman over the combined opposition of Governor Preston Smith, former Senator Ralph Yarborough, and Texas organized labor. Mr. Orr did not have the support of any major Democratic leader but won the post by a 32–30 vote. The victory was attributed by the *New York Times* to "the unwillingness of local Democratic leaders to take orders." [10] With Governor Smith at a low point in his public popularity, former Governor John Connally serving as secretary of the treasury in a Republican administration, and the late former President Lyndon B. Johnson in retirement at his ranch, no recognized party leader was in a position to control the vote for chairman. This is not an unusual circumstance in a party that is rife with factionalism.

In Indiana, John K. Snyder was elected Republican state chairman in 1970 over the active opposition of Republican Governor Edgar Whitcomb. Snyder's election resulted from a long-standing feud in the Indiana Republican party between the former state chairman and the Republican national committeeman, an ally of Governor Whitcomb. Snyder's election came about through the votes of ten state central committeemen, plus four who voted by proxy. The remaining eight boycotted the meeting by remaining in Governor Whitcomb's office across the street from Republican state headquarters.[11]

Snyder, immediately after his election to the state chairmanship, asked for party unity and urged all Indiana Republicans to forget the past differences and remember the future interests which should unite the party. In the rough-and-tumble world of Indiana Republicanism that goal was unlikely to be accomplished, but the statement represented the only kind of plea that the newly elected leader of a factionalized party could likely make.

John M. Bailey, Democratic state chairman of Connecticut for over a quarter of a century, was probably the best-known In-Party Independent chairman. Bailey played a major role in the election of four Democratic governors of Connecticut—Chester Bowles, Abraham Ribicoff, John Dempsey, and Ella Grasso. He continued to occupy his party chair during the two occasions when Republicans controlled the statehouse during his tenure. Never an autocratic boss in the tradition of Frank Hague, Bailey survived and often thrived on a combination of political alliances and tough-mindedness. As noted by one observer, he was not too proud to beg, nor was he too timid to swing a big stick when the need was manifest. In early 1973 he stated, "The only way I was able to make three different governors was to be tough and tell potential gubernatorial candidates, 'No, you can't be governor,' and then have the will to enforce it."

This statement was remarkably similar to one made by an equally well-known state chairman, Republican Ray C. Bliss of Ohio. Bliss stated in an interview that "The trouble with most chairmen is that they don't have the power base or the know-how to stand up to party leaders and tell them that they can't be governor or senator. A strong state chairman must be able to make that statement and to make it stick."

The In-Party Independent Chairman has considerably more flexibility in the exercise of his powers than does the Political Agent. He is not bound by the personal wishes of his governor, although he obviously must be interested in them. He operates at a different level and his power derives from sources within the party organization itself—not from the temporary holder of the gubernatorial chair. His fortune is tied to the success of the party and his goal is for *party* success. He is party oriented rather than candidate oriented. He often tends to be a "nuts and bolts" chairman who devotes many hours to organizational matters, candidate recruitment, and the efforts to influence the nominating process. This does not mean that the In-Party Independent can ignore the governor. Obviously, he must be interested in the fortunes of the chief officeholder of the party. Success in the statehouse is inextricably tied to continued success of the party. He is, however, clearly a political compatriot rather than a party retainer.

A long interview with one of the In-Party Independents caught him in a reflective mood. He described his role in this way:

I am on the best of terms with Governor ———. I helped him to get elected and he did not oppose my selection as state chairman. Nevertheless, I decided to run for the office and lined up my own support and brought about my own election. I then went to the governor and pledged to help him in any way that I could as long as it did not interfere with my plans for the party.

I think it is a mistake for a chairman to be tied too closely to the governor. It is damned hard to build a party if the whole thing is going to collapse when the governor is no longer in office. I think our traditional pattern here in ——— is much better. The chairman is truly independent and can concentrate his attention on party building. He does not tie his fortunes to any single candidate. I think it has permitted me and [my predecessor] to be more innovative and to do more with the party. The governor and I meet often and he consults me, but if I say, "No, Governor, we can't do that," he accepts it with good grace. Some of his staff get a little up-tight, but he understands.

I am absolutely convinced that the only way we can maintain an independent party is to continue maintaining an independent chairman.

Many of the In-Party Independents believe they have a more comfortable role than their brethren serving as Political Agents, and a more rewarding one than those who are Out-Party Independents.

The Out-Party Independent Chairman

The third type of state chairman is the Out-Party Independent who presides over a party that does not control the governor's office. He usually emerges from a personal power base or is elected as the choice of an unsuccessful gubernatorial candidate. In some states the party seldom, if ever, holds the governorship and is always presided over by an Out-Party Independent. This is the case in most southern Republican parties.

In other states the party may control one or more offices below the gubernatorial level or in Congress but does not control the governorship. In still others the problems associated with factionalized parties bring about the election of chairmen who can mediate factional disputes while attempting to build a party organization. In any case the failure to win the governorship is the key to this chairman's role.

Thirty state chairmen, 37.5 percent of the total, are Out-Party Independents. They are equally divided between the parties and represent states from all geographical areas. They represent the only category without a governor.

An example of an Out-Party Independent leading a party without major state officeholders is Caroline Wilkins, the Democratic chairwoman of Oregon, who was elected in 1970 and served until 1975. Wilkins succeeded to the office from the vice-chairmanship upon the resignation of the man who had been elected to the post. She was reelected to a full term one year later and to a second two years after that. She took over a party which was heavily in debt and which did not hold a major statewide office. Her stewardship of the Democratic party helped to overcome the debt and brought her recognition within Oregon and the nation as a political leader in her own right. She was elected one of two vice-chairmen of the Democratic National Committee in 1973 at the time of the election of Robert Strauss as national chairman.

A midwestern Out-Party Independent was elected to lead a party which had not controlled the governorship for over twenty years. Selected as chairman-designee by the most recent gubernatorial candidate, this man remained in office after his defeat. His most serious problem was the shortage of viable candidates for statewide races, and this, in turn, caused serious morale problems within the party hierarchy. The local organizations, county based, had deteriorated during the long office drought, and much of his effort was devoted to attempts to revive the substructure. This chairman was widely recognized as the *real* leader of the party. His major problem centered on re-creating a party to lead.

Other parties have traditions of electing chairmen with all the panoply and strategic infighting associated with an election campaign. Although the candidates for chairman sometimes are "sponsored" by leading public officials, they often win the position on the strength of personal support and by virtue of their own tactics.

California Democrats elected Charles Manatt state chairman in 1971 in a close election that was decided by a 428–418 vote. The delegates elected Manatt on a second ballot after he ran third on the first. Although

Senator John Tunney endorsed Manatt's opponent, former U.S. Representative George E. Brown, Jr., the senator's staff worked for Manatt, and the victory was considered to be strengthening to the Tunney organization. Brown, after having been defeated for the Senate nomination in 1970 by Tunney, had supported Tunney in the general election campaign. The state chairmanship of California is not a powerful office. Former Chairman Roger Boaz had once described it as a job that "chiefly involved the conciliation of competing factions and the organization of campaigns." [12] During the Reagan administration it clearly fit the description of an Out-Party Independent chairmanship. Manatt served out his term and, under California law, was unable to succeed himself. He ran for national chairman in 1972 and was defeated by Robert Strauss. In 1975 Manatt was again elected state chairman for another two-year term.

In October 1970, Harry Makris was elected Democratic state chairman of New Hampshire after the Democratic gubernatorial nominee, Roger Crowley, endorsed and supported another candidate for the job. The *Manchester Union Leader* editorially praised the loser as a man who "keeps [his] word" and "lives up to his commitments." [13] Makris faced the opposition of the powerful *Union Leader* throughout his term.

Several chairmen pointed out that the role of the state chairmen in their respective states depends in large part on whether or not the party controls the governorship. The status of a party as in or out is a crucial one. A midwestern chairman remarked:

In ———— the chairman must have the support of the governor and do pretty much what he says. Unfortunately, we lost the governorship two years ago and that casts us in a different situation. Without the governorship the chairman becomes the recognized political leader. We have both U.S. senators but they have neither one ever shown any real interest in the party. They leave us alone and we leave them alone. I am expected to do all the things that you would normally expect a party leader to do. If we had the top office, I would simply be the political arm of the governor.

Another chairman, from a western state, described a special set of circumstances which permitted the establishment of a strong party chairmanship to exercise political control in lieu of the governor's office:

Our new executive committee is really great. They were all hand-picked by me, and they know I'm the party leader and I know that I can count on them. The group who approached me to run told me that I could pick the people I wanted to work with, and I selected almost all of them. They are all new and enthusiastic and they know who is boss. We immediately established my personal control over all policy making in the party . . . and on the purely mechanical aspects of registration, voting, patronage, etc., they rely on me to keep them informed but they don't interfere with what I do.

The nature and importance of the chairmanship of the state party that is out of power depend in large part on the tradition of party government in the state, the availability of elected leadership (aside from the governor), the composition of the state committee, and the talent of the chairman. In some states the tradition of nonactivist chairmen is so strong as to preclude strengthening the office or even undertaking to strike out in new directions. Sometimes, the number of weak party identifiers who hold party office is virtually impossible to overcome.

Some state parties, notably those of the southern Republicans, occupy no state offices and have few if any state legislative seats. The fact that there is no elected leadership in the state forces the chairman to assume that burden. Approximately one-half of the southern Republican chairmen appeared to have adopted for themselves a role as party spokesman, but most of them did little else. The other half, undismayed by the perpetual failure to win local and state offices, act as though they play a real part in a competitive two-party system. They work at party organization, make speeches, raise money, and issue policy statements. They often voice the intention of building a party apparatus that can serve to translate southern Republican presidential votes into votes for state and local candidates. It is ironic that the area of the nation with the fewest elected state and local Republicans should occupy such a crucial role in the national party structure. It is doubly ironic that the leadership in that movement has come from the state chairmen, the group that most political scientists and journalists have dismissed as being of relatively little importance in American politics.

The attitude of the chairman toward his state committee is of considerable importance to his success. Most Out-Party Independents maintained that they had a good relationship, but one that was dependent upon the chairman's goodwill toward the committee. The state committee appears to be of considerably more importance to the out-party chairman, since it serves as his source of strength and it often is most responsible for his election to the office. Even so, some state parties have traditional nonactivist state committees. The members are often those who have contributed their money in years past but have preferred to remain relatively inactive.

The relationship to the chairman, once he is elected, is often perfunctory. One chairman stated: "I have meetings twice a year although the by-laws don't require more than one annual meeting. I quickly discovered that the members have nothing to offer and even resent being asked to attend. I keep holding meetings, though, because it gives the party some semblance of life." Another noted that his relationship to his committee was very good: "I try to keep them informed and I often ask their advice, but I never bring anything to a vote since I don't want to have to overrule them. I find it helpful to know what they think before I undertake something, though." Finally, an out-party chairman in a strong two-party state argued that state committee participation is most important. He noted:

I am very active with the state committee. It participates in all policy matters and meets monthly. We now have almost a full quota of members, and although they give me a free hand to carry out the day-to-day activities of the organization, I would never take a major action without consulting them in advance. They respect me for that and they seldom ever go against my wishes. They know that I will respect their wishes or try to convince them to change their minds. I think it is a good system.

The final determinant of the out-party chairman's power is most subjective. The talent and enthusiasm of the chairman are not things that can be measured quantitatively but are very important ingredients in determining the success of the party. One must talk with large numbers of the chairmen before distinctions in style and ability become apparent. Even then, there is great danger that an incumbent's true role may be misjudged. There are, nevertheless, marked distinctions between the abilities of the out-party (as well as the in-party) chairmen.

Some chairmen impress the observer as having taken to heart George Washington's warning to avoid the "baneful effects of the spirit of party." They have avoided those baneful effects by doing little or nothing to improve the out-party's fortunes. In some cases, and sometimes for legitimate reasons, they maintain no office, have no secretary, perform no duties, and carry out none of the responsibilities normally expected of a party leader. This is also true of some in-party chairmen, but in most cases they merely are following the role assigned to them by an incumbent governor. One long-time chairman noted with some pride that he had never attended a party meeting outside his state. Even though his party held no major statewide or congressional offices and he was the recognized titular leader, he did not consider it incumbent upon him to do more than preside over the existing dormancy.

Subjectively, the more impressive out-party chairmen are those who established goals for themselves, appear to have the native ability and experience to accomplish most of them, and worked doggedly to succeed. A surprising number in both parties singled out a particular individual state chairman as a model. One-fourth of all those interviewed, divided equally between the parties, cited former Ohio State Chairman (and later Republican National Chairman) Ray Bliss as the model state chairman; as one whom they would like to emulate. As might be expected, since Bliss was widely known as a "nuts and bolts" chairman, those who named him as their ideal considered organizational matters of uppermost importance.

Comparison of Role Types

Each chairman must approach his office within the boundaries laid down by party tradition, party law, and the political exigencies of the moment. The right personality elected to office at the right time can overcome the mossiest of traditions and the hoariest of laws. But to do so requires a goal oriented, ambitious, dedicated, and talented person willing to devote himself to overcoming the obstacles placed in his path.

The three types of state chairmen discussed in this chapter play very different roles. Their power is often, but not always, a product of the type of party organization that they represent. Control of the governorship is the key to their style and position. The power of a Political Agent may be as great or greater than that of the In-Party or Out-Party Independent. The Political Agent who serves an activist governer can wield considerable power and influence.

In-Party Independents are often viewed as "organizational" leaders while their governor is looked upon as the "political" leader. This may appear to be a meaningless distinction, but it is one that is sometimes cited. The Out-Party Independent is usually recognized as the *real* party leader and, if the party is more than a rudimentary collection of individuals, can be powerful in his own right. The measurement of power, in other words, is relevant. The degree of discretion given to the chairman may escalate from the Political Agent through the In-Party Independent to the Out-Party Independent Chairman. But examples could be found in each category where the degree of discretion available to the chairman escalates in the opposite direction.

Most of the Out-Party Independent Chairmen view themselves as *the* party leader. As such they assume a greater burden of responsibilities as party spokesmen, mediators between party factions, and campaign strategists. In a sense, this is an easier role in that they do not have to mesh the party organization to the governor's personal organization. But most of them would argue that it is a more difficult role because they do not have an elected leader to rely upon for advice and to provide the leadership and focus for party affairs. Some of them play the role of Out-Party Independent reluctantly and look forward to the day when they or their successors can become Political Agents or In-Party Independents. This attitude was exemplified by a southern Republican who said:

> I was successor to the office when the former chairman resigned. I have just been reelected to a term of my own. If we ever were to capture the governorship and I were still chairman, I would resign because I think the governor should have his own man in this office. Until that time I am forced to be leader of the party in ———. It is a difficult position to be in.

Regardless of role orientation, a new state chairman will be faced with certain expectations on the part of party officials and workers. These expectations will normally encompass some or all of the roles which are normally considered to be the substance of politics. In the next two chapters the roles assigned to state parties are discussed. Chapter 5 considers the traditional "old politics" practices of recruitment, patronage, campaigns, and issues. Chapter 6, on the "new politics," considers opinion polls, campaign finance innovations, data processing, professional consulting services, and intraparty communication.

5 The Political Role of the State Chairman: The Old Politics

Some things in politics never change. Jobs for supporters and candidates for the ticket seem to always be with us. Every chairman I have worked with for the past fifteen years has complained that those two things took up most of his time.
A midwestern governor

I have tried my best to get the [executive] committee interested in some of the newer techniques, but they think the party is only there to get jobs, run primaries, and attack the opposition. They aren't even interested in experimenting with some statewide polls. It's frustrating as all hell.
A midwestern state chairman

Since we tend to be a liberal party, we have been able to come up with a pretty good platform based on real honest-to-God issues the past couple of elections. Having seen how hard that was, I hate to think what some of these guys must go through when their factions are in disagreement.
A western state chairman

In 1896 when Zachariah Chandler resigned the management of the Republican State Central Committee of Michigan, he had been state chairman for ten years and had been connected with the committee for twenty. Arthur C. Millspaugh described his stewardship as follows:

[Chandler] almost never made speeches and rarely came into direct relations with the workers of his party, but he used money effectively, and was skillful in the choice of his subordinates and in the distribution of patronage. Tactful and conciliatory, he usually came to terms with his enemies, and he did not interfere in state contests unless his own prestige or position seemed involved. He was a boss; but, to use the words of one of his assistants, he was perhaps the "easiest boss that Michigan ever had." [1]

Millspaugh's description of Chandler's style might apply to many state chairmen today just as it applied in 1896. Chairmen are still practicing conciliation and mediation between party factions; still distributing patronage; still attempting to use money effectively; and still seeking to employ those skilled in the art of politics to build effective organizations and to win elections. The chairmanship of a state political party remains a highly personal office. Today's chairmen usually do not remain in office as long as Chandler and they can seldom be described as "boss." But they encounter the same types of problems, seek solutions, experience failure, capitalize on successes, and attempt to build organizational structures that will bring them credit at the conclusion of their service.

The political role of today's party chairman is a composite of those responsibilities viewed as "traditional" and those described as "modern." The traditional roles, those described here as the "old politics," include candidate recruitment, patronage, campaign strategy, and issue development. Modern party managers, however, have accumulated additional responsibilities of a more technocratic mold. Those in the forefront of the modernization movement are involved in public opinion measurement, scientific fund raising, the use of professional consultants, automatic data processing, and the technical intricacies of public relations management. It is of little consequence whether a chairman is a Republican or Democrat, agent or independent, in or out of power. There are chairmen representing every combination of type attempting to ride shotgun on marriages of convenience between the traditional and the modern. Zachariah Chandler, and other party leaders of his era, did not have technocratic responsibilities. They emerged during the latter part of the twentieth century and are, in themselves, a measure of the change which has occurred in the political art.

In this chapter and the next these two aspects of the chairman's role are explored. The chairmen themselves are in considerable disagreement over their role and scope. Each reflects individually those political weaknesses and strengths upon which he must build. Each, in a very real sense, is a prisoner of the history of politics in his state. They generally agree on the broad goals of their offices—namely, to improve party organization—but their approaches reflect vastly differing orders of priority.

Some attempt to treat the responsibilities of office in broad and sweeping terms. A southern Democrat, faced with a new growth of Republicanism, described the party's needs:

A chairman should be a good administrator if he is full time, or he should be responsible for selecting a first-class executive director if he is not. He must build a good organization from the ground up, something that we need desperately. He must serve as a conduit between the rank and file and the officeholders. He must take the heat off the officeholders, mediate disputes between them and the voters, communicate with elected leaders, . . . and make a lot of speeches. I truly feel that our parties are in danger of extinction and that we must make every effort to stabilize them. We must build party organizations that are issue oriented, not patronage oriented. One of the most disturbing things that I have noted during my months in this office is that people no longer trust the parties. Even our own Democrats don't trust us any more. I think that I will have to do whatever is necessary to overcome that feeling.

Another Democrat, in describing his organizational problems, cited party disloyalty as a prime concern:

We have some counties in which the entire county Democratic organization voted for Richard Nixon. Can you imagine that? That is just how bad our party organization has deteriorated. I am not really in a position to mediate between party factions because I am a part of one of the factions. . . . I'm not a policy maker because I really believe the state chairman should refrain from becoming involved in issues at all. In my state that could be disastrous. The job of state chairman, as I see it, is to devote all his energies to organizational matters and leave the issues to the candidates. I hope I can work with the county leaders to build up the organizations in those counties which have operated independently or where we are weak. Some of them have ignored the state committee for so long that I have little hope that I will be successful. I can't even rely on advice from national party people or other state chairmen because I don't know any well enough to ask.

Some chairmen have attempted, through informal delegations of power, to share political responsibilities that devolve upon the state committee. One northern Republican noted that various people in the party were active in carrying out a variety of assigned functions:

For instance, the national committeeman handles all the patronage problems and the national committeewoman does all the speaking engagements. This delights me because I don't enjoy doing either of those things and it gives them something important to do. . . . I normally let all officeholders be the spokesmen for the party, unless we don't have a top officeholder and then I think the state chairman does have to chime in and lead the party as far as making policy statements is concerned. In ——— we don't have much trouble with factional division. We are all generally moderate to liberal and get along pretty well.

Party chairmen from both parties agreed on the top five responsibilities associated with their offices: organization building, fund raising, developing campaign strategies, campaigning, and recruitment (table 5.1). Although ranked differently, the distinctions are easily explained.

Political patronage is a commodity that is of value primarily to the party in power. The Republicans controlled the White House and monopolized federal job dispensing during the entire time period covered by these interviews. They also held several governorships, including some pregnant with patronage such as those in Indiana and Pennsylvania. This would easily account for the considerable difference between the party responses regarding the importance of patronage as a chairman's responsibility.

The interview responses also suggest that the close relationship between the Democratic party and organized labor in some states accounted

Table 5.1   Responsibilities Rated "Very Important" by State Chairmen

Democrats (N39)		Republicans (N41)	
Party organization builder	92.1%	Campaign strategist	90.4%
Fund raiser	92.1	Party organization builder	82.9
Campaign strategist	84.2	Campaigner	75.6
Campaigner	68.4	Fund raiser	70.7
Recruiter of candidates	65.8	Recruiter of candidates	68.3
Mediator between factions	63.2	Patronage dispenser	51.2
Spokesman for party	57.9	Morale builder	46.3
Morale builder	50.0	Mediator between factions	42.5
Policy maker	50.0	Spokesman for party	41.5
Patronage dispenser	34.2	Policy maker	34.0
Liaison with private interests	31.6	Link between national and local	22.0
Spokesman for governor	18.4	Spokesman for governor	21.9
Link between national and local	15.8	Liaison with private interests	19.5

NOTE: During the course of a pilot study, interviews with selected state chairmen identified the above party responsibilities as the most important ones from the point of view of the chairmen. During the full study each chairman was asked to indicate his estimation of the importance of each item by designating it as "very important," "important," or "unimportant."

for the higher Democratic ranking of "liaison with private interests." Finally, the greater difficulty experienced by Democrats in fund raising probably accounts for their higher ranking of that responsibility. This was especially true between 1968 and 1972 when the Republicans controlled the national government and the Democrats were burdened with a $9.3 million national party debt.

The real significance to be noted in table 5.1 is the agreement between the parties on the importance of those roles having to do with organizational politics and campaigning. The recognition of the importance of political fundamentals by the leadership of both parties in the states is apparent from these responses. Organization building, fund raising, campaign strategy, and candidate recruitment are the recognized responsibilities that have traditionally been associated with good party management.

James MacGregor Burns maintains that state party leaders are impotent and that the state political systems are really run by elected officeholders and candidates. There is little doubt that some state officeholders exercise significant, even total, political control over party affairs in many of the in-party states. But that accounts for only half of the political parties at best and ignores the differences between In- and Out-Party Independent Chairman.

Burns contends that candidates for state office have a major role in running their parties; however, most candidates for major state offices have political clout only so long as they are viable candidates. Their influence diminishes rapidly once they have been defeated. As noted in chapter 3, one of the principal reasons for the premature resignation of state chairmen is the defeat of their patron.[2]

Without question some elected public leaders exercise enormous power over the affairs of their state parties. Governors Nelson Rockefeller and Ronald Reagan and Chicago's Mayor Richard Daley readily come to mind. During his terms as governor of Arkansas, Winthrop Rockefeller *was* the Republican party in that state. Numerous other lesser-known elected officers have exhibited tight, albeit temporary, control over their party's operations. It is easy to select examples to illustrate Burns' point. But it is unrealistic to ignore those states in which elected leaders have shown little interest in party control or those in which the out-party leaders do provide effective opposition. The principal difference is one of constituency. The public official, whether he be a governor, senator, or mayor, exerts power in the name of the people—not just those who voted for him but the general public. The party chairman, on the other hand, may serve an equally important constituency representing those inside the party who elected him. As has been noted, if the chairman is simply carrying out the political mandate provided him by an elected governor, the two constituencies have merely merged and can be treated as one. In parties out of power, however, and those where an incumbent governor maintains an apolitical stance, the elected party chairman may, in fact, be *the* single most powerful political leader serving a party constituency. These chairmen often occupy politically strategic positions from which to direct their party's affairs. Given the necessary resources, many of them have demonstrated beyond question that they are the party's boss. In such cases they are responsible for those components which make up the old politics: candidate recruitment, patronage, developing campaign strategy, and the exposition of issues. These activities have always been charged to the state chairman or equivalent party officers. Efforts to carry them out have not always been effective, but they will ultimately serve as the crucible from which the chairman's record will be forged.

Recruiter of Candidates

Many authorities have contended that the recruitment and nomination of candidates for office are the most important functions of the political party. Lester G. Seligman has noted that the "recruitment of political candidates is a basic function of political parties" and concludes that "a party that cannot attract and then nominate candidates surrenders its elemental opportunity for power." [3] Professor E. E. Schattschneider states unequivocally that "whatever else they may or may not do, *the parties must make nominations.*" [4] That being so, the officials of the party should, by implication, make every effort to control the recruitment machinery which governs the selection of candidates for office.

Commenting on the recruitment process at the state level, V. O. Key, Jr., noted: "Perhaps the most important function that party leadership needs to perform is the development, grooming, and promotion of candidates for statewide office. Although striking exceptions may be cited, it is in its inadequacy in this role that the most grave shortcomings of party leadership is to be found.[5]

Complaints about the direct primary system of nomination from party leaders are, by now, an old refrain. The emergence of a self-starter candidate running in opposition to a recruited choice can spell havoc for party cohesion and for strong leadership control. Yet the primary system encourages candidates to run regardless of whether or not they have party backing. One party leader described the problem his party faced in 1970:

My recruitment committee and I worked for weeks to talk a particular individual into running for the state senate. We visited his place of business, invited him to party strategy discussions, asked his friends to work on him. He was very reluctant to undergo a campaign that was, at best, a 50–50 chance. Now, he was quite frank in saying that he would like to be in the Senate. He just needed to be persuaded to make the run. We finally made him some promises of campaign help that he couldn't resist. He agreed to run. And, damned if a guy none of us even knew didn't announce three weeks later. We had practically promised —————— that he would go through to the nomination without opposition. Well, I had to do something I do not normally like to do; that is, intervene in a primary. The chairman and I both put our necks on the line by personally endorsing our man. Fortunately, he won, but we were a little worried.

Among chairmen of both parties 73.8 percent engaged in some form of regular candidate recruitment. Due largely to party-building efforts in the South, Republicans tended (80.5 percent) to be more active in recruitment than Democrats (66.7 percent). Considering the number of states where self-starting has become the common method of entry into candidacy, these figures represent surprisingly high levels of recruitment. Most chairmen concentrated on ticket filling at the county level or in state legislative races.

Recruitment takes a variety of forms. Some chairmen are personally involved in all efforts while others concentrate on those offices at the head of the ticket. Thirty-six percent of the chairmen, the same number in both parties, personally engaged in candidate recruitment. Sometimes the prospective candidate was approached by the chairman in his capacity as party leader while at other times the added prestige of the governor or another high-ranking elected official was invoked. As one chairman put it: "It is hard for a prospective candidate to say no if you speak in behalf of the governor."

At times recruitment demands months of work. A Democratic chairman from a competitive state noted that his recruitment efforts for the state legislature begin as much as two years in advance:

When we see a young man or woman that we think would be a good candidate for the legislature, particularly the House, we begin to groom him. I see that the individual is appointed to party committees in order to increase exposure and establish some limited name-identification. We send him out on the trail to speak at dinners and other events. If he stands the test we then approach him about running for office. I don't think that some of them ever realize that we consciously groomed them for office.

Other chairmen do not believe it appropriate (or good politics) to engage in recruitment activities themselves. They assign others to do it, thus permitting the chairman to remain above the battle. A western Democrat described an intricate system of recruitment which

permits me to stay out of it entirely. I guess I would have a veto over a candidate, but I never exercise it. I have the county chairmen recruit at the county level; the urban chairmen in our largest cities recruit at the urban level; and our congressional district chairmen recruit at that level. We don't often have an opening in Congress since we have incumbents in all the seats. If we should, I believe I would intervene with the district leaders to try to get the strongest candidate we could. I bet the real problem would be to beat people away from seeking the nomination.

In seeking candidates for statewide or congressional office, some believe that recruitment should be left entirely to elected officials. After preliminary screening and sifting has taken place, the governor (or other respected official) is asked to contact the prospective candidate personally.

Many chairmen use a recruitment committee chosen from among members of the state committee. Some of them are traditional and are equivalent to standing committees. Others are appointed ad hoc, usually providing more direct control for the state chairman. Typical of them was one described by a southern Republican:

I have a recruitment committee that has been very effective in getting candidate lists together. They have been immensely effective in fact. We have sixty-five candidates running for state legislative seats this year. That is spectacular when you consider that six years ago we had less than fifteen. We are trying to base our appeal with the voters on attractive, young, articulate candidates, and we have been particularly successful in encouraging Young Republicans to take the plunge, both men and women.

Most chairmen express the belief that they should assume an active role in the recruitment process. To some, this means more than successful persuasion. As often as not in some states, it is just as important to dissuade self-starters without alienating them. This was illustrated by a Democrat who noted:

I actually recruit at all levels. The only way to guarantee good candidates on the ticket is to recruit them yourself. It's important to recruit because that is the only way you can keep self-proclaimed candidates from gaining a spot on the ballot, and that can do you in. You simply have to have the clout to tell a self-starter, "No, you cannot be a candidate and if you go ahead and try we will give you no support at all." I have gone so far as to imply that the party will work against a guy if he persists in running. One has to be brutal about it with some of them.

That recruitment has become a year-round job in election years was explained by a Republican:

I definitely think that the chairman should have a very active role in all phases of recruitment. I have now gotten the rules changed so that the chairman is elected in January precisely for that reason. Candidates must file by April 1st, and we'll start . . . demanding reports on how the county leaders are doing filling their tickets as early as the January meeting of the state committee. I think this added pressure from a chairman who has just been elected or reelected, and who will be continuing in office through the election, helps us to fill our ticket. In the past we have sometimes had candidates on our ticket and sometimes we haven't. We are even trying to fill our ticket in the cities even though the candidates haven't much chance. We don't always get particularly good candidates, but it is more important to fill the ticket and show that you're alive than it is to field a list of good candidates.

A tightly structured party system, such as that presided over by Chicago's Mayor Richard J. Daley, may combine the processes of recruitment and nomination. Often, in order to earn a position on the ballot, a candidate must have demonstrated his loyalty through long years of party support and diligent effort. When he is "ready," the leadership will encourage him to present himself to the Democratic "slating committees" which meet to interview and debate the merits of various candidates for office. Meeting first in Springfield and then in Chicago, the slating committee hears each contender for office present his case in a tightly guarded closed session. The Chicago meeting is presided over by Mayor Daley himself, acting in his capacity of Cook County chairman. After long debate the slating committee emerges to announce the party's slate of candidates for the upcoming election. These candidates are still not officially nominated until they are ratified by the voters in the state's primary election, but the Illinois Democratic party has seldom been troubled by serious primary opposition. It can happen, however, as was demonstrated by the challenge of Democrat Daniel Walker in 1972 when he filed against the slated gubernatorial candidate, Lieutenant Governor Paul Simon. Walker not only went on to defeat Simon in the Democratic primary but was elected governor over the Republican incumbent.

Recruitment is important if new blood is to be transfused into the political system. As an isolated process, recruitment is one of the favorable catchwords of politics. But even the most avid and successful of recruiters can become enmeshed in webs from which he cannot extricate himself. Some political situations are fraught with danger. One such danger occurs when a party is divided and factionalized and expects the chairman to serve as mediator and conciliator. Recruitment of new candidates is often impossible without creating even greater dissension. If the chairman attempts to carry out his recruitment responsibilities, any approach to a prospective candidate may appear to be favoritism. Some have sought to recruit candidates who have not previously been involved in politics. But the limits of that approach are apparent. Others have merely abandoned any recruitment efforts at all for fear of alienating one faction or the other. One of them stated:

> You can't take any part in encouraging one candidate over another in ———— without jeopardizing your position. Our party is a highly personal one with three major groups led by three old-time leaders. Every state chairman is a member of one or the other of the groups, and every one has been elected by a coalition of some of the members of more than one. As chairman, I can't take any part in recruitment or nomination without sacrificing my role as mediator between the factions. I keep a strictly hands-off policy. Anyone can make a run for it who wants to.

A second danger arises not so much from recruitment activities as from the post recruitment period of the primary election. Each respondent was asked: "In a primary fight between two or more party candidates for the same nomination, do you feel that the state chairman should become involved?" The open-ended responses are shown in table 5.2. In both parties combined, 57.5 percent indicated that they would intervene at least provisionally. Most (28.7 percent) said that they would involve themselves if necessary to protect the caliber of the ticket. Others felt that intervention would be desirable only if the candidate had been officially endorsed. Approximately the same number in both parties (28.8 percent) said that they would not intervene under any circumstances.

The penalties for backing the wrong candidate were illustrated by the following incident described by one chairman who intervened regularly in primary contests:

When ——— was chairman in 1966 he announced his support for ——— for governor. Now, that did not seem to be an important problem at the time because everyone expected him to win hands down. Unfortunately, he proved to be a dull and lackluster candidate, and a relative unknown, ———, actually won the primary. Just about everybody ran for cover, but the chairman was left standing there holding the bag. He was immediately asked to resign, which he did, and ———'s campaign manager was designated as chairman. They went on to lose the election but that wasn't much consolation to [the former chairman].

The direct primary system of nomination is a spur to self-starting candidates. Individuals may file in most states without clearing their intentions with anyone. Some, of course, have no alternative because of the weaknesses inherent in some local party organizations. But a state chairman who desires to build a ticket and wishes to recruit and groom candidates to be a part of it can be severely undercut by self-starters. Unless there is some form of party endorsement procedure, the leadership has

Table 5.2   Chairmen's Attitudes toward Intervention in Primary Contests

Response to Question: Should Chairmen Intervene?	Democrats (N39)	Republicans (N41)	Total (N80)
Yes, only if candidate is endorsed by party	7.7%	7.3%	7.6%
Yes, if necessary to protect caliber of candidates	25.6	31.7	28.7
Yes, but only by recruiting strong candidates	7.7	4.9	6.2
Yes, open intervention	15.4	14.6	15.0
No, never under any circumstances	28.2	29.3	28.8
No, in local races; yes, in state races	0.0	4.9	2.5
No (but has intervened when necessary)	5.1	0.0	2.5
NA/DK	10.3	7.3	8.7

no way to signal its choices to the workers and the voters. Some endorsement systems are quite informal, though at the same time effective. One Democratic leader in a metropolitan county tried and failed to get legislation passed which would permit the party to indicate preferences for each office on the primary ballot. He was particularly concerned that the lower-income white and Negro voters have some guidance in choosing among candidates on the primary ballot. He described his solution to the problem:

we simply go into each precinct in the problem areas early on election morning and mark our choices in lipstick right on the machine. We usually go back about noon to freshen up the mark.... It has been quite effective in helping us educate our voters in choosing among good Democrats.

Most endorsement procedures are not so easy, nor are they so effective. Consequently, the party's leadership is sometimes faced with one or more nominees who owe the party nothing. They run under, but do not carry, the party's banner. Of the numerous horror stories related by party leaders, this one best serves as an example:

I have tried for three years to get it across that we cannot expect to have a good organization until we get control of our ticket. We just had another setback that makes me want to quit.... I worked long and hard to put together a list of candidates who might give us a chance at some legislative seats in one key county. But in two of the three districts we got an outsider who had never been involved in party affairs.... The primary was held about three weeks ago and we got a Bircher nominated in one, a housewife with no experience in another, and we got our own guy nominated in the third. How in hell are we to go to the people with that? To make matters worse, the Bircher is probably going to win and will be around to embarrass us for the next two years, if not forever.

The recruitment of candidates is simply one means of channeling political aspirations. Very few state chairmen, or other party leaders, hold sufficient power to decline to let a prospect run. Some—a Ray Bliss or a John Bailey or a Richard Daley—have been able to exercise that degree of power, but most must rely solely on empty threats or personal persuasion. Some chairmen have developed a candidate screening committee to serve as the litmus paper through which prospective candidates must pass as a check on their mettle. Such devices also help to take some of the heat off the chairman, thus providing him with a greater degree of freedom with which to operate.

On the whole, those state party organizations which have increased their strength in recent years have experimented with more formal recruitment and candidate screening processes. Sometimes these have worked and at other times they have not. In general, the weaker systems, and those led by less active chairmen, have permitted nature to take her course. In effect, they rely on voter judgment to select candidates from among the self-starters. That is no way to build a party though it may fill a ticket.

The development of more closely contested two-party.systems in some states has enhanced the desirability of affirmative action in the selection of candidates. Even in old established party systems there appears to be more interest in recruitment. Most chairmen and other party leaders have concluded that active recruitment is the crucial underpinning of party building.

Dispenser of Patronage

Job patronage is the use of appointive governmental and political positions as a reward for past or future party work. It still is an important commodity in which many state chairmen regularly trade, despite the advent of civil service and merit systems. Federal patronage positions are available to the president's party. State patronage positions are available to those who are members of the governor's party and in some cases to those active in the opposition party. The positions involved are generally of two types: paid government positions involving the public's business; and unpaid honorary memberships in various party councils and committees. The former are the most important, since they bring the employee personal emolument as a reward for party service. Jobs, in short, represent a principal currency of politics. The second are of lesser importance in terms of monetary reward but carry with them honor and prestige. In either case a knowledgeable state chairman with the cooperation of his party's congressmen and governor can use patronage appointments as a means to maintain control over party affairs and to engender loyalty from those who are appointed.

For the party in power, federal patronage positions are a means of rewarding the party faithful with paid jobs or honorary memberships. Control over them almost always rests with the White House, but the actual appointments are usually channeled through the state party organizations. Since this study was completed during a Republican administration, there was virtually no federal patronage reported by the Democratic state chairmen. Some administrations have treated the dispensation of federal jobs casually and have attempted to down-play the "reward" aspects. Others have insisted upon highly structured systems of clearance and have demanded absolute loyalty of those receiving job awards. Many Republican state chairmen complained that the award of patronage jobs in the federal government was counterproductive—doing the party more damage than good. They often voiced an old complaint that for every successful applicant there were several unsuccessful ones who blamed the party for their failure to secure the position. On the whole, the state chairmen in both parties considered federal patronage to be a mixed blessing.

Systems for clearance of federal patronage ranged from casual conversations between the state chairmen and members of Congress to highly structured committee clearance involving party personnel from the precinct through the state to the Congress. One eastern Republican noted:

> We haven't had much Federal patronage—not nearly as much as I expected when we took over the White House. What we have had has been mostly middle-level commission appointments, and they have been handled by Senator ———— and myself. He simply calls me up and says that there is a vacancy and that he has been thinking of nominating some particular person for it and what do I think. I usually check with that person's county chairman to see if his party credentials are in order, if I don't know him, and if they are, give the senator my approval and the appointment is submitted. That does not necessarily mean that we will get it, but Senator ———— has quite a bit of influence with some of the people in the White House and has done pretty well in this sort of thing.

A number of states use a more structured system of clearance, usually involving a patronage committee composed of state party officials, members of the governor's staff, and members of the House and Senate. A prospective appointee is cleared in his precinct and county and considered by the patronage committee before being recommended to whichever member of Congress serves as that party's liaison with the White House. A typical example of a state patronage committee at work was that of the Republican party of Idaho. During the first six months of the Nixon administration that committee was composed of the state chairman, the national committeeman and woman, the governor, lieutenant governor, two congressmen, the U.S. senator, and three Nixon campaign officials in the state. This group acted upon the recommendations of a three-man screening committee composed of the state chairman, the governor, and one Nixon man. In order to receive a favorable recommendation, an individual seeking federal appointment was required to show the signatures of his county chairman and precinct leader on his application. Once approved by the screening committee and the full patronage committee, the nomination was carried forward by Idaho's Republican U.S. senator (a member of the full committee).

This system lasted for six months until the June 1969 Republican National Committee meeting in Washington when White House aide, Harry Dent (former state chairman of South Carolina), met with the RNC and asked that each state select a single contact man to deal with the White House on patronage matters. At that time the earlier patronage committee arrangement in Idaho was abandoned, and it was agreed that the national committeeman from Idaho would serve as the official patronage contact. Recommendations henceforth flowed directly from the national committeeman to the U.S. senator to the White House, once they had been cleared with the proper local party officials by the committeeman.

This change in procedure was the culmination of a hectic six months during which the Nixon administration came under heavy fire from Republican officials throughout the nation. In many states, Nixon campaign aides sent nominations for jobs directly to the White House, while state party officials were either uninformed or in the process of clearing and submitting entirely different names for the same positions. The turmoil and hard feelings that ensued were responsible for Dent's visit to the national committee meeting and for the change in procedure in Idaho and many other states. Patronage affairs ran more smoothly in the later years of the Nixon administration.

In the past half-century many states have adopted legislation placing most state jobs under a merit system. Many local governments have also sought to reduce political influence in "nonpartisan" governments by instituting merit appointments. Some states, however, still maintain large numbers of patronage positions which are used in the brokerage of political power. Robert H. Salisbury, in a 1966 study of urban party organizations, found the Democratic party of Saint Louis has been able to reward more than 40 percent of its members with patronage jobs of one kind or another.[6] And Mayor Richard Daley of Chicago still retains control over an estimated 35,000 patronage jobs with which he regularly oils his political machine. A former state chairman of Pennsylvania noted that the governor of that state has 65,000 patronage positions to award, while in Indiana about 8,000 of that state's 22,000 public employees are patronage appointees. In West Virginia a Democratic party official reported that his party controlled all state offices except the governorship and could distribute 300 state jobs. However, he noted, if they had control of the governorship there would be 15,000 jobs to distribute. These are exceptional cases but illustrate the importance of patronage as a political system.

Most state chairmen report that they have few, if any, state jobs to distribute, and that, of course, depends upon whether or not they serve the in-party. One midwestern Republican In-party Independent said that during his three years in office he had been able to recommend the appointment of less than 100 individuals to all types of positions. He further noted that in the process of making these appointments he had probably angered 500 to 600 others, either because they themselves wanted the job and didn't get it or because they were unhappy with the individual who was appointed. In short, he felt that the availability of jobs does not always carry a reward that justifies the internal political turmoil. Another chairman noted that those jobs available are often low-paying and low-prestige positions which are awarded to people who contribute little to the party organization except their vote. In his state the important patronage positions were high-prestige but unpaid memberships on state commissions.

Most states have some patronage positions that must be filled. They range from a few controlled by the governor to thousands controlled directly by the party. As noted in table 5.3 the role of the state chairman in dispensing state jobs is varied. In some states he has no control over patronage, the entire matter being handled in the governor's office or the office of some other elected political officer. In other states he has total control over the distribution of jobs and need not check with anyone regarding them.

Complete control of patronage by the chairman was apparent in 11.2 percent of the state parties. An illustration was provided by a midwestern Democratic chairman:

I have total control over state patronage appointments. No one of the many thousand state jobs can be awarded without my approval. I normally give my approval, but I have an absolute veto. It doesn't matter who recommends; I have absolute veto with state patronage appointments. Even if we are out of power, I have over 2,000 state patronage appointments over which I have control.

In some cases the chairman's control over patronage is tied to his role as fund raiser. Three chairmen—two Democrats and one Republican—

noted that those who received patronage jobs must contribute to the party. One of the Democrats noted:

I have had about 125 appointments to make since I have been here and in every case I called the man in and said, "All right, you placed well in the Civil Service test and I am willing to recommend you but I want $300." And in every case I got the $300 for the party. I'm not embarrassed about it at all. That's the way we have to do it to get money. In effect, I sold the position.

Another such instance was reported by a Republican chairman who responded to his governor's appointment of a new chairman of the State Fish and Game Commission by calling the appointee and saying to him:

You know, you've been appointed and I'd like to have a contribution of a couple of hundred dollars from you for the party. This guy [the appointee] said, "Why, I never engage in party politics. I don't think I can give you anything." I retorted, "If I'd been asked I would have called you up and said, 'Say, you're about to be appointed; we expect a $200 contribution from you.'" And I'd have gotten it, but this way we're out of the money. He doesn't owe us anything.

Most state patronage, as noted in table 5.3, is controlled by the governor's office; 52.6 percent of the state chairmen reported that their

Table 5.3   Role of State Chairman in Dispensing State Patronage

	Democrats (N39)	Republicans (N41)	Total (N80)
Has complete control	12.8%	9.8%	11.2%
Is member of patronage committee composed of party leaders	2.6	12.2	7.4
State executive committee clears appointments	5.1	2.4	3.8
Makes suggestions but has no voice in final decisions	25.6	9.7	17.6
Governor controls; chairman does not participate	46.2	58.6	52.6

NOTE: Columns do not total to 100 percent due to multiple responses. These percentages may be inaccurate due to the lack of control over the selection of states. For example, the figures may be overrepresentative or underrepresentative of the states as a whole, because there was no method to control the distribution of states between those with merit systems and those with patronage systems.

governor maintained operating control over all patronage appointments. The following were typical:

Governor ———— doesn't check with us at all. He makes the appointments and we read about it in the paper the next day.

There is a great deal of state patronage in ————, but the governor handles all of it through his own staff. Sometimes they call on me and ask what I think about somebody, but it's usually a decision that's already been made and they are simply going through a perfunctory courtesy.

The governor handles it. There is no clearance at all. He simply makes the appointments.

In terms of state patronage, the governor handles everything and they never contact me. They never ask for my advice or inform me what they're doing with regard to jobs.

Several state chairmen (17.6 percent) reported being called upon for suggestions in patronage decisions but acknowledged that they had little voice in final decisions. Ordinarily they were not unhappy with this system, since many of those whom they suggested were actually appointed.

Cooperation between the governor's office and the chairman is of considerably more importance in those states where the minority party controls the governorship. Several chairmen reported that this was a particularly sticky problem because many opposition officeholders were good at their jobs and there were no available members of the party in power who could perform the jobs as well. One said:

We have a special problem, in that we had to keep the Democrats happy because there are so many of them. We have many Democrats in office. We simply can't fire them, and since there are not many Republicans around we have to hire a great many Democrats. As a general rule, I make recommendations to the governor on appointments, and the governor and his staff consider the recommendations seriously. They don't always follow them, but they give them serious consideration and I would say that generally they follow them. This is particularly important in the case of the reappointment of Democrats to jobs because you can really set off a hornet's nest in some counties.

In another state both parties have traditionally divided patronage responsibilities between the chairman and the governor, regardless of which party holds the governorship. Judgeships, which neither the chairman nor the incumbent governor believes should even be under the patronage system, are handled exclusively by the governor on a nonpartisan basis, while all other patronage appointments are presented as recommendations from the chairman for appointment by the governor.

Sometimes the party's executive committee serves as a patronage committee to screen and make recommendations, and in other states a special patronage committee of the type described earlier in Idaho is used for this purpose. Patronage committees normally are composed of the state chairman, the governor or a representative of the governor's office (if the party is in power), the national committee members, and selected other individuals. In every instance the chairman serves as a member and in most tends to play a dominant role.

Many party officials have mixed feelings about patronage. On the one hand, they fear that an appointment will create more problems than it solves and make more enemies than friends. On the other hand, the jobs are there to fill and all political leaders recognize the need to enhance party morale and encourage party workers by filling available jobs with party people. There are usually few precautions that can be taken to guarantee effective job performance by patronage appointees. Some have proven embarrassing to the parties. One Democratic chairman described such a problem:

On state appointments we tell every appointee that we will bring charges against him if he gets in trouble. We think it is better to do it ourselves rather than have the Republicans do it, so we make it quite clear to them that if there is any chicanery and we run across it we will ourselves bring charges against them to protect the party's good name. On all state judgeships we turn the names over to the ———— Bar Association and get a written letter of clearance. Then if the Bar refuses to clear because of a competence question, that takes some of the heat off the governor and myself. I have had to call prospective judicial nominees in and say, "Why, we were happy to appoint you, but the Bar Association in this letter I have here refused to clear you and didn't give you a high enough endorsement and we're just not going to be able to make the appointment, because, as you know, we've come to depend on these Bar Association clearances." This makes the candidate quite unhappy but he's unhappy with the Bar Association and not with the party organization. It has an added benefit, in that if the Bar Association cleared an individual and he later got in trouble it takes some of the heat off the governor. We can simply say, "Well, the state Bar Association cleared him and we did everything we could; it isn't our fault he got in trouble." That's why we have written letters of clearance. We can prove everything if we get in trouble with an appointee.

Patronage remains an important commodity in which a political party can trade. Even though jobs are not as important to the success of party politics as they once were, patronage still greases many state and local machines. Those who take part in the process often express ambivalent attitudes toward patronage politics. If pressed, however, most of them, both chairmen and governors, still view prospective jobs as an important incentive to party workers.

Campaign Manager

In its broadest sense campaigning is the process of developing resources and putting them to advantageous use with the goal of winning elections. Most candidates employ a manager to assume overall direction of their campaigns, relieving them of the day-to-day responsibilities. Campaign managers normally accept the burdens of scheduling, fund raising, public relations, speech writing, tactical planning, and issue exploitation. There may be other campaign aides with specific assigned duties, but the manager has overall responsibility.

It was not, however, in this sense that the state chairmen ranked "campaign strategist" (table 5.1) so highly. Over 90 percent of the Republican party leaders collectively rated the management responsibility as "very important," ranking it above all others. Eighty-four percent of the Democratic chairmen ranked it as highly. These are extraordinarily high rankings for a specific function associated with the state chairman's responsibilities.

Since few incumbent state chairmen actually serve as the campaign manager for a particular candidate, it is apparent that the role of campaign manager and strategist is viewed by them in a different context. As noted in chapter 2, over one-fourth of the chairmen had run for office themselves and many others had earlier served as manager of another's campaign. The state chairmen's view of their campaign responsibility must be considered in that light. They are far more likely to see themselves as campaign manager of the state party's total ticket with general responsibility for getting as many persons elected as possible. Their management interest is not limited to a single candidate but is more likely to embrace the efforts of the whole party.

Three patterns of management activity are apparent. First are those chairmen who, with the approval of the state committee, concentrate party resources on a single statewide race. This is usually the case in one-party states where the minority party does not run a full slate but channels available party resources to a single top-of-the-ticket candidate. Although some of these efforts are little more than symbolic, the fact that the minority party is running a candidate at all has psychological significance. A number of southern Republican chairmen acknowledged that virtually all their resources were channeled to a single candidate for governor, U.S. senator, congressman, or state constitutional officer. The chairman himself served, in effect, as the campaign manager for the candidate and, through him, for the party. One of them put it this way:

We have not elected a statewide candidate in a hundred years or more. We are just beginning to get some Republican organizations in the suburbs of ———— and we thought it was important to give them something to work for. So we talked ———— into running for governor. We put all our effort into his campaign. I was his manager, and the finance chairman [of the party] was his fund raiser. We lost badly, of course, but, by God, we proved that we are alive.

Another variation on the same theme was described by a chairman who convinced his party to emphasize a single statewide race as a means of providing assistance to the whole ticket. He personally assumed management of the governor's campaign, in effect accepting it as a responsibility of the state chairmanship. He explained:

Almost all of our officeholders were up for election last year, and the most important of them was governor ————, who was running for a second term. His popularity is such that we decided to tie the entire statewide campaign to him in hopes that his coattails would be broad enough to pull everybody else into office. Even though we were not as successful as I had hoped, I do believe it was a good strategy, since we did elect the governor and a significant number of our people down lower on the ticket. The decision to tie ourselves to the governor was not universally popular. Quite a few of our legislative candidates felt that we neglected them and, of course, everybody always wants more money, more speakers, and more help than you can actually give. I was criticized pretty widely for, in effect, managing the gov-

ernor's campaign, but that was because the others didn't see that the strategy
was to use him to help the whole ticket. . . . However, in view of the fact that
we picked up three seats in the legislature, I think we did pretty well.

The second, and by far the largest, group of chairmen viewed campaign management much more broadly. All the regular functions of the
chairmanship and the headquarters team were combined to campaign for
the party itself. Resources were expended so as to maximize party benefits. Assistance included recruitment, voter registration, fund raising, public relations, and issue development. All the candidates were viewed as
potential beneficiaries of a party-oriented campaign managed by the state
chairman. The campaign role became a party function. A representative
comment serves as an illustration:

> The chairman in ———— has traditionally avoided becoming involved too
> greatly in any particular campaign. Most of our candidates had their own
> managers and organizations. Our headquarters concentrated on legislative
> races. The top candidates [for attorney general and U.S. Senate] wanted to
> run their own campaigns. . . . We put out party policy papers, speech kits,
> organized a speakers' bureau, and did things like that to serve all the party's
> candidates. We were also able to give each of the candidates some support
> through a series of statewide ads pushing the whole ticket.

Theoretically, such campaign efforts become a part of the chairman's
regular responsibilities. In a real sense their success or failure reflects on
the general evaluation of him in his chairman's role. That this is the case
is demonstrated by the high rate of resignations or defeats of incumbent
chairmen within three months after each election. The 20 to 35 percent
who leave office after each biennial election often depart in a cloud of
kudos but are in actual fact forced out of office because their efforts as
campaign chairmen were not reflected in an expected payoff at the polls.
This appears to be particularly true in highly competitive states where
expectations may run higher.

Finally, a third group of chairmen do not engage in any aspect of campaigning. They do not have the resources at their command to support a
campaign or they place greater emphasis on others of their roles. In the
South, even the majority party chairman is sometimes not involved seriously in campaigning. Many commentators have reflected upon the highly
personal politics that prevail in the southern states. Party organizations
have, in some instances, atrophied because party leaders have opted for
a personal campaign devoted solely to their election or reelection. The

leitmotif of southern political history has been one of personal factions (the Longs, Talmadges, Russells, Faubuses, Bilbos, and many others) dedicated to electing individuals, not devoted to the party per se. These factional leaders ran as Democrats, but they did not rely on the Democratic party for their success. Although not as numerous as they once were, this traditional form of politics still precludes organized party campaign efforts in some southern states.

Table 5.1 offers convincing evidence that state chairmen believe they have an important role in campaign management. Defining that role and determining the extent to which they should become involved are problems that are not easily resolved. Most chairmen have opted for active participation but are aware of the personal dangers resulting from a poor election showing. The postelection resignation rate provides convincing evidence of the relationship between campaign management and election success. To remain uninvolved and above the battle generates considerable risk. It is most difficult to attract campaign workers and volunteers when the leadership itself is isolated from the conflict. Campaigns are used to involve people. They are vehicles for attracting new voters and campaign workers. The party which does not become involved risks cutting off nourishment and sustenance to the organizational apparatus. At the same time some state chairmen are properly concerned over the effect of a highly personal commitment to the campaign. It is likely that increased organizational strength and improved headquarters operations will encourage chairmen to assume greater management responsibilities. It is also true that the limited tenure of the chairmen will be counterproductive, emphasizing once again the importance of resolving that pressing dilemma.

Issues, Ideology, and Party Platforms

Campaigns provide the occasion for candidates and parties to state their case publicly, to agree or to disagree, and to provide the electorate with a variety of reasons for supporting them. In spite of the fact that there is a widely held view among candidates that one must speak to the issues if one is to win, the evidence suggests that few in the electorate listen to issue-oriented campaigns. Yet, at the same time, the voters have repeatedly demonstrated their fear of candidates who appear to take extremist positions on the issues. This is a paradox that party leaders and campaign managers are forced to address. Their campaign responses have taken several tacks. Some down-play issues, attempting to lose them as individual brush strokes on a broad ideological canvas. Others attempt to control the use of issues by channeling debate to limited specific topics. And still others rely on platform generalities as the anchor upon which to moor the campaign.

Most chairmen identified their parties as "moderate," "moderate conservative," or "moderate liberal." This effort to occupy the ideological center is in keeping with the conventional wisdom which holds that parties must appeal to the broad range of voters in the middle of the road. This electoral norm was apparent when only 16 percent of the chairmen identified their own parties unequivocally as "liberal" and only 10 percent as "conservative."

The fact is that most chairmen view distinctly ideological commitments as a deterrent. Except in the South, where both parties are often committed to "conservatism," there is an inclination to build campaigns around programmatic issues. This strategy permits the party leaders to exercise some control over those issues which emerge, while at the same time avoiding ideological identifications which might cause voter alienation. It is preferable, in their view, for candidates to discuss taxes, highways, schools, welfare, or environmental questions and not become involved in debates over degrees of conservatism and liberalism.

Issues are conceived in a variety of ways. Some merely emerge, often unexpectedly, during the campaign. At times they are of such an emotional nature that they dominate the campaign period and play an important part in the outcome. Others develop out of a conscious effort by the leadership to direct the attention of the voters by carefully selecting the policy matters around which the statewide campaign will be built. And still others avoid involving the party organization at all, leaving the development of issues to individual candidates. Finally, a number of chairmen viewed the party's platform as the most legitimate means of going on record while protecting the candidate's personal prerogatives.

Sometimes unexpected issues emerge to dominate a campaign. Since they are usually unanticipated, they can lay waste to well-laid plans. A case in point in the early 1970s was the question of busing to achieve racial balance in public schools. One Republican chairman described the effect:

It was my intention to run a generally issueless campaign. We only had two important races and none of the candidates on either side greatly differed in their views. We were really planning to sell personality. . . . But the busing issue hit us hard and forced our people to adopt positions against forcible busing that some of us didn't even agree with. It was largely neutralized, though, because the opposition took the same position. The real damage was caused by the total dominance of that particular problem over the campaign. We were never able to get ——'s position across because busing always seemed to intervene.

Most party leaders attempt to select the issues around which the campaign will be built. The choice may be that of the state chairman, a party committee, the governor, or a campaign manager. The issues selected may be included in the party's platform or they may not. More than half the state chairmen described a process of informal discussion among party leaders and candidates in which various issues were considered for their voter appeal and decisions were made as to the best way to exploit them. A Democratic national committeeman who was involved in the process in his state described it this way:

Before every campaign . . . we sit down and discuss what we hope to say to the voters. [When asked to identify the participants he listed the two national committee members, the state chairman, the executive director, finance director, research director, and a representative from the only state office held by his party.] I remember one time when we decided to say as little as possible because we couldn't reach an agreement. Generally, we are able to devise a short list of positions which we then encourage our candidates to adopt. We have no way of making them do it, but we have them available if they are needed. In the last couple of elections we have had the benefit of a straw vote that is run by the [statewide newspaper], and we would like to have an early poll but we can't afford it.

Another strategy is to allow the candidates to develop their own positions on issues. In effect, this requires the party to remain uninvolved. It is a form of laissez-faire politics that can result in political anarchy as various candidates, running under the same party banner, adopt conflicting and contradictory positions. Nevertheless, if the issue conflict within the party is so great that no common ground is possible, it may be the only way to play the game.

Those chairmen playing the role of Political Agent or In-Party Independent often look to the statehouse for leadership on issue formulation. An incumbent governor may wish to maintain control over the policy positions adopted by his party. He may wish to broaden support for his programs by binding candidates to his own position on major issues. As explained by one chairman:

The state chairman should not make public statements on issues in ———— unless he has discussed it with the governor and determines that he wants the statement made. In that case, it is all right. He might put up a trial balloon or something of that sort, but he would never make a statement on his own so long as we have the governorship. This applies to campaign statements as well as issues that crop up between campaigns.

Another respondent drew a distinction between the chairman's role as an in-party or an out-party leader:

I have a hand in developing issues. I did much more when we were out of power because now I think it is up to the governor to do this, and he and his staff think so too. Nevertheless, I am in on most major pronouncements, if for no other reason than I need to be informed so that I can handle the press or the county people.

Some organizations develop issues as a matter of long-range party strategy. For example:

We as a party have advocated the income tax because we realize that in order to finance the state the governor is going to have to advocate an income tax before the legislature within the next six months. We feel it is better to have the party take responsibility for it than it is to make the governor catch all the hell. It gave us time to build party support for the income tax before the proposal had to be made. We began building up to this over two years ago.

Many chairmen viewed the party platform as the most convenient and accepted means of treating issues as well as ideology. Platforms are used regularly in 89 percent of the state parties. They are formally adopted by the state convention or the state committee. Most platforms originated in draft form in an incumbent governor's office or from an ad hoc committee of party leaders. The state chairmen almost always are involved in platform drafting. In any case the draft document is presented to the state convention or to the party's central committee for final approval. It then becomes an official party document.

A party platform represents the confluence of many streams. The original sources of many of the ideas contained in it are often difficult to trace. Ideas, phrases, paragraphs, and sections may have emanated from such disparate sources as the governor's office, legislative caucuses, party workers, public opinion polls, and earlier platforms. Sometimes it is little more than the governor's campaign pledges imposed upon his party. The patterns are infinite, as reflected in these descriptions:

The platform has always been written by Governor ————. It goes through a very complicated and detailed process of being approved, but the process is not very important since it was written in ————'s office and everybody knows it.

Since the ———— Company dominates politics in this state, the platform is drafted by us but we must meet with their approval. The "company" inevitably cuts across our platform positions, so it insists on having anything cut out that crosses its interests. In return they pay our way. It looks like we sell out, I know, but you have to realize that it is a small price to pay since no one ever pays any attention to the platform once it is released.

We use the governor's campaign issues as our platform. That's all.

Our platform is adopted by a platform committee which is really a subcommittee of the state committee. We use it as a campaign document and make every effort to adopt it into law. We take our platform very seriously. We even try to hold our candidates to it. We apply what pressure we can to make our legislative candidates pledge support.

The platform committee actually wrote the platform sixty to ninety days before the convention. It was cleared with all relevant individuals including all three gubernatorial candidates. We had open-forum meetings across the state for contributions from the public end. At most of these, local party officials testified and in some cases tried to get county platforms incorporated into it. As state chairman, I am then responsible for shoving the platform through the legislature. We take the platform very seriously, and so do the Republicans.

I personally write the platform in my office with the assistance of Professor ———— who helps us with research occasionally. It reflects the governor's views, and we try to insist that our legislative candidates embrace it as theirs. If they refuse, there isn't really anything we can do about it though.

Once adopted, the state platform provides party leaders and candidates with a convenient source for political positions on the issues, and it also offers a reasonably effective means for them to dodge taking personal positions. If some of the candidates choose to run non-issue-oriented campaigns, they can refer questioners to the platform without personally endorsing it.

Approximately one-half of the chairmen expect candidates to support the platform while 36 percent do not. Most of those who demand candidate support have few weapons with which to enforce sanctions against those who refuse. Those who succeed are usually those who assist the candidate in paying his campaign expenses.

Uses to which platforms were put were varied. Some 26 percent of the state chairmen reported not using the platform in the campaign at all (table 5.4). Its adoption is a formality which the leadership fears not to carry out. The document is used primarily as a public relations device in 27 percent of the parties as represented by these comments:

We give the platform to the candidates, and it usually gets one or two days in the newspapers but that is about all. We use it as a basis for publicity releases.

We try to publicize our platform a little bit but that's about it. I wouldn't dare try to run on it. The people who draft it are not always the best judges of what to say.

We published ours last year and it got pretty wide distribution as a campaign document. Unfortunately, it got us in real hot water. The young kids got an abortion plank added, and we ended up with many of our Democratic candidates disavowing or abandoning the platform.

Few state parties attempt to convert the platform into legislation. Among the 7.5 percent that do, one party converts the entire platform into bills to be introduced at the time the legislature convenes. One

Table 5.4   Use of the Party Platform

	Democrats (N39)	Republicans (N41)	Total (N80)
Not at all	23.1%	29.3%	26.2%
Primarily as a public relations campaign document	25.6	29.3	27.5
As a basis for legislation	10.3	4.9	7.5
As a vehicle to sell governor's program only	2.5	2.5	2.5
Slight or undesignated	10.3	9.8	10.0
More than one of the above	7.7	9.8	8.8
DK/NA	20.5	14.6	17.5

county leader who served as chairman of the platform committee for his party reported:

We have had a tradition of trying to adopt our platform into law. In fact, the other party does too. One of the things we keep in mind while the platform is being drafted is whether or not a plank can be translated into a bill we can support. I remember one year our guys introduced about 175 bills based on our platform. We drafted them over at headquarters, and they picked out the ones they wanted to drop in.

One chairman expressed concern that his party's platform had been adopted into law but by the wrong party:

We adopt a platform and we try to use it in the campaign, but our problem right now is that Republican Governor ——— is more liberal than anybody in the Democratic party ever thought of being, and he has adopted into law practically everything we've stood for in the past few years. He has been very successful in getting our good Democratic platform turned into a good Republican record.

In view of the general irrelevance of issues to campaign outcomes, it is interesting to note the searing battles that take place in state conventions over adoption of the platform. In 1970 the Texas Republican State Convention erupted into an "internecine battleground" during consideration of platform planks condemning school busing and marijuana, according to the *San Antonio Light*:

The party's platform committee has considered platform requests of 40 different groups, ranging from the Texas AFL-CIO to the Texas Association of School Boards. They went into a huddle early Monday to settle an upper echelon dispute over whether the party should embrace specific statements of goals, or adopt a platform so broad-based it would ease party candidates through hurdles in rural areas or metropolises.

The lid blew off when Harris County Chairman Mrs. Nancy Palm declared she is "sitting on 650,000 votes" (and 570 of the convention delegates), and put State GOP Chairman William Steger of Tyler on notice that, "If we do not get a platform with planks, there will be a floor fight." [7]

Other conventions, however, are quiet, uneventful, and open. Robert C. Ingalls, editor and publisher of the *Corvallis Gazette-Times* reported that during the 1970 Republican Convention in Oregon every one of the 238 delegates was allowed to float around, to speak at any of the ten platform subcommittees, and to vote in each of them. Even guests were allowed to speak, and some of them cast vocal ballots. Ingalls ended his account with his view of party platforms as political documents:

There are some who say, with justification, that party platforms are only an exercise in futility, anyway. What do they mean? Who is bound by them? Few people ever see the whole thing in print, they add, and here in Oregon people vote for the candidates, not for the platform on which they are supposed to be standing.

Perhaps the most good comes from the interchange of ideas of people from various localities, coffee klatches, fellow workers, PTAers and other sections of our population. Getting ideas from all these voters and consolidating them into a platform gives those who are elected to run our state a pretty good idea of what the people are thinking.[8]

It would seem that the development of issues for campaign or platform purposes is one of the most unscientific and unexplored areas of campaigning. The difficulties involved in reading the public's mind at any particular moment are a source of considerable consternation to many campaign managers and party officers. Many expressed a desire to have more emphasis on issues during the campaign period but fear the consequences of permitting the adoption of four-square statements which might alienate voters.

When asked where issues should originate, as opposed to where they do originate, the chairmen divided into four groups. Twenty-four percent believe that issues should be the exclusive prerogative of the candidates; 20 percent feel that the state chairman should be responsible for issue development; 20 percent suggest leaving the emergence of issues to the drafters of the platform; and 16 percent expressed their willingness to leave the problem in the hands of the in-party governor or out-party gubernatorial candidate. The remainder preferred combinations of these four alternatives.

The Old Politics and the New

The old politics still consumes more of the chairman's time than does the new. The political aspects of recruitment, patronage, campaign strategy, and the development or control over issues are highly personal in character, involving either the chairman's or the governor's power. These are not matters that can be left to others. They require firsthand knowledge of the party and are often intricately entwined with the personal relationships which always exist in political affairs. The old politics is, in short, a highly personal form of politics.

The new politics, as used here, includes public opinion measurement, organized fund raising, data processing, professional consultative services, and the various means through which party leaders communicate with party members and workers. It is not altogether new, but it is largely non-traditional. Chapter 6 is devoted to its exploration.

6 The Political Role of the State Chairman: The New Politics

Quite simply, I could not get along without polls. I have convinced the state committee of their worth, and we have contracted for at least three in each campaign. We design our whole statewide campaign around them.
A midwestern Democratic chairman

The crew that was in before me put in a lot of expensive computer stuff. Well, as long as I know who my county chairmen are I don't need that stuff. Hell, I can't even read the damn things. Also it was expensive as hell. I got rid of it pretty fast.
A midwestern Democratic chairman

Money may be the mother's milk of politics but it also is the worst part of the job of chairman. I hate that part of it. Maybe . . . because I'm not very good at it.
A western Republican chairman

In the twenty years since Stanley Kelley, Jr., called the attention of political scientists to the "new" profession of political public relations and campaign management,[1] the activities of experts in political campaigns have become commonplace. For more important contests it is now considered a virtual necessity to employ a campaign management firm to get the candidate's name and message to the voters. In 1970 a *National Journal* study of sixty-seven contested elections for the U.S. Senate showed that only five did not employ professional consultants. Thirty hired professional media consultants, twenty-four contracted for the services of national opinion polling firms, twenty employed public relations and campaign management firms, and sixty used commercial advertising companies.[2] One by-product of such political entrepreneurism is a diminution of loyalty by the candidate to the party. This has been particularly true in senatorial, congressional, and gubernatorial races. It is in these contests that the stakes are the highest. They represent powerful offices and are likely to attract dedicated candidates willing and able to spend the time and resources necessary to win. Such effort is costly and requires expertise in the "new" politics if it is to be successful.

Consequently, for very high office, electioneering is no longer centered in the party organization but has become, instead, candidate centered. In order to mobilize for a victorious campaign, many candidates have turned to commercial public relations, advertising, and management consulting firms as a means of selling themselves to an expanding and an increasingly independent electorate. The rapid and extensive growth of public relations in politics followed the explosive impact of the electronic media. The early growth of political public relations and campaign management firms in California developed out of the need for media expertise in campaigns for political office in a geographically large and populous state. They were also a product of the multitudinous issue questions which materialize during every election. Whitaker and Baxter, Spencer-Roberts, and Baus and Ross, three of the best-known national firms, all began in the Golden State and are headquartered there. Their reputations and successes were quickly noted by other politicians in other states. It is estimated that there are now over 300 political public relations firms throughout the nation. They provide management or consultative services to a wide variety of candidates of both parties, including general advertising, public opinion polling, and general campaign management. The cost is so high, however, that most contracts are for the more important and more powerful public offices.

While the more dramatic senatorial and gubernatorial contests have attracted widespread attention to the use of private consulting firms, a large number of state parties have been engaged in similar activities but with far less visibility. Public opinion polling was the first such activity to be adopted in strategic planning by party organizations. By 1972, 65 percent of the state party organizations were engaged in some form of polling, often pertaining to less notable offices such as state legislative races. Over half the party organizations had adapted the computer to fund-raising efforts. Automatic data processing was also being used extensively in the larger states in the typing of personalized letters, generation of voter lists, dial-selected telephone canvassing, voter and precinct analysis, and for printing mailing labels. Some data banks include information about every registered or potential voter within the jurisdiction. The importance of computer politics has been long recognized, but its great cost has prevented it from coming of age.

Of the 100 parties surveyed, 62 published an official newsletter or newspaper as a means of communicating with voters and workers. An analysis of these documents demonstrates the wide variety of uses to which they are put. Newspapers fall under the general rubric of the chairman's role as party spokesman. The mail that he sends or receives is also a part of the interparty communications process although it appears to have been largely displaced by the telephone.* Technically, neither of these could be described as new to politics. Nevertheless, some of the uses to which they have been adapted are closer to the new politics than to the old.

The development of new campaign strategies and stratagems has been slow. It had to await the scientific development of television, computer hardware, polling techniques, and other social and technological inventions of the mid-twentieth century. Although each of these innovations was created primarily for other purposes, innovative partisan tacticians eventually saw the enormous political possibilities implicit in their conception. There is little doubt that we have embarked upon an era of technocratic politics, and there is considerable evidence that numerous state party organizations have demonstrated a quick interest in their potential. The Republicans and Democrats at the state level have both trailed their respective national organizations in initiating the use of the new techniques. Furthermore, the immense costs involved have limited the more expensive efforts to wealthy or large-state parties.

Public Opinion Polling

The scientific measurement of public opinion began in the mid-1930s, came into its own in the 1940s, and was accepted by the public in the 1950s. Modern polling had its origins in newspaper straw votes, market research, and the application of the mathematical laws of probability and

---

* Two chairmen and one chairwoman were asked to monitor personal mail for a period of a week. The original intention was to demonstrate the centralist role played by the chairman as a conduit between the national and local parties as well as to horizontal state party units. One of the chairmen received virtually no party-oriented mail during the week but noted that most of his party business was transacted by telephone. One state Democratic chairwoman kept a daily log of incoming mail for the week of August 28, 1972. The results were as follows: letters, official, 8; letters, miscellaneous, 6; notices of meetings, 3; party publications, 5; nonparty publications, 1; requests for information, 3; financial contribution, 1; copy of telegram, official, 1; advertisements, 8. The incoming mail received by the third chairman was of the same nature. The mails appear to be used for official notifications, but political matters are more often reserved for the telephone and personal meetings.

sampling to human behavior.[3] Except for the remarkable setback of 1948, the polling organizations have moved steadily ahead to prove their value as campaign instruments.

There has always been a degree of suspicion toward polling by political leaders and candidates. Polls have often been misused during campaigns—loaded questions, faked results, and leaked outcomes often being the rule rather than the exception. At the same time, political strategists have increasingly come to rely on polls as tools of campaign decision making. Most no longer need to be convinced that a properly structured, carefully conducted, and accurately analyzed poll can be valuable to the candidate in seeking public office.

Polls first came to public attention in presidential campaigns. After the debacle of 1948, the major polling organizations steadily improved their techniques and, consequently, their accuracy and acceptability. They eventually overcame their embarrassment over 1948 and by 1960 were in considerable demand, both at the presidential level and in the states and congressional districts.

Polling, as a regular tool of state party management, began in earnest during the mid-1960s. Spurred by their successful use in congressional, senatorial, and presidential races, candidates for statewide office began to use polls as strategy-generating devices, and their popularity spread rapidly. Nationally known political leaders, such as Governor Nelson Rockefeller, made widely publicized use of polls as campaign tools. Candidates and managers throughout the nation began to clamor for prompt and reliable campaign information. Polling organizations developed well beyond the original restricted group of national concerns, and most states and regions emerged with opinion analysts of their own within the space of a few years.

Early experimenters with local and state polling were often more interested in predictions of electoral outcomes than in campaign strategy. The costs of polling, which are always substantial, were quickly absorbed by some party organizations, while others sought to raise funds earmarked for that specific purpose. By 1972, 65 percent of the state political parties were engaged in some form of polling activity as a function of the official party mission. An additional 20 percent of the state chairmen acknowledged that they would use polls if money were available. Many candidates contracted for polls on their own and at their own expense, but the true measure of their strategic use was in the party headquarters.

Party officials use political poll data in three ways. Most of the chair-

men (81 percent) see it as an aid to general campaign strategy development (table 6.1). An example was furnished by a western Republican:

As you know, we only began to win in this state a few years ago, and we
did it then by commissioning a poll to show us what was concerning the
voters. We discovered that certain issues were bothering people, but more
importantly, we discovered that the then-governor was considered to be un-
responsive. We determined to field a candidate, concentrate on those issues;
and we did and we won. We have used polls regularly ever since.

The long-range future of the party may be of more importance than
the more transitory short-range campaign. Some party officers, aware
of the importance of party image, have attempted to use opinion polls
to determine what that image is and, if it needs refurbishing, what can
be done to polish it. One state chairman reported:

I've just gone through a statewide poll. The Republican party in ———
is tainted as being owned by industry, and it was at one time, but most of us
don't think it is now. In fact, the biggest industries have been supporting the
Democrats, and some of them have been doing so for a long time. We wanted
to find out if this link to industry was a true image of our party with the public, and we thought a poll would help, and it did. We just completed it—
using the best polling operation in the state—and we found out that the public *does* see the Republican party as a creature of industry and, in fact, as
being based primarily in industry. Since we know that isn't true, we have
hired a new public relations firm and advertising agency to change that public image by telling the truth about the party as well as by pointing out the
true situation between industry and the Democrats. I think that is the kind
of thing polls should be used for.

A midwestern Democratic party which currently occupies the governorship uses polls as a regular off-year election tool. "We use Central

Table 6.1   Use of Poll Data by Party Organizations

	Democrats	Republicans	Total
To develop issues	65.8%	73.2%	69.6%
To ascertain standing in race	34.2	61.0	48.1
To assist with campaign strategy	71.1	90.4	81.0

NOTE: Multiple responses.

Surveys of Iowa," the chairman reported, "with three or four polls during each campaign and one or two during the off years." He explained that the major goal was to develop long-range campaign strategy based upon factors such as issues, the popularity of the party's officeholders, and the reaction of the voters to governmental and public affairs. For an expenditure of from $8,000 to $18,000 for each statewide poll, the party collects valuable information that is used in effecting political strategy.

One of the mysteries of political campaigning is the process by which particular issues emerge to shape an election. Political leaders are fearful of the impact of a spontaneous issue which might arise to damage their campaigns or candidates. It is understandable that 70 percent of the chairmen expressed the view that polls should be used primarily as tools through which issue politics might be exploited. In 1968 one headquarters contracted for a series of polls designed to provide candidates with up-to-date opinion data on those issues of most concern to the electorate. Party leaders credited the series with their substantial success on election day that year. A western Democrat reported that the issue poll done for his party had "enabled us to take a stronger stand on gun control legislation when we found that an overwhelming number of Democrats in ———— opposed it." He noted that the party not only capitalized on a popular issue but reaped a favorable press reaction because of its forthright stand.

A common practice among candidates and managers is to leak favorable polls to the press. This not only builds morale but places the opposition on the defensive. There is some risk of overconfidence among campaign workers, but most managers consider it a risk worth taking and aim for a bandwagon response. One recounted a bitter lesson when

we hired ——— to do a poll for us in two waves. The first was to be six weeks before the election and the other one week before. Both polls showed us winning all major offices by wide margins, and the poll manager informed us during a strategy meeting that our best bet was to sit out the remaining days of the campaign. Whether he was just plain wrong or our people became overconfident, I don't know, but on election day we lost everything. I mean *everything*. I really think the poll was about as inaccurate as it could be. He was so wrong that his business didn't survive.

In spite of occasional misfires, polling has become an accepted and necessary part of state political campaigns. Forty-five percent of the chairmen were pleased with the polls taken for them, while only 5 percent were displeased. An additional 20 percent stated that they would use polls extensively if the party could afford to.

Among those who do not employ scientific polling (usually because they lack the money), efforts are sometimes made to engage in an unscientific effort at little cost. One Republican chairman was enthusiastic about the results of his experiment with Young Republicans as public opinion pollsters. He reported that

the use of Young Republicans to conduct polls for us was begun under my predecessor. He paid a university professor a consultant's fee to develop a polling strategy and to offer some interviewing pointers to a select group of YR officers. At first they were not very useful, but they have become surprisingly accurate in the past two years and we are most pleased with them. It saves us a lot of money and builds a lot of enthusiasm on the part of the YR's. I will try to hire an agency to do one major poll for us each election, but the use of YR interviewers enables us to go into the field every two weeks.

Another technique was described as follows:

We do not use professional polls. We have never used them since I have been in office. I give the big counties fifty phone calls to make at random from the telephone book and the small counties get twenty-five calls. If one legislative district has ten counties I assign ten phone calls to each county in the district. Now this is obviously not scientific. It's really just a telephone straw vote, but we have found it to be very effective and reasonably accurate. It told us, for instance, that ———— was in serious trouble and was probably not going to make it. It was extremely accurate in that prediction almost county by county.

The great expense of public opinion sampling precludes the use of scientific professional polls by many party organizations. Some candidates allow the state party to add "piggyback" questions to privately commissioned polls, and others permit party leaders to study "leftovers" after the candidate who commissioned the poll is finished with the data. Neither of these solutions has proven to be very satisfactory. The poll results are often keyed so closely to the individual candidate's campaign that their applicability to general party efforts is limited.

On occasion a candidate's success with a personal poll has convinced party officials of the benefits to be derived for the party as a whole. A new Republican chairman in a state with a new Republican governor reported:

The party didn't do anything in the line of polling. This was strictly a ———— operation geared to the governor's race only. The governor's poll

showed him winning by 500 votes. It was such a narrow majority that I
pretty much discounted the poll. Every poll taken showed the same thing—
we would win by a bare majority. I really thought the pollster just was telling
us what we wanted to hear. But when the election was over, the poll was so
close to being accurate all over the state right down to percentage by percentage that it made believers of all of us. I was tremendously impressed and,
as chairman, have budgeted money for party organization polling next year
by the same guy. It will be the first time that either party in this state has
undertaken regular opinion sampling.

Opinion polling has assumed an important place in the strategic arsenal
of many state party organizations. Approximately one-third of the state
organizations have budgeted money for polls since 1970. The successful
adoption of polling to state party affairs, plus the increasing use of data
processing by both the national and state parties, has brought the scientific revolution to politics at a rapid pace.

Automatic Data Processing

The ability to make effective operational decisions is one of the major
keys to successful campaigning. This has become more difficult, however, with the increasing mobility, sophistication, and complexity of the
American electorate. Information is the principal need in campaign
planning. The political decision maker needs to know the social, economic, and political composition of the electorate within his constituent
jurisdiction. He needs to have some understanding of the issue interests
of the voters. And, above all, the strategist is dependent upon up-to-date
precinct lists which can be used during the campaign itself as well as on
election day. Each of these information needs is ideally suited to computer technology. It was not long after its development that political
leaders recognized the value of automatic data processing in election
campaigns and party organizations. Indeed, some academic experts see
a perceptible shift of "political power from party leaders, political
brokers, and special interest group leaders to those who are information
and communications experts." [4] The marriage between politics and elec-
tronics began at the national party level in the mid-1960s.

The Republican National Committee, under the chairmanship of Ray
C. Bliss, authorized a study of centralized data processing in 1966. The
committee produced a handbook to explain computer technology in lay
terms, undertook a pilot program based on test precincts, and sponsored

two "training conferences" designed to "update information and exchange views on political EDP (electronic data processing) for Republicans with limited or no experience." [5] The goal of these conferences was to demonstrate to the state party leadership the benefits to be derived from data processing in terms of demographic data, voter behavior, mailing, opinion polling, and the use of media.

The Republican headquarters produced a total of sixteen manuals and eleven computer programs offering to the states standardized techniques and approaches, and by mid-1968 twenty state Republican organizations were using data processing in one form or another.[6] The RNC also published a series of technical manuals on developing demographic analysis, voter histories, use of voter name files, and establishment of computerized finance systems.

As outlined by Bliss,

The primary goal of the National Committee in the electronic data processing field is to provide competent leadership and guidance to state and local organizations as they explore possible use of this device in their own operations. During 1968, direct consultative services were given to eighteen states, and the series of nine technical EDP manuals developed specifically for the state and local finance systems and voter name lists were continued.

In addition, secondary EDP goals were established for the first time in 1968. These included:

(1) Pre-packaged computer programs for Republican organizations having proper financing and competent technical support on location. This new concept was successfully implemented in the finance and voter name list fields and was designed to save GOP committees the financial burden of "start-up costs."

(2) A centralized election statistical "data bank" for projecting election long-term trends by counties, thus providing speedier election reports for and by the National Committee.

(3) Sponsorship of a consortium of professional survey and electronic data processing research firms that work for Republican candidates to discuss, advise and lend support to RNC special EDP projects. One such project in 1968 was the plotting of the normal vote and swing vote for all counties in the "key state" areas for the Nixon-Agnew campaign.[7]

After providing addressing and mailing services for state and local organizations and congressional candidates in the mid-1960s, the Democratic National Committee turned to more sophisticated services in 1969.

Through EDP equipment, the DNC began to furnish computerized mailings, largely for fund-raising purposes. In more recent years the DNC moved into voter identification activities, for which they charge a fee to the user.[8]

Approximately one-half of the state party organizations, mostly those in large and/or competitive states, currently use computers. Those who do not tend to represent small states (often without a permanent headquarters) or noncompetitive parties. Many of the chairmen in the states without computer facilities indicated a desire to have data processing capability but were unable to, due usually to inadequate financing.

Computer use ranges from the printing of mailing labels and address lists to sophisticated analysis of voter reaction to candidates and issues. EDP becomes operative in some states only at election time, while others use it on a regular year-round basis. Most of the parties that have adopted EDP contract with private firms for the service. In a few states, however, both parties have been permitted to use "free" time on equipment leased or owned by private industry. As one Republican from a western state described the arrangement:

We barely have enough money to operate headquarters, but we approached the ———— Corporation and asked permission to use their computers. The president of the company is a member of the executive committee and was very sympathetic. He took it up with the people in the company, and they offered both the Democrats and us two hours a week of computer time plus the use of programmers. They knew full well that the Democratic state people would not be interested. They are barely able to stay alive. Anyway, we have been using their services for over a year, and the output has been fantastically helpful. For the first time we have some knowledge of where our voters are, who will contribute money, and other information of that kind. With the expansion of the company, I keep worrying that they will cut us out, but so far, so good.

Most experts in the field acknowledge that the Republican party is several years ahead of the Democrats in the development of technocratic politics. That is certainly true of party sponsored and supported activities. It should be noted, however, that the Democratic party, both nationally and in many of the more important states, has had access to the extensive and sophisticated technology developed by organized labor. COPE, the political action arm of the AFL-CIO, has computer systems operating in California, Maryland, Pennsylvania, Ohio, Texas, Oklahoma, Colorado, Michigan, Connecticut, and the District of Columbia. The major operating goal is voter registration, and COPE has over five million names stored in its system. This data base serves as the foundation of the election-year voter identification and registration drives which work almost exclusively to the advantage of state and national Democrats.[9]

Saloma and Sontag note that the gap in technical capabilities between the parties may be more apparent than real. They report that some state Republican organizations have learned to their dismay that the Democrats have greater consultative resources than their restricted finances might suggest. Democrats tend to use consultants more in developing media strategy than in organizing more efficient services for the state parties. With the support of organized labor in voter registration and of the National Committee for an Effective Congress in bringing about the marriage of political consultants and party politics, the Democrats may not have to do as much to gain the same degree of effectiveness.[10]

Most party officials do not believe that the use of electronic data processing and campaign consultants will displace the older forms of political activities. Most use them as tools to make the older style of politics more viable and more flexible. Party leaders sometimes express fear that private profit-making consultants might displace the political party, and most would not like to see that happen. One national committeeman, during the course of a long critique of his incumbent state chairman, declared:

I think it is a mistake for the party to go into computers and media campaigns to the extent that it has. [The chairman] is in love with these gadgets, and I will admit that they have their uses, but I fear that we can overdo it and will end up eventually with the profiteers dictating to the politicians. To me, there will never be a substitute for the good old-fashioned seat-of-the-pants campaign.

State political parties are just at the threshold of modern campaign development. So far there is no substantial history of success or failure by which these efforts can be judged. There is little doubt, however, that the next few years will witness a major push in the direction of campaign technocracy. The political party organizations will, of necessity, be in the forefront or they may ultimately be displaced by private political campaign consultants.

Fund-Raising Activities

Every state political party must have money if it is to successfully accomplish its mission. Money is necessary not only for campaigns but for normal day-to-day operations of the party headquarters. The difficulties associated with the raising of political money are often apparent in a casual reading of the daily press. In mid-1971 the *Pittsburgh Post Gazette* reported: "The State Republican party is $500,000 in debt, and one may ask, 'What happened to the big industrialists, people like the Pugh and Mellon families?' " [11] In late 1970, the *Albuquerque Tribune* reported that "State GOP Treasurer George McKim said after the meeting that a statewide party deficit of $20,000 exists." [12] The *Springfield Union,* reporting on the problems of the Massachusetts Democratic party, said:

David E. Harrison, Chairman of the Democratic State Committee, will leave his job in May following an attempt to solve the committee's problem of heavy indebtedness.

Harrison, a former state representative, has been party chairman for more than two years. During that period the party has gone through lean times. . . . Debts have increased and fund-raising efforts have not kept pace.

Rent and telephone bills have escalated and the committee must move its headquarters. Although the State Committee voted to pay its chairman $16,000 a year, Harrison . . . has never been paid.

The deficit has mounted to about $45,000 excluding Harrison's back pay.[13]

In late 1972 the *New York Times* began a story about potential changes in the New York Democratic party with this statement:

The Democratic party in New York is broke, its state treasurer said yesterday, and he blamed the situation in part on the "lavish spending" of the state chairman, Joseph F. Crangle.

The party treasurer, Abraham Hirschfeld, said that . . . "We do not have the money to pay the rent," [and that] "Money is being spent at such a pace that we will soon be out of the money we borrowed.". . .

Mr. Hirschfeld, asked about "lavish" spending he had criticized, cited the shift of the state headquarters here from a hotel basement to a Madison Avenue office building at "four or five times as much rent."

Mr. Crangle said in reply, "We've always had trouble raising money in New York but we're meeting our current bills and we've taken the party out of the basement, added staff serviced the 62 counties, for which we spent some money." [14]

Neil Staebler, chairman of the Democratic State Central Committee of Michigan from 1950 to 1961, and Michigan finance director for the Democratic National Committee in 1949–50, has noted:

A chairman gets spread quite thin over the many aspects of party activity, but one field which he can never neglect is money-raising. A disproportionately large amount of his time is inescapably committed to meeting the need for funds. It should not be assumed, of course, that he does all the work himself, or that he is the most active party worker in the field of finance. Every chairman finds one or more trusted lieutenants to work in this field and encourages the formation of a finance committee to give them support and assistance.[15]

Responsibility for Fund Raising   As shown in table 6.2, the primary responsibility for fund raising falls into four patterns. Sixty-one percent of the Democratic chairmen and 29 percent of the Republican chairmen reported that they were principally responsible for raising the money with which the party had to operate. This was often not an assigned responsibility but one that had devolved on the chairman because of the failure of other systems to work. On the whole, the chairmen passionately dislike the fund-raising chore but assume responsibility for it as a matter of party survival. Some representative comments from various state chairmen follow:

I am *de facto* state finance chairman. Our finance chairman used to be very good, but he has gotten tired and jaded and he no longer does very much. As state chairman I am primarily responsible for putting on our dinners and for raising whatever money I can by phone calls. It takes a great deal of time but there is no one else to do it.

There seems to be an awful lot of money raising. Raising money is probably 60 to 65 percent of my job as chairman. The finance director is OK but he's nothing great. I have to spend a great deal of my time and effort in raising money and I really shouldn't have to.

Since 1966 we have had exactly two contributions of over $100. I spend 60 percent of my time and 60 percent of the money that we raise trying to raise more money. I have a staff man who serves as finance chairman, but he doesn't have the time, with all of his other duties, to devote to it, so I end up doing it.

At the other extreme are those states (16.2 percent) where primary responsibility for fund raising rests with a party finance committee and/or a finance chairman. The finance committee is sometimes elected by the state committee and sometimes appointed by the state chairman. The finance chairman is usually appointed by the state chairman but is sometimes selected by the finance committee. Twice as many (21.9 percent) Republican chairmen as Democratic chairmen (10.2 percent) assign primary responsibility to a finance officer. A general rule of thumb in state party finance holds that the solicitor should be the financial peer of the people he solicits. He should already have donated a substantial sum himself, at least an amount equal to that which he is asking others to donate. Several chairmen noted ruefully that they had personally been unsuccessful in raising money because they were not personally wealthy and were unable to negotiate on the same level with those who were. One Republican chairman from a small state said:

I haven't had to be too involved in state party finance. In fact, I do very little other than speak at county fund-raising dinners when asked. I appointed a very good person as our state finance chairman. This person is a millionaire and has all kinds of contacts and has no trouble raising money. I tried two years ago to do it on my own but found that the party's wealthy benefactors would not talk to me, knowing full well that I have no money and work for a salary.

And another chairman, a Democrat, said:

I have been able to raise money in small amounts, but this party has traditionally had to rely on large contributions. . . . The large contributors . . . will only contribute to those who are as wealthy as they are. Consequently, I got Mrs. ———, who is wealthy in her own right, to contact these people for me and they were quite willing to give to her. Between my $1 and $5 contributions from lots of people and her large contributions from a few people, we have kept the party going.

Almost three times as many Republican as Democratic chairmen reported that fund-raising responsibilities were shared between the state chairman and the finance chairman (see table 6.2). In most instances, a

Table 6.2   Responsibility for Fund Raising

	Democrats	Republicans	Total
Chairman responsible	61.6%	29.3%	45.0%
Finance committee/finance chairman responsible	10.2	21.9	16.2
Shared responsibility: state chairman and finance committee	17.0	41.5	29.1
Governor responsible	0.0	7.3	3.8

NOTE: Based on responses of state chairmen to a question asking for a description of *actual* fund-raising responsibility as opposed to legal or normative responsibility. Columns do not total 100 percent due to deletion of minor categories.

somewhat formal division of labor had been worked out between the two, with the finance chairman usually representing wealth and prestige and concentrating his efforts on those likely to make large contributions, and the state chairman concentrating on fund-raising dinners, small contributors' sustaining programs, and the imposition of quotas upon the county and congressional district parties. Shared responsibility appears to work well in most states, due to the enormous time consumption involved in fund raising and because it permits contact with different levels by different solicitors. The state chairmen, however, appeared to be more likely to understand mass collection techniques and to have the advantage of controlling the administrative machinery to make them work.

A midwestern Republican stated:

We have a finance committee and a very good finance chairman. He knows where most of the big money is in this state and is able to pull in sizable contributions every year. I have no contact with these kinds of people, but I did learn how to run a sustaining program for small contributors while attending a national committee meeting in Washington and have spent much of my time this year implementing such a scheme. We are just about ready to send our first mail-out and are very hopeful that it will give us a return that will allow us to sustain our operations on a continuing basis so that we can place the larger contributions in a campaign fund for next year's elections.

A Democrat, describing his relationship with the state finance director, said:

I am getting professional help in building a solid financial base for the party. I have a good finance chairman and he makes the plans, and the state headquarters, under my leadership, carries them out. For instance, he has drawn up elaborate plans for a $100-a-plate dinner that we're going to have in February, has made all of the arrangements, and the headquarters operation is sending out 1,800 invitations and making phone calls and whatever else is necessary to make a success of it.

Finally, in three Republican parties the governor served as the chief fund raiser. In two, the respective governors were millionaires and supported their parties out of personal funds year after year. The chairman representing one of these parties reported that he and other leaders were trying to break loose from the governor in order to help the party to stand on its own feet financially. The third governor, who was not a millionaire, assumed responsibility for raising all party monies and had apparently been quite successful.

As noted in table 6.2, twice as many Democratic chairmen (61.6 percent) as Republicans (29.3 percent) were responsible for the actual money-raising operations of their respective parties. Furthermore, 41.5 percent of the Republican chairmen shared responsibility with a finance committee (usually including the finance chairmen) while only 17 percent of the Democrats did. This is probably due to the long-standing practice of the Republicans of maintaining a National Finance Committee (RNFC) to coordinate national fund raising. The RNFC is independent of the Republican National Committee, a status which ostensibly permitted it to operate outside the Hatch Act reporting requirements for "party" committees. The chairman of the RNFC, who is appointed by the Republican national chairman, works through a network of regional vice-chairmen, state finance chairmen, and volunteers spread throughout the fifty states. Chairmen of the state finance committees have traditionally worked closely with the state party committees and state chairmen to determine the amounts of money to be raised and the budgetary allocations to be made. This system has integrated state finance people into national fund-raising efforts and accounts for the greater Republican responses suggesting shared responsibilities.

Methods of Raising Money   The methods of raising political funds fall into six categories. Most money for the state parties is raised through dinners, small contributors' sustaining programs, large contributor clubs, special personal appeals, a quota system, or a special tax. (See table 6.3.) One of the most popular methods of raising money and one that is almost universally used is the political fund-raising dinner. Many of these

Table 6.3   Methods of Raising Party Funds

	Number of parties using		
	D	R	Total
Dinners	19	20	39
Quota system	1	6	7
Clubs for large contributors	4	6	10
Sustaining programs for small contributors	16	12	28
Direct appeals, phone or mail	10	12	22
Special tax or levy	3	1	4
Several methods combined	11	12	23

NOTE: These figures represent actual numbers of parties, since multiple responses were prevalent.

events center around Lincoln Day and Jefferson-Jackson Day celebrations. The cost of attendance ranges from $5 to $500 but with an average cost of around $100 a plate. The state chairmen use a variety of means of attracting people to such dinners. One midwestern Democrat, at the time he was interviewed, was in the process of lining up an annual Jefferson-Jackson Day dinner and was calling Democrats throughout the state to encourage them to purchase tickets. A big-name television entertainer of some years before was under contract to appear, and the chairman was fretting because his telephone discussions had convinced him that the star attraction was no longer popular enough to attract a large audience. On the other hand, a Democratic chairman reported:

Two years ago we had a fund-raising dinner at $100 a plate: 13,000 state employees, all of them appointed by party officials and cleared by me, and each of them contributing in effect $100 to the state campaign chest. We raised nearly one million dollars at this one dinner.

The Democratic state chairman of New York, John Burns, described a fund-raising dinner at Toots Shor's Restaurant, during which the Ali-Frazier prize fight was broadcast over closed-circuit TV. Many prominent New York Democrats attended, and although the party paid $16,000 for the TV rights, the charge of $250 per person brought a substantial windfall to the party.

Many state organizations approach the use of dinners at a more mundane level. One party regularly brings in approximately $15,000 through a series of $25-a-plate dinners, while in a western state another fledgling party suffered a substantial loss in sponsoring a barbecue at $25 per person, failing to break even. It would be an exaggeration to say that the political dinner is the mainstay of state party funding. However, virtually all parties use dinners at one time or another and rely extensively on them to produce operating revenues. Some have used dinners for a long enough period of time to be able to actually predict income and budget on the basis of the expected revenues.

One Democratic and six Republican parties rely on a quota system for fund raising. In general, the state finance committee or the central committee, operating on the advice of the state chairman or the finance director, constructs a system of quotas to be assigned to each county and/or congressional district. These units are then theoretically responsible for raising that amount of money to send to state headquarters. One state uses a quota based on the number who voted for the party's candidate for governor in that county in the last election, combined with the amount of taxable income. Theoretically, this formula suggests that a rich county can contribute more to the party than a poor county can. Ultimately it is the state chairman's responsibility to collect the quotas, a duty easier to plan than to carry out. Some county organizations pay their quotas as a matter of course while others pay little attention to the demands of the state party for contributions.

A relatively recent phenomenon in party finance, an outgrowth of national party fund-raising efforts, is the development of small contributors' sustaining programs in a number of states. Most of the state parties using a sustaining program are following the pattern established by the Republican National Committee in 1962. Through this program millions of people, Democrats and Republicans alike, receive letters from national party officials asking for small ($10) contributions in return for which the contributor would become a "sustaining" member of the Republican party. The remarkable success of this program encouraged state and local parties to follow suit.

The 1970 budget of the Colorado Democratic party, for instance, projected an income of $24,000 from the sustaining fund program of small contributions; $50,000 from the Century Club composed of large contributors; and, $100,000 from a program based on county quotas and called "Capitol '70." [16]

The April 1972 issue of the Illinois Republican newsletter described the "1200 Club of Illinois," a sustaining program:

Members of the 1200 Club have been mailed notices in recent days informing them that the small donor club has been re-activated for the 1972 Republican campaign.

The 1200 Club is composed of persons donating $12 to the party for funding of the GOP at all levels in the State. The Republican State Central Committee, County Committees and the candidates they support, and the statewide Young Republican organization benefit from the funds, according to State Chairman Victor L. Smith.[17]

The Oregon Democrats, under Chairwoman Caroline Wilkins inaugurated a state sustaining program called "7 for the 70s." Under this program an Oregon Democrat could contribute $7 per month to the state party, either by a single check for $77 or by having the $7 donation charged to his BankAmericard or Master Charge account until personal revocation of the authorization was received. A separate program for "Contributing Members" enabled an individual to contribute $12 per year, $10 as a contribution to the party and $2 for the monthly newsletter. Families could join for $22.[18] (See illustration.)

PARTY MEMBERSHIP AND NEWSLETTER SUBSCRIPTION

☐ Please continue to send me the newsletter for the coming year. My subscription of $2.00 is enclosed.

☐ Please enroll me as a Contributing Member of the Democratic Party of Oregon for the coming year. I enclose $12. ($10.00 membership and $2.00 newsletter.)

☐ Please enroll my family as Family Members of the Democratic Party of Oregon for the coming year. We enclose $22.00. ($20.00 Family membership and $2.00 newsletter.)

Name_____
                Please print

Address_____

_____

DON'T RIP OFF THE DEMOCRATIC PARTY OF OREGON! Tear and send with appropriate amount to: Democratic Party of Oregon, P.O. Box 189, Corvallis, OREGON 97330

> 7 for the 70's >

STATE SUSTAINING FUND

☐ Please enroll me in "7 for the 70s". My contribution of $7.00 is enclosed and you can expect a similar amount from me each month.

☐ You may bill my BankAmericard or MasterCharge account _____ #_____ for _____ per month ($7.00 or more) until I revoke the authorization.

☐ My check for $77.00 is enclosed or you may bill my BankAmericard or MasterCharge account _____ #_____ for $77.00. Please jog my memory a year from now.

Signed _____

Address _____

_____

Mail to Caroline Wilkins, Chairman, Democratic Party of Oregon, Box 189, Corvallis, OR 97330

As a sustaining member of his party, a contributor usually receives a membership card or a letter of appreciation from the state chairman. The sustaining programs have one important benefit: they provide a steady, predictable source of income. The money is used both for campaigns and headquarters support in most states.

At a different level a number of parties have followed the lead of the Democratic National Committee which established the $1,000-per-member "President's Club" in the early 1960s. Several state Democratic parties, under impetus provided by the national committee, have created Century Clubs at $100 per year and, in one case, $500 per year. In return for a contribution of $100 each year, the club member receives a club membership card, a subscription to the party newsletter or newspaper, special benefits at the state conventions, and invitations to a select, party-sponsored cocktail party or dinner. Some party leaders acknowledged that a contribution also eased the way for patronage contract awards from those parties in power.

In four political parties, three Democratic and one Republican, a system of tax levies has been developed to provide continuing income to the party. No doubt the best known of these was that used by both parties in the state of Indiana. Beginning in 1933 during the administration of Democratic Governor Paul V. McNutt, state employees were requested to contribute 2 percent of their net wages to the political party in power. As described by the *Wall Street Journal* in 1971:

Each month Mrs. Marietta Mercer, a receptionist with the Indiana State Highway Commission here, dutifully contributes two per cent of her net wages to the state Republican party.

Her faithful money-giving doesn't stem from any avid interest in the party's fortunes; Mrs. Mercer pays because she fears she'll lose her job if she doesn't. "It's a real financial burden, but you learn pretty fast that it's pay or get fired," she grumbles.

Mrs. Mercer and some 40,000 other patronage workers with state, county and local jobs in Indiana, are forced to kick back part of their salaries to the party in power, even in non-election years. Known as the two per cent club, the group includes everyone from low-paid city garbage men to highly-paid professionals.*

* *Wall Street Journal*, April 8, 1971, p. 1. In May 1971, Republican Governor Edgar B. Whitcomb announced the abolition of the "kickback" system because, he said, "The Republican National Committee had informed him recently that Indiana is the only state in the nation still maintaining the system." According to in-

Contributions in 1973 accounted for about $400,000 to the Republican State Committee and about $50,000 to $60,000 to the Democrats. As might be expected, most state party officials support the system as an easy and proper means of collecting money with which to run the party. It enables the party to budget on a regular and predictable basis under which the Republicans, the party in power, maintain a headquarters staff of twenty-six while the Democrats employ a staff of nine. One key Republican noted that employee contributions are not required and that they have little to do with who gets a job. Participation may be crucial, however, in the determination of who gets promoted if the candidates for promotion have equal qualifications. The qualified candidate who contributes will usually be chosen for promotion over the qualified candidate who does not. Generally speaking, informants in both parties in Indiana maintain that there is no serious effort to enforce the system of contributions, as evidenced by the number of the total work force who do not take part.

Finally, one of the most productive sources of political money to be invented in recent years has been the telethon experiments of the Democratic National Committee. The 1974 telethon lasted twenty-one hours and was studded with performances and appearances by headline entertainers and politicians. Although it cost $2.5 million to produce, Democratic officials expected to net approximately $4.5 million in contributions. In order to gain acceptance by the state Democratic committees, $3.0 million of that amount was pledged for distribution to the state parties. Even so, some state party leaders were not pleased with the idea. William Holzman, executive director of the Democratic party of California, which led the states with $800,000 in pledges, said, "I hope it's the last one. I don't think the people will buy it any more." [19] He was

---

formed Republican leaders, the real reason for the governor's action was his desire to force the GOP state chairman to resign. The chairman refused and the state central committee would not take action to remove him. The governor abolished the 2 percent kickback system as a pressure tactic to force the chairman's resignation. After several months, the party's coffers were at low ebb and the chairman resigned, at which point Governor Whitcomb reinstated the system of employee contributions.

In a related development, U.S. Comptroller General Elmer B. Staats has referred the Indiana patronage collection system to the attorney general because a sample GAO audit of sixty-four employees of the Indiana State Highway Commission showed that 10 percent of them were compensated from federal funds. Staats has asked for a determination of the legality of requiring such employees to contribute a portion of their salaries for political purposes.

partly correct. The 1975 telethon produced considerably less revenue than expected, although it did make a good profit.

There is little question that the chairmen see fund raising as an important, if somewhat baffling, part of their responsibilities. As noted in table 6.4, when asked to designate the degree of importance assigned to fund raising, 81.4 percent said that it was "very important," with 92.1 percent of the Democrats designating it as such. The fact that the Republican chairmen rated it of somewhat lesser importance reflects the greater ease with which the party controlling the presidency can raise money. The 9.7 percent Republicans who rated this aspect of the chairman's job as "unimportant" were completely free of fund-raising responsibilities because of a system of patronage contributions, guaranteed receipt of fees, or, in two cases, a governor who picked up party expenses.

Most state chairmen dislike the fund-raising aspects of their jobs. Money is raised under enormous handicaps in some states, and party leaders spend considerable time thinking about new ways to finance the political enterprise. Century clubs, small contributors' sustaining programs, remitted filing fees, credit card contributions, and some quota systems are all products of fertile minds seeking solutions to this perennial problem. They are all aspects of the "new politics" that did not exist before the modernization of state parties began. Nevertheless, it is hard to escape the impression that political fund raising remains one of the more unscientific aspects of politics. Debt-ridden parties find it virtually impossible to convince contributors that there is virtue in paying old debts left from earlier campaigns. If the party is debt-free, the reaction to its money-raising efforts may depend upon the potential contributors' personal assessment of the chances of electoral success.

National events can drastically affect state solicitations. The Watergate

Table 6.4   Importance of Fund Raising as Role for Chairman

	Democrats (N39)	Republicans (N41)	Total (N80)
Very important	92.1%	70.7%	81.4%
Important	7.9	14.6	11.3
Unimportant	0.0	9.7	4.8
NA/DK	0.0	5.0*	2.4

* Each of these Republicans who were unable to answer the question had taken over his respective party fairly recently and had, as yet, not gone through a fund-raising campaign.

affair, which dominated the news through 1973 and 1974, had many unanticipated repercussions at the state level. Some reported substantial increases in contributions as money normally given national parties was funneled to the states instead. Others reported losses of large contributors but offsetting gains from small contributions. Some leaders reported an upsurge in small contributors responding to an attitude that "state politicians are more honest and more deserving than those in Washington."

Contributions to both parties declined in some areas as people turned away from parties, blaming their disaffection on the prevalence of scandal. State financial disclosure laws were blamed by some for the drop in contributions. Finally, the general decline in the economy was thought to be partly responsible for declining party income.

Attitudes toward Public Finance of Politics

The years 1973 and 1974 saw an upsurge in support for the public financing of federal elections—"an idea whose time had come," according to Senator Hugh Scott. Most of the proposed financing plans concentrate upon the presidential, senatorial, and congressional levels of politics. None of the plans under consideration includes state offices within the framework to receive public monies. Some of them are directed only to the presidential level, embracing both primaries and general elections, while others include general election funding only for presidential, senatorial, and congressional offices.

The reaction of state party officials to public funding has been varied, as has the reaction of political leaders at all levels and in both parties. One southern Democratic chairman has said, "I am emotionally opposed to public finance but see no practical alternative due to the widespread abuses that have developed through private finance." Another, a western Republican, argues that public finance would "wipe out the political parties by discouraging public involvement in politics and by eliminating any feeling of accountability on the part of elected officials." Some see public finance as the only possible means through which a minority party can ever successfully compete with a well-funded majority party. Furthermore, some fear that any public finance scheme will incorporate some form of mandatory private finance but that contributors will not give to the party if they are aware that tax money is going to be forthcoming.

In August 1973, *U.S. News and World Report* polled all 100 state chairmen regarding their attitudes toward tax support of political campaigns. Thirty-one Democrats and twenty-three Republicans responded.

The survey revealed a strikingly partisan division on the issue. Twenty-five of the Democrats and one Republican responded affirmatively to the question, "Does the U.S. need a new system of financing political parties?"; twenty Republicans and five Democrats answered negatively. None of the Republicans and twenty Democrats responded favorably to the question, "Should the Federal Government pay the costs of political campaigns?" Among the respondents, Democratic critics of private finance argued that politics has become a rich man's game and that the little man is outweighed by the special interests. Republicans expressed criticism of the present system, too, but generally favored it over the alternative of funding from the public treasury. Many expressed support for tightening loopholes and limiting contributions and expenditures rather than more drastic proposed alternatives.[20]

At the federal level, changes in the income tax law now permit tax incentives to encourage political contributions. The use of tax credits and deductions provides encouragement to those who wish to increase the ratio of givers from the present 11 percent. For a tax credit, the tax-payer can subtract one-half of any political contribution up to $25 from the tax bill; for a deduction, those who itemize can list contributions to political candidates or parties up to $50. Tax credits tend to benefit lower-income taxpayers while deductions favor those in higher income brackets. Federal tax credit and deductions should increase the number of citizen contributions to the state and local parties.

The tax check-off provision of the 1971 Federal Election Campaign Act permits the taxpayer to instruct IRS to put $1 of his or her tax payment into a Presidential Election Campaign Fund, either earmarked for a particular party or to go to a nonpartisan general account. For a variety of reasons, only 3 percent of the 1973 taxpayers chose to allocate a dollar for this purpose. By 1974, however, taxpayer response had increased fivefold. The 15 percent who participated added $17.5 million plus an additional $8.4 million collected retroactively from taxpayers who missed the first year.[21]

Whatever the outcome of the debate over public financing of elections, the fact is that several states have, in one way or another, adopted a form of public finance. The 1973 Maine legislature passed a bill permitting taxpayers in that state to participate in their own tax check-off by contributing $1 to the political party of their choice by checking an appropriate block on the state income tax return. The check-off, unlike the federal system, increases the Maine taxpayers' tax liability by $1. One party official was quoted to the effect that it would be three to five years before either party realizes a significant amount of income from the check-off.[22]

Oregon permits a tax credit for political contributions. An Oregon taxpayer filing a joint return may take one-half of his or her contribution up to $25 as a credit against both their U.S. and Oregon income taxes. In effect, as much as $50 can be contributed to a political party at no cost.* Another chairman described a system through which county clerks include a party contributor envelope in their mailings of primary election ballot instructions.

Florida law directs that qualifying fees from candidates for office be distributed to the two parties according to a complicated formula dividing the proceeds between the state central committees and the county commissions. Qualifying fees amount to 5 percent of one year's salary, and the entire proceeds are earmarked except for 15 percent retained by the state for administrative expenses. In 1972 the Florida Democratic State Committee received approximately $600,000 from this source while the Republican share was proportionately less since there are fewer contests in that party.

Alabama also earmarks filing fees for the political parties. The Democratic party in the state receives approximately $150,000 per election from this source. A recent three-judge district court found the filing fee law in Alabama unconstitutional because it did not permit candidates who could not pay the fee to run for election in the state. The court upheld the concept of filing fees and did not interfere with the right of the Democratic party to conduct primary elections but insisted that serious candidates who could not pay the filing fee be permitted to run anyway. The decision is not expected to have much impact on the earmarking of filing fee monies for the Democratic State Committee.[23]

The number of states experimenting with various forms of public finance of politics is small. The experiments, in most cases, have not been carried on long enough for many conclusions to be drawn as to their effectiveness as fund-raising devices or their impact on political parties in general. Virtually no discussion has been held at the state level of public financing of elections from the general treasury. Most state chair-

* Caroline Wilkins, state Democratic chairwoman of Oregon, regularly published a tax credit table in her party's newsletter. The table provided to the potential contributor a specified dollar amount that could be claimed under either a state or federal tax credit and also showed the net cost to the contributor for each donation. For an example see *Democratic Party of Oregon* (newsletter), published at Corvallis, Oregon, November 1973, p. 5.

men and other party officials maintain a preference for retention of private financing of state elections combined with strong disclosure laws. This appears to be the pattern established in most of the states and is likely to prevail for the immediate future.

Political fund raising has undergone important changes within the past two decades. Sustaining programs, large contributors' "clubs," earmarked filing fees, income tax credits and check-offs, and telethons are all new to politics. They have not replaced traditional methods of fund raising, but their impact in terms of contributions as well as citizen participation has had a profound effect on the political parties. Of the three major sources of party money currently being used, two—sustaining programs and telethons—have been developed within the past fifteen years. The third, fund-raising dinners, has been a staple of political solicitors for many years. The enormous increases in the costs of running party organizations and campaigns, including the money necessary to fund the innovations of the new politics, have forced the parties at both national and state levels to search for new sources of revenues. Some of them have shown considerable ingenuity in that search.

Party Communications

Intraparty communications has been an inhibiting factor in party growth from the inception of the party idea. Decentralization of party organizations within each state, lack of up-to-date membership rolls, and rapidly changing party leadership all combined to create artificial barriers between party leaders, workers, and members. It has always been a difficult barrier to breach. The means to inform party members and call them to action on behalf of the party's candidates and ideals have never been easily available. Nevertheless, the American parties have traditionally relied on two methods of maintaining contact—official party newspapers and the regular mail. A third communications vehicle has been added in recent years as some state headquarters have contracted for Wide Area Service (WATS) lines opening channels of almost unlimited statewide telephone contact.*

Obviously, the use of the mails, party newspapers, and extended tele-

---

* The American Telephone and Telegraph Co. instituted multiband Wide Area Telephone Service in 1961. A subscriber, for a set fee, can have unlimited use of telephone service within a contract area. Those state party organizations which subscribe normally contract for statewide service.

phone service is not a technological innovation in the same sense that polling, automatic data processing, and management services are, but the great expansion in their use during the past two decades suggests that they are being viewed in a new light. Although they are not new techniques, they are being used on an expanded basis and in more innovative and sophisticated ways.

The problem of intraparty communications has been a thorny one from the beginning. One of the original reasons for the creation of the Committees of Correspondence during the Revolutionary period was to provide a means of communication between far-flung party outposts. These committees served as the principal means of organizational party building as ideas were exchanged, information was collected, and issues of the era were debated. Before the campaign of 1800, Republicans in New York and Pennsylvania had perfected a system of "committees of correspondence." They were composed of active party members who, among themselves, published newspapers or newsletters with a political interest. This method of reaching the populace and winning votes soon became an accepted means of political action and spread across the country. As Donald H. Stewart described the phenomenon:

With all their gifts for leadership, and all the popular topics that arose, Madison, Jefferson, and their companions could not possibly have worked this miracle [the defeat of the Federalists] without the aid of the newspapers. Devoted Republican editors and tireless correspondents, oftentimes more intemperate and enthusiastic than judicious and accurate, acquainted voters with candidates' abilities, aroused citizens to the real or imagined dangers of Federalist policies, and developed the issues and reasoning that came to spell Jefferson's ultimate success.[24]

This need for communication, more for political proselytizing than anything else, led to the establishment of the first party newspapers. The first of these was probably the *Gazette of the United States,* published from 1789 to 1800 by John Fenno, who usually printed what the Federalist leaders told him to. His goal was to use his paper to gain support for a strong central government, a view shared by George Washington and Alexander Hamilton. With his well-known dislike for party factions, it is doubtful that Washington would have encouraged the development of a political press if he had known where it would lead, but Hamilton quite properly saw it as a key to the maintenance of Federalist hegemony. To insure the continuation of the *Gazette,* Fenno benefited from printing patronage channeled his way by the Treasury Department. Secretary Hamilton also loaned Fenno operating money on occasion.[25]

In 1791 Thomas Jefferson prevailed upon a renowned poet, writer, and journalist, Philip Freneau, to undertake the publication of a newspaper to deal with the issues of the day. In order to provide Freneau with a living while the paper was beginning, James Madison brought him to Philadelphia as a translator in Jefferson's Department of State.[26] Unlike the Fenno enterprise, Freneau's *National Gazette* was a balanced paper which presented more than one viewpoint on political matters. It also aspired to, and gained, national coverage and scope.[27] To insure the widest possible circulation for the Freneau prose, his friends actively solicited subscriptions in many states. Jefferson and Madison worked to enlist readers in Massachusetts, Georgia, and Kentucky, while Henry Lee offered subscriptions to the citizens of Richmond. The readers of the *National Gazette* were promised news and essays that would "promote the general interest of the Union." Its publication was prior to the establishment of state political parties, but it is still considered to be the first national party newspaper and served as a model for state political papers which were to follow.

It was at this time that the first of the state political newspapers appeared. The Republican followers of Jefferson were the first to enter the field since they were out of office and needed a vehicle for political attack. Some of the more notable papers were the *New London Bee, New York City Republican Watchtower, Portsmouth Republican Ledger,* and the *South Carolina State Gazette.* Each of these papers devoted space to attacks on the opposition, presentation of Jeffersonian views, and exhortations to vote for Republican candidates. No purpose would be served in carrying this brief history of party newspapers further. A magnum jump from the eighteenth century to the present, however, might demonstrate that the goals of party news dissemination have not changed very much. The first issue of the *Pennsylvania Democrat,* March 1969, spelled out its purposes:

You are now reading the first edition of our new monthly newspaper, *The Pennsylvania Democrat.* . . . We aim to make this newspaper as lively and as informative as its predecessor. . . .

But despite the many problems involved with producing a newspaper, Chairman Thomas Z. Minehart feels that it is essential now that the State Committee re-establish lines of communication and information exchange with Pennsylvania Democrats from the precincts to the State Capitol. . . .

It will carry stories to provide Democratic workers with detailed information on the governmental and political issues of the day so that they are better able to carry the message to the voters.

It will also serve as a vehicle to the nitty gritty of precinct work, to committeemen and women. It is our hope that the committee people will exchange ideas and techniques they have found to be successful.

And it will give us an opportunity to present to you in depth stories on Democrats recording significant achievement, whether it be on the floor of the House or Senate in Harrisburg, in local government, or in precinct activity.[28]

The Modern Party Newspaper / Newsletter

At any given time the number of regularly published state party newspapers will vary widely. Whether or not a party publishes is a question that is often controlled by the current financial condition, the attitude of the chairman toward intraparty communications, and the availability of staff to handle the actual production. By 1972, sixty-two parties published a newspaper or newsletter in one form or another, thirty-two did not publish, and six were not accounted for but probably did not publish. Every party in the midwestern area except the North Dakota Democrats published a newspaper or newsletter on a somewhat regular basis, and most of those in the middle Atlantic and New England states did also. Almost half of the southern parties, primarily Democratic, did not publish a paper, and half of the western parties did not. A follow-up two years after the initial contact revealed that at least two papers had ceased publication and three new ones had begun. This kind of fluidity is constant, but it should be borne in mind that some party newspapers have published on a regular monthly basis for long periods of time, including at least one for ten years or more.

Approximately one-third of the papers examined are professionally produced on mechanical printing equipment. They are offset printed with extensive use of photographs, and they normally contain from six to eight pages in each issue. Another third are published in the format of slick-paper magazines with considerable use of photographs; these are normally about four pages in length. A final third, the least professional in appearance, are mimeographed and stapled, sometimes printed on both sides, and usually two pages long.

Most party newspapers are published monthly although several are weekly or biweekly and one is published every six months. A few bear seasonal dates such as Winter, Spring, or Summer. Normally the publisher is listed as the state committee, and usually the articles and news items are not attributed. Several chairmen indicated that the state committee was legally responsible as publisher.

Sample papers from sixty-two state party organizations were collected and later content-analyzed, following the process through five stages: (1) the research propositions were formulated so that relevant sampling procedures could be selected for coding; (2) the sample was selected and content categories were identified; (3) the documents (party newspapers) were read, coded, and condensed to special coding sheets developed for the purpose; (4) the items in each category were totaled and scores assigned; and (5) interpretations of the findings were made in the light of a series of propositions which were constructed earlier.*

At this point, the following content categories were selected to assure reproducibility:

1. All articles or letters written by the state chairman and so designated, either by title or name

2. Articles written to furnish information, give praise, or engage in self-criticism about the state and local party

3. Articles written in a manner that demeaned or criticized the state opposition party

4. Articles relating the local party to the national party or furnishing information about national politics

5. Critical articles designed to demean the national opposition party or some political event involving that party

6. Articles generally directed to the young people in the party

7. All uses of space to publicize a fund-raising event or to direct an appeal for funds to the party members (including paid advertising)

Since one area of particular interest concerned the use to which the party newspaper was put regarding the publicizing of the state chairman

---

* The newspaper collection was compiled by the author through personal visits and letters to state chairmen. Sixty-two organizations furnished a single copy, while ten chairmen placed the author on the mailing list to receive copies over a one- or two-year period. Six of these were later selected for detailed content analysis over a selected time frame. The actual analysis was done by Robert E. Jednak, a graduate research assistant in the Department of Political Science, Florida Atlantic University, under the author's direction. The study resulted in a master's thesis entitled, "A Content Analysis of State Political Party Newspapers" (Florida Atlantic University, August 1970).

or the governor, two additional items were coded as multiple responses. They were:

8. Articles, regardless of general theme, which mentioned the state chairman by name or title

9. Articles, regardless of general theme, which mentioned the governor by name or title

The composite average of all analyzed newspapers and newsletters is shown in table 6.5. It is clear that the largest amount of space is used to provide information about the party to the members, workers, and officials throughout the state. The importance of this cannot be over-emphasized as it is often the only regular means of contact between the various echelons of the party. Articles praising the national party, its leaders and policies, as well as those concerned with fund raising and finance, constitute the only other substantial uses of space.

Every article in each paper was analyzed and, depending upon the purport of the article, was designated with the appropriate content category number. After these designations were made, the total column-inch space was tabulated for each category. This, in turn, was converted into a percentage of the total column-inch space. The sum for content categories 1 through 7, then, equals 100 percent. Through this means Jednak showed how the editors distributed content emphasis.

Table 6.5   Composite Average for All Newspapers Analyzed
(Percentage of Column-Inch Space)

Content category	Score
(1) Chairman's letter	3.29%
(2) State party information	46.64
(3) Critique of state opposition	9.39
(4) National party support	18.86
(5) Critique of national opposition	3.79
(6) Youth	4.26
(7) Finance	13.77
Total: Content Categories 1–7	100.00
(8) Mention of state chairman	17.89 *
(9) Mention of governor	22.63 *

* These items were also included among the seven primary content categories.

Two particular themes ran throughout all coding categories and, as noted earlier, were eventually singled out and assigned supplementary category numbers 8 and 9. They were the column-inch space devoted to activities of the state chairman and of the governor. The space assigned to these two categories was tabulated separately from the seven primary coded groups.[29]

State party newspapers and newsletters serve the party and its leaders in a variety of ways. They are the chief source of internal party news for the workers and members and, as such, are often directed toward the accomplishment of specific ends. As shown in table 6.5, at least 3 percent of the column-inch space was devoted to each of the primary content categories. The two categories of space which mentioned the state chairman and/or the governor in some way cut across the seven primary categories and were coded separately. Therefore, a single reference to the state chairman might be coded twice, once as a content reference in a principal content category and once as a specific reference to the chairman in category 8. There is little doubt that state party newspapers are used extensively to publicize the activities and personal qualities of the state chairmen and their governors: almost 18 percent of the column-inch space singled out the chairman for reference while nearly 23 percent mentioned the governor, a significant number in view of the fact that only half the papers represented parties in power. One paper, over a one-year period, included a picture of the governor in every issue; another included a picture of the chairman in all but one issue; and sometimes, as in the case of the Illinois and Ohio Democrats, the entire issue of each paper was printed on a letterhead bearing the chairman's name.

Examples of categories 8 and 9 are not especially meaningful, but the following items serve as illustrations:

At the November meeting of the York County Committee, State Chairman Cyril M. Joly, Jr., met with the group . . . [*GOP Newsletter* (Maine), December 1969, p. 4]

Pennsylvania's big four Republicans have been named co-chairmen of the new Republican Progress Squad by Republican State Chairman John C. Jordan . . . [*Newsletter* (Pennsylvania), November 1969, p. 1]

Accomplishments by the 1970 legislature demonstrated the teamwork by Gov. Frank L. Farrar, legislators, and GOP officials . . . [*South Dakota Republican News,* February 1970, p. 1]

Gov. Robert Ray has worked successfully to see that Iowa's immunization program against German measles (rubella) gets started immediately... [*Newsletter* (Iowa), December 1969, p. 4]

It was hypothesized that the state chairman would use the party newsletter to build or sustain his own position in the party hierarchy. In view of his relatively short tenure and the contradictory pressures generated by the job, it seemed reasonable to assume that the chairman would use those means at his disposal to strengthen his personal role in the party. An obvious way in which to do so would be to publish a signed personal letter, memorandum, or column in each issue, either in his official capacity or in his role as editor of the paper. As noted in table 6.5, few chairmen actually did so; only 3.29 percent of the chairmen employed a personal message of any kind. Examples were as follows:

This has been a busy month for both myself and state headquarters. The two-day Washington fund-raising trip has created a lot of interest. . . . Each time I go to Washington I am more and more impressed with the leadership of Rogers Morton [Republican National Chairman]. ["Comments from Chairman Crittenden," *The Florida Republican Challenger,* November 1969, p. 2]

In our efforts to strengthen the party so that we can recapture the highest office in Arkansas, as well as fill with Democrats many other offices that will be contested, we must be sure that our party encourages the meshing of the activities of all these groups of people toward objectives which will make our state reach greater heights. ["From the Chairman," *The New Democrat,* October 1967, p. 2]

State party papers are normally state party oriented in their coverage. They serve as a combination news-dispensing and enthusiasm-generating organ, and they should not be evaluated on the same scale and with the same criteria used to assess public newspapers. Even so, an important share of space (46.6 percent) was devoted to state party information and news, suggesting that the editors did recognize the fragility of the information link between state party leaders and members. Items fitting within this particular category usually came closest to the traditional "news" function of a paper. Thus, two examples:

Allen Overcash of Lincoln is serving as Chairman of the State Candidates Committee. His job: to see that a qualified Democrat is filed for every race in Election Year '70. [*Nebraska Demo-Gram,* January-February 1970, p. 2]

Douglas County Democrats will host the State Central Committee meeting in Roseburg, Saturday, December 1. Reports will include a Rules Committee proposal for by-laws changes, suggested methods for selection of delegates to the 1974 National Conference, finances and Telethon II, and State Fair Booth. [*Democratic Party of Oregon,* November 1973, p. 2]

Just as there are recurrent controversies between the national and state governments in our federal system, there are also disagreements between national and state party organizations and leaders. Conflicts over money, speakers, public policy, and organizational responsibilities are commonplace, but discords such as these usually proceed to their ultimate conclusion behind the scenes. Surface evidence suggests to most party members, as well as to the opposition, that the national and state party people are cooperative and supportive of each other. National committee publications in both parties often extol the virtues of elected state officials. State party newspapers, in turn, devoted almost 19 percent of their column-inch space to praise of one or another aspect of national party events or personages. That category (table 6.5) ranked second among all the categories in space allocations.

The *Utah Republican,* in early 1970, included a story with this lead: "The Salt Lake City Commissioners sent President Nixon a resolution affirming their support of the President's Vietnam policy" (*Utah Republican,* December 1969–January 1970, p. 2).

Another example of praise for a national party action appeared in late 1973:

The Democratic National Committee will establish training programs for the 1974 and 1976 campaigns to upgrade the organizational, fund-raising, communication and research skills of campaign managers, candidates and state party organizations.

Conferences will be held in Boston (January), Chicago (late January and early February), . . .

This sounds like a great idea and *The Spokesman* hopes it is the start of regular efforts along such lines. [*The Spokesman: Wyoming's Democratic Voice,* December 1973, p. 1]

Fund raising, as has been noted, is always an important activity in party politics, and it is reflected in the 13.7 percent of space devoted to it in party newspapers. Direct appeals for funds, the publicizing of fundraising events, and direct advertising for contributions were all used by a variety of papers. Some appeared to devote a very large percentage of their available space to fund raising. The *Colorado Democrat* devoted an average of 37.99 percent of each issue to articles about fund raising or advertisements for contributions or to official advertising. The *Democrat* is one of the few party papers designated as an official medium for publication of state legal notices and collects considerable revenue therefrom. Of the total linage allocated to fund raising in the *Democrat,* 77 percent was in the form of official advertising. The remaining 23 percent was made up of articles describing fund-raising events.

The November 1973 issue of the *Democratic Party of Oregon* (newsletter) devoted the entire front page to an article describing the September 15, 1973, Democratic Telethon II. It also contained a story describing a fund-raising dinner with Senator Henry (Scoop) Jackson of Washington as featured speaker, an advertisement asking for contributions of from $2 to $15 as a "member" of the Oregon Democratic party, and an article explaining legislative action to increase the tax credit available for political contributions. In a two-page section containing nineteen short items from various Oregon county Democratic parties, twelve of them dealt with local fund-raising events.

Only a small amount of space (3.79 percent) was devoted to criticism of national opposition candidates and parties. Examples included:

According to a copyrighted news analysis in the Los Angeles Times, Madison Avenue techniques may be leading the Nixon administration in a short cut to skid row. [*Hawkeye Democratic Leader* (Iowa), November 1969, p. 2]

For President Nixon the year 1968 will be remembered as the "year of promises"; 1969 as the "year of forgotten promises." [*Demo-Memo* (Missouri), January 1970, p. 3]

As might be expected, more column-inch space (9.39 percent) was devoted to criticism of the state opposition party and opposing candidates.

The Senior Senator from Indiana is a model for students of inconsistency! Vance Hartke has changed his position on Vietnam so often that it is doubtful tonight if he remembers where he stands. [*Trunk Line* (Indiana Republican), December 1969, p. 3]

Minnesota Republicans are doing their best to hide the fact, but it looks like a few squabbles are erupting behind their placid image. Third District Congressman Clark MacGregor is claiming party "bossism." [*State DFL News* (Minnesota), January 1970, p. 4]

Finally, 4.26 percent of the space in party newspapers was devoted to articles oriented toward youth. Both political parties at the national level have devoted a good deal of time and money to wooing young people over the past decade, especially since the approval of the eighteen-year-old vote. Examples of youth-related articles were as follows:

Joan Wall, a 22 year old MIT student, is the youngest state chairman in the history of the Massachusetts Young Republican Association. [*Target* (Republican), May 1969, p. 6]

Kentucky Young Democrats have a statewide goal of 120 new clubs. [*The Democrats,* October 1969, p. 2]

State party newspapers and newsletters will continue to occupy an important communications position in state party politics. They represent one of the few means of regularly reaching out to the party workers and officials, and the need for them is attested to by the increased number being published. It should also be noted that a sizable number of county and city party organizations also publish newspapers on a regular and continuous basis.

Subscriptions, earmarked budgeted funds, and advertising provide enough money so that most of the newspapers and newsletters are self-sustaining, and some have proved to be sufficiently profitable that their style and appearance have been enhanced through new formats. Most party leaders believe that every effort should be made to keep the party's news organ alive and to broaden its circulation, although a few argue that the benefits do not match the costs. One, who originally considered the party newspaper to be an "expensive adornment and a frill," later changed his mind:

When I came in we were putting out a four-page offset paper. I found that it was costing almost $100 an issue more than it was bringing in and the postage bill was eating us up. I discontinued it because of that. The research director had been editing it and it wasn't a bad little paper, but I just decided that I couldn't afford it. We got so much flak, though, that the executive committee insisted that I reinstate it, and one of them covered the deficit until we could get it on a self-sustaining basis. I began charging a minimum subscription fee of $1, and we now have it on the black side of the ledger. In fact, when we began to charge for it we increased our circulation. I think, in retrospect, it was a mistake to kill it. A lot of people apparently read it with interest. For a lot of them it is their only regular contact with headquarters.

Some Ideas Whose Time Has Come

Political scientists point out that evidence accumulated over a long period of time suggests that voting behavior is relatively unaffected by campaign strategies and appeals. Voter loyalties are, on the whole, more important in the long run because most voters consistently support candidates of the party to which they maintain an allegiance. It has also been demonstrated that most voters make up their minds prior to the opening of the campaign.[30] Those candidates who win attribute their victories to superior campaigning while those who lose assign the blame to forces beyond their control.[31]

At the presidential level the advent of new techniques of campaigning has probably diminished the role of the national party organizations in national campaigns. Presidential candidates normally create their own parallel campaign staffs and employ professional consultants and campaign management firms to undertake the national effort necessary to secure a nomination or the election. The national party organizations have been slower than presidential candidates to adopt the new techniques of politics, but both national committees began experimenting with information retrieval systems, computer analysis, and data-based financial plans in the 1960s.[32]

Agranoff's statement that "Contemporary party involvement in the new campaigning can best be described as evolutionary and peripheral" is particularly appropriate to state parties.[33] For a variety of reasons, as noted earlier, state party organizations have been slow to adapt to the new politics. But considering the precarious health and vitality of the state parties two decades ago, the fact that many of them have begun to experiment and to implement new approaches to their responsibilities is cause for some rejoicing by those who wish to see the organizations strengthened.

It is ironic that the politics of California demonstrates both sides of that equation. Professional campaign management got its start in the Golden State in the 1930s and 1940s when political conditions provided a testing ground for professional political services. The parties were weakened by the influx of a transient population with little knowledge of and small interest in state and local politics, and the impact of the nonpartisan movement was greater in California than in most other states. The emergence, during the period, of a highly volatile initiative and referenda syndrome, plus an increasingly issue-oriented voting electorate, opened the way to the initial development of political advertising which later led to the early nurturing of professional campaign management. Many of the early management firms got their start in California, but most of their contracts have been with the campaign organizations of candidates and issue-oriented groups. State party organizations have generally been unable to employ their services because of the costs involved and, in some cases, because of a failure to appreciate their significance. Thus, the irony: the new politics got its start at the state level—but with individual candidates, not political parties. The circle has now begun to close as, thirty years later, state party organizations begin to adapt to the new style of politics and electioneering.

Public opinion polling in a political milieu first attracted national attention in the presidential campaigns of the 1940s. It, too, was adopted by national parties and private candidates before state organizations demonstrated much active interest. Polling by the state parties was slow to develop because the cost was high and local solicitors discovered considerable antipathy toward contributing money for polls. Only the immediate strategic need of the campaign situation convinced party leaders that money should be spent for measuring the public's attitude toward candidates and issues.

Automatic data processing was another innovation in politics that filtered down from the national to the state party levels. The use of ADP at the two national committees is not especially sophisticated but is rapidly becoming so, while its implementation by the state parties is still in its infancy. The fact that ADP has not progressed much beyond the experimental stage is due to its high cost plus a general lack of knowledge of its applications to everyday politics.

The only campaign or organizational aid discussed in this chapter to which the adjective "new" does not really apply is the party newspaper or newsletter. Even so, the early development of this intraparty communications device was followed by 150 years of neglect. Only recently have state party organizations again begun to publish newspapers and has their acceptance as political tools been demonstrated, albeit on a somewhat limited scale.

Both national parties have undertaken programs to instruct party leaders in the intricacies and uses of modern political techniques. For instance, the September 1969 meeting of the Democratic National Committee included agenda items specifically designed to familiarize state chairmen and other state party leaders with technical applications in politics. Workshops were scheduled to address the uses of the media, fund raising by direct mail, the use of computers, and public opinion polling.

The workshops were scheduled to allow each chairman to attend all four. Such programs have become commonplace in the intervening years.

State party organizations have been slow to adopt new techniques. Party leaders appear to have been dominated by a conservatism which prevented them from exploration, and reevaluation took place only after political events overcame organizational reluctance. The breakdown of strong party loyalties and party identification plus the growing need to appeal to the expanding "independent" vote forced party leaders and candidates to seek new ways to attract voters and contributed to the re-vitalization of the movement to improve campaigning. Independent voters, in order to be won over, were made the targets of carefully constructed campaign efforts which required modern political techniques if they were to be successful.

The tendency of presidential, senatorial, and gubernatorial candidates to commit themselves to personalized, separately financed, and independently managed campaigns often left state and local party organizations with inadequate resources. In order to survive, some state party leaders realized that stringent efforts had to be expended if the traditional role of the party was to be preserved. The old politics, although familiar, was not effective in the mass market. The need for new approaches coincided with the rise of the new political techniques as well as the increasing availability of the hardware to put them into effect.

Finally, the cost of experimentation was prohibitive. As the personalized campaigns for high office developed, the costs of winning elections in the electronic era multiplied many times over. While the candidates at the top of the ticket could raise the enormous sums necessary to mount a modern campaign, the state party organizations often found themselves holding an empty moneybag. Nevertheless, as the state fund raisers were shown how to adapt new techniques to fund raising, money began to be more plentiful in some of the larger states and the adoption of modern campaign technology was underway. As these expenditures prove themselves to be justified in some of the larger states, more state party leaders will overcome their reluctance and no doubt will move to adopt them.

The increasing impact of the electronic media, rapidly growing and constantly changing populations, the availability of hardware, and fear of party atrophy, combined with improved revenue collection schemes, have provided the evidence necessary to convince most state party leaders of the efficacy of the new politics. The use of political technology is clearly an idea whose time seems finally to have come.

One of the by-products of a federal system of government is a decentralized party structure. Because of decentralization, state chairmen were unable to cope for years with their geographical isolation from Washington and from each other. They were unable to develop as a cohesive force in politics and could not even exchange ideas on a regular basis. Chapter 7 describes the efforts of the state chairmen in both parties to organize laterally. These efforts, having proven successful, could provide the basis for a new force in American politics.

7 Lateral Organization:
The Struggle for Power

We will never get power in the Democratic
party until we can demonstrate our muscle.
We may get on the national committee, but
we will have to fight every inch of the way
to get there.
A Democratic state chairman

Some of the Republican chairmen aren't
interested in power in the party. They are
active in their regional associations because
they pick up ideas and learn how to undertake new problems from other chairmen. I
think that is the principal benefit to be
gained from association together.
*A western Republican national
committeewoman*

If we can achieve the influence in our party
that the southern Republican chairmen have
in theirs, I will consider us successful. The
amazing thing is that they don't win anything and have no parties to chair, but they
are listened to as though they won all the
apples all the time.
A New England Democratic chairman

Only in the past two decades have the
state party chairmen as a group come to occupy a more powerful and
responsible position in the American political hierarchy. In spite of their
strategic position midway between the national and local organizations,
they were unable until recently to garner much attention. Some chairmen,
acting individually, were able to put their own personal brand on their
own particular party organization, but, collectively, the organizational
importance of the state chairmen was minimal.

A number of factors have contributed to this generally limited impact.
Most of them can be traced directly to the decentralized nature of the
American party system. The state parties are scattered geographically
across the continent, a fact that has made concerted action difficult in the
past. Because they are widely dispersed, interrelationships have been slow

to develop, and until they were granted membership on the national committees, there was no formal means for the chairmen to congregate in one place. Every four years most of them, but not all, would meet at their respective national nominating conventions, but even that limited contact was dependent upon each individual being selected as a delegate. Furthermore, the very nature of the convention institution, built as it was on a foundation of state caucuses and candidate entourages, tended to prevent chairmen from moving outside the limitations of caucus and candidate politics. As a group they simply were not a force with which to contend in either party.

An additional hindrance was the demonstrated reluctance of both national committees and a succession of national chairmen to provide the means for the state party leaders to become a more potent political force. The national committees have historically been president-directed in leap years and Congress-directed in off years. They seldom have found the time or resources to be state-directed in any year. To be sure, some state party organizations made clear their own determination to resist "interference" by the national committees. Consequently, both parties have demonstrated considerable uneasiness over efforts of state party leaders to carve themselves a more important niche in the national arena. The Republican National Committee agreed to the creation of the Republican Governors' Association in the early 1960s only after individual governors became a force of such influence that they could no longer be ignored. The GOP leadership, without the presidency, the Congress, or the electorate, could not ignore the Rockefeller brothers in New York and Arkansas, Scranton of Pennsylvania, Love of Colorado, Evans of Washington, Romney of Michigan, Smylie of Idaho, and Rhodes of Ohio. Therefore, the association was established with national committee support. The long efforts of the Democratic state chairmen to organize into a formal association are detailed in this chapter. Their eventual success came after years of frustration caused by the reluctance of the national committee leadership to cooperate in the venture.

By 1974 all the state chairmen in both parties were voting members of their respective national committees, and both the Democrats and Republicans were organized nationally into state chairmen's associations. They meet frequently at national committee meetings and conventions of their own. They are key participants in regional party organizations and are no longer forced to figuratively press their noses against the window of party affairs. They are on the inside looking out. Let us turn to how this change in fortune came about.

The Republican State Chairmen's Association

In the early years of party development, the state chairmen operated as independent political entrepreneurs, doing for their individual state parties what they could but doing nothing as a unified group. There is no record of any kind of concerted effort by party chairmen prior to this century. The earliest suggestion that a group of chairmen may have jointly taken action toward a common goal was included in the minutes of a meeting of the Republican National Committee held during the period 1917–24. Jo Good, convention director, Republican National Committee, has recalled a set of minutes for an RNC meeting during that period in which it was reported that the national committee had given the Republican state chairmen special permission to sit in on a meeting of the RNC to hear a discussion of some topic of special interest to the states.[1] There is no indication that any substantive action came of this meeting, nor is there any record of further joint endeavors during the next twenty-five years.

In 1948, after the unexpected defeat of Thomas E. Dewey in the presidential election, there was considerable agitation in the Republican party to get back to the "grass roots." On March 13, 1949, a meeting of all Republican state chairmen was held in Chicago. Called by A. T. Howard, Nebraska state chairman, who was at that time chairman of an embryonic midwestern association of state chairmen, the meeting was attended by twenty-eight chairmen. Leading women from each state party, most of whom held office as vice-chairman, were invited, but few came. The substantive outcome of that meeting was a resolution which read as follows:

... that we organize as a committee of state chairmen and vice-chairmen; that we ask the National Committee to designate us as a Committee of the National Committee; that we recommend that the Chairman of the Republican National Committee be requested to act as chairman of this important committee; that the chairmen and vice-chairmen of each regional group be a vice-chairman of the National Committee of State Chairmen and Vice-Chairmen; that we meet at least once a year in off-election years and at least every six months in election years; that we urge each region to organize as soon as possible and hold regional meetings as frequently as consistent with conditions in such region.[2]

Nothing came of this resolution, although it was discussed briefly at the national committee meeting in August of that year. During this period the state chairmen engaged in considerable gentlemanly agitation for membership on the Republican National Committee. The vehicle through which this effort was carried on was an unofficial organization of mid-western and Rocky Mountain state party leaders which had been inaugurated in 1948 or 1949. The states represented in this regional organization were Arizona, Colorado, Idaho, Illinois, Indiana, Iowa, Kansas, Michigan, Minnesota, Missouri, Montana, Nebraska, New Mexico, North Dakota, Ohio, Oklahoma, South Dakota, Utah, Wisconsin, and Wyoming. At a later date West Virginia and Nevada were added.

The issue was finally joined at the 1952 Republican National Convention during debate and final passage of a rules change proposed by the Committee on Rules. The new rule provided that a state chairman would automatically become a voting member of the RNC if his state had cast its electoral votes for the Republican candidate for president at the preceding election; or had a majority of Republicans elected to seats in the U.S. House of Representatives and Senate from that state; or had elected a Republican governor in the last gubernatorial election. This bonus system, providing for a third member of the national committee for those states electing Republican officeholders, resulted in a flexible membership depending upon how the party did at the polls in any given election. Over the next few years approximately forty state chairmen qualified at any given time for membership on the RNC.

The two delegate groups which led the fight against membership for the state chairmen were female delegates and those from the South. Some female delegates argued that the addition of state chairmen, almost all of whom were and always are men, diluted the strength of the women on the national committee from one-half to one-third. The southerners feared that their inability to elect Republicans would continually diminish their collective power in the councils of the national committee. Mrs. John E. Messervy, a delegate from South Carolina, spoke for both groups when she said:

For too long the Southern states have been treated as stepchildren at family reunions. We have to stand up against the Democrats in our states, because we do wear a badge of Republicanism bravely and hold our banner high, and at Republican gatherings and conventions we hope for sympathy and understanding and not discrimination.

We in South Carolina have met our quotas in the past financially, and I have myself written checks for $1,000 year after year for the National Republican Party and have said to them, "Spend it in the states where you can win."

Are we to be beaten down with the weapons we put into your hands after we have, in a small way, helped to give you this power to be used against us? . . .

This proposed change in the rules creates inequality between men and women. How can you as Republicans appeal to the great majority of women voters in America, thirty million in number, when you ruthlessly propose discrimination against us? [3]

Debate was almost nonexistent, the delegates having exhausted themselves in the nomination battle between Dwight D. Eisenhower and Robert A. Taft. The roll-call vote in favor of the rules change was 683 to 513 with ten delegates absent. Virtually all of the southern and border state votes were cast against changing the rules while most of the large populous states, with the exception of Pennsylvania and Illinois, voted to admit the state chairmen. It is ironic that in later years the southern Republican chairmen have emerged unofficially as the most cohesive and effective regional group operating within the framework of the national committee.

In 1968 the rules were again changed, this time to include all state chairmen as members without qualification. In 1972 the convention added the chairmen of the District of Columbia, Guam, Puerto Rico, and the Virgin Islands, bringing the total membership of the RNC to 162. Admission of the Republican state chairmen to full national committee membership and participation was reasonably easy to achieve. The growth of the chairmen as a distinct organizational group within the Republican party developed almost simultaneously.

By 1952 the Midwest and Rocky Mountain State Chairmen's Association had generated additional strength. Its third chairman was Ray C. Bliss of Ohio, and part of the favor with which it was viewed by national party leaders was due to his presence and leadership. Bliss usually managed to have a special meeting of the member chairmen a day prior to each national committee meeting and, at times, regional strategy was agreed upon during those sessions.

Early in the 1960s all the state chairmen were invited to attend a reception given by the Midwest and Rocky Mountain State Chairmen's Association, and from that gathering party leaders from other regions began to discuss formation of other regional groups. There exists a record of a meeting of the western chairmen in 1961 with those attending representing the far western states plus Alaska and Hawaii.

On December 6, 1962, William E. Miller, Republican national chairman, announced formal recognition of a Republican State Chairmen's Association under the chairmanship of Ray Bliss. Miller said that the group would hold one national meeting plus regional meetings throughout the year. These conferences were to be organized with the assistance of the national committee and its staff. Subsequently, association meetings have been coordinated with national committee meetings so that the state chairmen could attend both with less expense in time and money. The conferences usually include an evening reception, regional breakfasts, and day-long workshop sessions, which cover a wide variety of matters ranging from formal speeches to campaign advice and technical stratagems.

From the national group there gradually developed four distinct regional organizations, identified as the Midwest, Western, Northeastern, and Southern State Chairmen's Associations. Each group developed its own by-laws, collected dues, and elected officers. Just prior to the 1964 National Convention, Chairman Miller asked the chairman of each of the regional associations to serve as a member of the newly created Republican State Chairmen's Advisory Committee. This action was taken without formal ratification by the RNC. The order creating the advisory committee specifically directed that it consist of the chairman of each of the regional state chairmen's associations with the chairman to be appointed from among the four. The first chairman of the four-member group was Ray Bliss. In 1972 the chairman of the advisory committee was designated as an ex officio member of the executive committee of the Republican National Committee. In common practice the Republican State Chairmen's Advisory Committee is synonymous with the Republican State Chairmen's Association. The chairman of the former is always considered to be the leader of the latter.

At the same time Miller also announced formation of the Republican Governors' Association with Governor Robert E. Smylie of Idaho as its first chairman. Miller believed that by creating these two new organizations of state political representatives in the year prior to the 1964 elections he would have an easier time holding a divided party together as Governors Rockefeller, Scranton, and Romney and Senator Goldwater competed for the presidential nomination. Coincidentally, Miller himself emerged from that convention as the Republican vice-presidential nominee.

After the Goldwater election debacle, in April 1965, Ray Bliss was named national chairman to try to pull the party together. Bliss resigned as chairman of the Republican State Chairmen's Advisory Committee as well as state chairman of Ohio. At his first national committee meeting in June, Bliss met with the four regional leaders and named Dr. Gaylord Parkinson of California as chairman of the advisory committee. Parkinson was succeeded in turn by Robert D. Ray of Iowa, Ody J. Fish of Wisconsin, and John Andrews of Ohio. Upon assuming the mantle of party leadership in mid-1973, George Bush appointed John McDonald of Iowa as chairman of the advisory committee. Thus, four of the first five appointed chairmen have been representatives of the Midwest State Chairmen's Association. This attests to the power of the midwestern states in the Republican party as well as to the generally strong party leadership which emerges from that area.

Chairmanship of the Republican State Chairmen's Advisory Committee is considered to be of some importance although it has little apparent real power. David Broder, then of the *Washington Evening Star,* noted in 1965 that the race to succeed Ray Bliss as chairman of the group included Wirt A. Yerger, Jr., of Mississippi, an early and ardent Goldwaterite and one of the leaders of the new-generation southern GOP bloc; Craig Truax, Pennsylvania, a former newspaperman who was one of the strategists of the abortive 1964 Scranton-for-President campaign; and tempted to straddle the battle waged between the warring factions of his Dr. Gaylord Parkinson of California, a physician-politician who at-state party. As Broder noted:

> The job they are vying for has had little actual power. Under Bliss the state chairmen met twice a year to talk over such practical problems as finance, organization, and publicity. He rigidly barred any discussion of party policy or personalities from their sessions . . . but Yerger, Truax and Parkinson believe that the association could develop more importance in coming years.[4]

Ten years later Broder's assessment of the impact of the association is still essentially correct. The influence of the state chairmen on the Republican party has been a product of their leadership rather than their collective power. The semiannual meetings of the group have tended to be formal and unidimensional. In June 1971 a Denver meeting of the group heard a report on the Supreme Court's activities in the realm of legislative districting and another on the emerging youth vote. Six months later in Washington the chairmen heard formal presentations from the national chairman and co-chairwoman, a report on planning for the 1972 national convention, various reports of ongoing activities of the national committee, and a discussion of White House patronage problems. The latter, the only substantive issue on the program, was one of a series of follow-up meetings with White House aides to further refine patronage clearance after the initial difficulties described in chapter 5.

The real benefits derived from the semiannual meetings do not arise from the formal program sessions themselves. In both parties the program serves merely as a device to bring the state chairmen together in one place and at one time for informal political intercourse. As shown in table 7.1, 49 percent of the respondents suggested that the most valuable advantage of these conferences was as a vehicle for "the exchange of ideas and information." * As "ideas" the chairman cited such things as innovative fund-raising techniques, voter registration programs, and the political uses of automatic data processing. As "information" they included anything from political rumor to participation in internecine conflict. One Republican chairman summed up both advantages in this way:

I go to the speeches because it is noticed if I am not there. Some of them are pretty good, but most of them are rah-rah stuff. I don't need to have somebody from the national committee tell me that it is important that we elect more Republicans to the House. The real advantages come from the informal discussions I have with other chairmen in the bars. You not only pick up new ideas of a political type, but you pick up the latest rumors and inside dope on what's going on and who is doing what to whom. I first found out that you can let people charge political contributions to their credit cards in a bar with another chairman. And he got the idea from the Democratic chairman in his state.

Meetings of the chairmen's associations during the early 1970s often developed into strategy sessions for dealing with intraparty controversies. Democratic chairmen, caught up in their efforts to gain DNC membership, convened a number of times to plan strategy. Republicans, cut off and isolated from the Nixon White House, discussed ways and means of penetrating the iron wall that presidential aides built between the party and the president. On at least one occasion, after their dissatisfaction and unhappiness became public knowledge, they were invited to a White

* As noted in Table 7.1, 62 percent of the Republicans cited "exchange of ideas and information" as the principal advantage of association membership while only 36 percent of the Democrats did. At the same time 22 percent of the Democrats registered "no opinion" while only 9 percent of the Republicans did. Both of these responses can be attributed to the greater maturity of the Republican State Chairmen's Association as opposed to the relative newness of the Association of State Democratic Chairmen.

House cocktail party given to assuage their injured feelings and to demonstrate that the president was available to them.

It is clear from table 7.1 that neither group of chairmen, the Democrats or the Republicans, viewed their participation in their respective associations as particularly advantageous other than as a vehicle for the exchange of ideas and information. No other advantage was cited by 13 percent of the respondents in both parties. Even so, 80 percent of the Republican chairmen described their participation in association activities in favorable terms while only 7 percent used unfavorable terms. Some of the remainder had not attended an association meeting at the time they were interviewed and thus had no opinion.

On the whole the regional Republican organizations received stronger endorsements from the chairmen than did the national association. Of those who had attended and taken part in a regional meeting, all but one found them helpful. In addition to exchanging ideas and information, the respondents frequently noted that regional problems, either of a political or a substantive nature, could better be discussed in a localized setting. The southern and western chairmen in both parties view themselves as having distinctly different problems from those of their brethren in other regions. Westerners are tied together by mutual concern over water resources and the difficulties associated with the open primary. Southern chairmen of both parties share concerns over regional conservatism, school busing, and problems of integrating blacks into the party structures. Southern Republicans must contend with the problems of perpetual minority status in a one-party system while southern Democrats wrestle

Table 7.1   Advantages of National State Chairmen's Association

Principal advantage	Democrats (N39)	Republicans (N41)	Total (N80)
Exchange of ideas and information	36.0%	62.0%	49.0%
Morale building	13.0	13.0	13.0
None (opposed to association)	13.0	7.0	10.0
Social outlet	6.0	5.0	5.5
Stronger competition with national committee	5.0	0.0	2.5
Miscellaneous	5.0	4.0	4.5
No opinion	22.0	9.0	15.5

with the difficulties associated with reconciling divergent views as expressed by the national party establishment in Washington.

Although the Republican State Chairmen's Association has been dominated by midwestern leadership, the southerners are more often singled out by their colleagues for their role in party affairs. The southern Republican party leaders, representing little organizational strength, have had a remarkable impact upon the national Republican establishment, as witnessed by the following comments:

The State Chairmen's Association has been a very useful group. I've gotten to know a lot of guys and have gotten a lot out of it. One of the things I have gotten out of it was watching how the southern chairmen operate. They know what they want and they are not afraid to twist some arms to get it. All the other regions could learn a lot from them. I think competition between the regional groups is healthy, and I see more of it now than I used to. This is due primarily to the southerners—particularly to Clarke Reed, Harry Dent, and the Texans.

I am opposed to the southern chairmen and their use of power politics. I've watched Clarke Reed and his boys operate and they are effective, but I don't think we should use the regional associations as vehicles to tie the party to political elites which will carry all of us down to defeat. Nor do I think they should be allowed to get away with enunciating conservative right-wing policy which hurts us everywhere outside their area. I wish they would concentrate on building their party organizations and leave policy statements alone.

I don't believe the national Republican State Chairmen's Association has been worth a tiddledy-damn. It's not constituted in such a way that it can do anything. In fact, the only state chairmen's group that I have seen do anything is the southern group under Clarke Reed. I don't think it is because of their having a similarity of interests at all. Rather, it is due to their being one-party states and not having to worry about their actions alienating their voters.

Most Republican chairmen expressed opposition to the adoption of policy stands by their association. Their reluctance to enunciate joint policy decisions came from their fear that an association position might alienate local voters. Furthermore, they had been pressured to take positions on some occasions, and in retrospect, many had concluded that their refusal to do so had served the interest of the Republican party well. One example was described as follows:

I don't think the State Chairmen's Association should take policy positions. We were asked [by the White House] to take a policy stand in favor of the Haynesworth nomination and later on the Carswell nomination to the Supreme Court. We refused. We were also asked to endorse the work of the Young Republicans and again refused. I think that those were proper positions to take. Once we, as state chairmen, begin to take positions on controversial matters we will suffer as a party. In every case the White House exerted tremendous pressure on us to support their stupid decisions. I don't think we should all jump on every sinking ship the White House sets afloat.

The Republican State Chairmen's Association has had considerable success in exercising influence within the national party. The Republican National Committee was quite willing to permit the chairmen to organize and, in fact, took the initiative in bringing their leadership into the higher councils of the party. Their acceptance was accomplished with considerable finesse and with little fanfare. In this respect they differed from their Democratic counterparts.

The Association of State Democratic Chairmen

The Republican State Chairmen's Association developed through an evolutionary process and with the cooperation of national party leaders. The Democratic counterpart, founded eight years later, was the product of intraparty skirmishes and political turmoil. The ideal for the Association of State Democratic Chairmen, which has been attributed to a number of Democratic leaders, emerged from the conviction of some chairmen that their role had been unnecessarily small and uninfluential. One of the earliest to consider the plan was Chairman Clark Rasmussen of Iowa, who discussed it with John Mitchell of Nebraska. The two then joined forces to push the idea. At approximately the same time, in March of 1969, the Young Democrats' national convention was held in New Orleans, and R. Spencer Oliver, the organization's president, invited the state chairmen to attend and hold a separate meeting in congruence with the Young Democrats. Although there are no records of that meeting, those in attendance were Chairmen Pat Thomas of Florida, Robert Vance of Alabama, Severin Beliveau of Maine, Elmer Baum of Texas, Robert Rose of Nevada, Eugene O'Grady of Ohio, as well as Mitchell and Rasmussen. This informal group began to discuss establishment of a national state chairmen's association and agreed to meet again in September during the Democratic National Committee meeting in Washington. That meeting took place with the same group in attendance, plus Salvatori Bontempo of New Jersey, Crosley Lewis of South Carolina, and Henry Topel of Rhode Island. Reports of some of those who attended suggest that Mitchell and Rasmussen dominated the meeting. They both were party officers from adjoining states in the Midwest and were in agreement on the need for a chairmen's association. There was considerable maneuvering to be chairman of the proposed group, and it was conceded by most that Clark Rasmussen would be selected as chairman. However, a decision was made that the officers should represent different regions, and Mitchell and Rasmussen, both being from the Midwest, could not both serve, so Rasmussen gave way to Mitchell, who was then elected chairman. Eugene O'Grady of Ohio made an impassioned plea to include representatives of the urban states on the steering committee and was himself elected, making it impossible for Rasmussen to serve even in that capacity. Interestingly enough, Rasmussen resigned shortly thereafter as state chairman of Iowa, and Mitchell resigned as state chairman in order to run for national committeeman from Nebraska. He was not successful and served out his term as leader of the state chairmen's association without holding any formal state party office.

The Democratic state chairmen were generally unhappy with the Democratic National Committee and its chairman, Senator Fred Harris. They were convinced that Harris and his staff were actively discouraging the organization of the state chairman's association because they saw it as a further threat to the power of the national committee. Several respondents received calls from DNC staff people attempting to discourage their participation in the organization, but the pressure merely consolidated their determination to organize. At the spring 1970 meeting of the embryonic association, the national committee did furnish rooms and provided some staff assistance. However, after Mitchell resigned as chairman in 1971 and Severin Beliveau of Maine was elected to replace him, Beliveau placed a call to a senior staff man at the national committee, identified himself as the chairman of the Association of State Democratic Chairmen, and heard the telephonic response, "There is no such association!" This attitude on the part of the top staff at the national committee brought more determination than ever to the state chairmen to succeed in their organizational efforts. R. Spencer Oliver, a former president of the Young Democrats National Federation, was hired as part-time executive director of the state chairmen's association, and was furnished an office in the Watergate complex, then occupied by the Democratic National Committee.

The next meeting of the association included as speakers every presidential candidate identified at that time, Senators Muskie, McGovern, Jackson, and Harris. Forty-two out of the fifty state chairmen attended the meeting in Washington, although opposition from some DNC officials and staff continued. Robert Strauss, then chief fund raiser for the Democrats, reportedly sent a memo to the staff reneging on the DNC promises of office space and staffing for the state chairmen. The memo also noted that even though the state chairmen had scheduled leading speakers the staff of the DNC was not to leave work to hear the candidates because they could not afford the time away from their jobs. Many members of the staff were unhappy, and many of them left their jobs and attended the program anyway. During the course of the meeting, Gordon St. Angelo, the Democratic chairman of Indiana and one of the senior members of the group, stood and read the Strauss memorandum to the assembled state chairmen. This action reportedly generated so much hard feeling on the part of the presidential candidates and the state chairmen that National Chairman Lawrence O'Brien and Robert Strauss both appeared before the meeting to apologize. The state chairmen were then invited to meet with O'Brien and the staff regularly, and O'Brien furnished them with a $40,000 annual budget. In addition, the organization was furnished a secretary and a two-room office. The opposition of many members of the Democratic hierarchy continued, but Chairman O'Brien continued his support and cooperated to carry out the original obligations that had been made. Strauss and O'Brien withdrew from the battle, and the new state chairmen's association generally received cooperation and support throughout the remainder of O'Brien's term. Even so, O'Brien, in league with the association, had to maintain constant pressure on the national committee and its staff in order to gain acceptance for the group.

Controversy between the association, its officers and staff, and the national chairman continued after O'Brien left office and was succeeded by Jean Westwood and then, after the 1972 election, by Robert Strauss. Even the contest for the national chairmanship was cast in competitive terms as two of Strauss' major opponents for the position were state chairmen, Joseph Crangle of New York and Charles Manatt of California. In addition, the Watergate break-in caused a major rupture in the relations between some of the staff people at DNC and the state chairmen's association. The purpose of the break-in, as discovered later, was to remove electronic eavesdropping equipment from two offices—those of National Chairman O'Brien and of the executive director of the state chairmen's association, Spencer Oliver. Oliver had made a number of enemies in the DNC hierarchy in the preceding two years by his unflagging advocacy of positions in behalf of the association, and fights over office space, budgetary allotments, staff, national convention participation, and membership on the DNC had caused considerable internal strife. Shortly after the arrest of the Watergate burglars, O'Brien filed suit against the Republican National Committee for one million dollars in damages. Oliver filed a separate suit and in the process further alienated O'Brien and other top Democrats. In 1973 O'Brien won his suit with a court judgment amounting to $600,000 damages to be paid by the Republican party. Oliver's suit was still pending, but the public conflict between O'Brien and Oliver had strained the relationship between the DNC high command and that of the state chairmen's association. Oliver retained the support of most of the chairmen's association hierarchy throughout the controversy, but he did not take as much part in day-to-day operations as he had previously.

The controversy continued in mid-1974 as the state chairmen jockeyed with a somewhat reluctant party hierarchy for more power. On April 2 a memorandum from Robert Vance, president of the chairmen's association, to each of the state chairmen and vice-chairmen reported that the "Charter Commission has overwhelmingly endorsed the extension of full voting rights to all state chairmen and vice-chairmen on the Democratic National Committee." Vance went on to describe the voting and the debate that surrounded the decision, including an observation that, "Despite initial objectives of reformers, labor representatives, and Chairman Strauss," the amendment which had been offered to the commission's document was approved.

The reference to Strauss drew a rebuttal from the national chairman two days later in a letter to Vance:

I have just finished reading a memorandum sent out under your name on April 2 which could conceivably lead some of the members of your Association to think that I have not consistently supported the representation of the State Chairman's Association on the DNC. . . .

I am perfectly satisfied with the alternative which was reached on this question at the recent meeting of the Charter Commission, and so far as I know, there should be no difficulty in maintaining it in the final Charter document. . . .

My concern with further enlarging the National Committee was that it has become quite difficult for full expression and participation of the Committee as it is constituted with 303 members, and further additions might serve to further dilute the deliberative nature of DNC meetings. . . . However, I am delighted that the Chairmen and Vice-Chairmen will be receiving full votes in the future, and feel that the size of the new body will not be unmanageable.[5]

Other controversies between national party leadership and the state chairmen concerned the use to which the $600,000 settlement won from the Republicans would be put. The chairmen's association bid for some of the money to use in helping develop ongoing campaign services for state and local party organizations. National committee leaders, although uncertain as to how the money should be used, were more inclined to retain control over its distribution through the DNC. Chairmen's association spokesmen contended that this attitude merely reflected the traditional DNC favoritism to the congressional and presidential interests in the party. National committee officials argued, on the other hand, that the goals of the party were broader than the chairmen's association wished to recognize. This disagreement merely brought into clearer focus a long-standing conflict between the two groups as to which was going to provide primary services to the state parties. Obviously, the relationship between the Democratic National Committee and the Democratic state chairmen has not been a smooth one at any time. It is somewhat astounding, therefore, that the chairmen gained DNC membership in a relatively short period of time.

The 1968 national convention convinced many Democratic state party leaders that there was need for drastic action to reform and revitalize the party. Some of the Democratic state chairmen had long chafed from the knowledge that their Republican counterparts had full membership with voting privileges on the Republican National Committee. Not only was this true, but it had been achieved many years earlier without great intra-party trauma and with the active cooperation of national party leaders. One of the first goals agreed upon by the chairmen who began planning the formal organization was to gain membership on the DNC. This quickly developed into the major goal of the organization and was a subject of major discussion at every subsequent meeting of the association.

Most of those who participated in the early organizational meetings which led to the Association of State Democratic Chairmen cited as their principal motivation the need for more visibility within the national party. One means of getting that attention was through full membership on the national committee.

A key meeting in the history of the Association of State Democratic

Chairmen was held in Washington in May 1970, with forty-two of the fifty chairmen attending. There was quiet discussion of the best strategy through which to pursue DNC membership, and at a September meeting at the Balmoral Hotel in Miami Beach the first open discussions of the role of the chairmen and their future with the national committee were held. On May 12–14, 1972, at a meeting in Hollywood-by-the-Sea, Florida, matters began to resolve themselves, and a resolution, drafted by Spencer Oliver, was passed. It read as follows:

A resolution be offered to the Democratic National Convention to create a Democratic National Committee which would consist of the National Committeeman and Committeewoman of each state and territory, the State Chairman and highest ranking party official of the opposite sex from each state, all Democratic governors, ten members of Congress (five from the Senate, five from the House), twenty Young Democrats (the seven national officers plus thirteen to be elected at large by the National Committee), and twenty at large members to be selected by the aforementioned members.

This would create a National Committee of approximately 300 people and provide for representation of the various levels of party and governmental activities.

There would be 1200 votes apportioned among the states on the same formula as that which applied to the committees of the 1972 Democratic National Convention. The votes for each state would be apportioned equally among the members of the Committee from that state. The Committee would meet immediately following the Democratic National Convention and elect a chairman, vice-chairman, secretary and treasurer.[6]

The group also went on record to request special national convention facilities for state chairmen, including office space and furniture for the association in the headquarters hotel, a reception room near the convention floor, a section of the gallery of the convention hall for those chairmen and vice-chairmen who were not delegates, a car and driver for each chairman, as well as assignment of pages and floor passes. For the first time the Democratic chairmen were going on record with specific demands for party services at a national convention.

Although not adopted in that precise form, the Oliver Resolution had a clear impact upon the final recommendations forwarded to the national convention by the McGovern-Fraser Commission. On Thursday, July 13, Representative Donald Fraser of Minnesota, who chaired the McGovern-Fraser Commission during its latter stages, presented the commission's official resolution for party reform to the convention at Miami Beach. He explained the resolution, as it affected state chairmen, as follows:

We also strengthened the National Committee by adding the State Party Chairman and the ranking officer of the opposite sex, both being added to insure closer ties between the State Party and our National Party. The total maximum vote on the new committee will be 234, the total memberhip 303. The difference between the total vote and the total membership is explained by the fact that some members of the committee will have a divided vote.[7]

The question of the divided vote was a crucial one for the state chairmen, because it was their vote that was to be divided. There was considerable negotiation within the ranks of the chairmen between those who believed that one-half vote was better than nothing and those who wanted to force Fraser to provide the chairman and ranking member of the opposite sex with a full vote. The Minnesota state chairman, Richard Moe, sided with his friend and party colleague, Congressman Fraser, throughout much of the discussion, while Oliver and ASDC president Severin Beliveau of Maine led the fight to hold the chairmen together in behalf of their demands.

The Fraser Resolution also called for a conference on Democratic party organization and policies to be held in 1974, the purpose of which would be to adopt and implement a new party charter. This part of the resolution was made necessary when the contending elements at the 1972 convention were unable to reach agreement upon a compromise party organizational reform and finally agreed to additional study, with action to be taken in 1974. The Fraser Resolution, including the newly structured national committee and the call for the 1974 conference, passed on a roll-call vote of 2,418.45 to 195.10.[8] The half-vote for chairmen was retained in the final document.

After the convention, DNC General Counsel Joseph A. Califano, Jr., was given the task of codifying the rules of the newly constituted Democratic National Committee. That codification, dated August 6, 1972, described the membership as follows:

(a) the chairman and the highest ranking officer of the opposite sex of each recognized state Democratic party;

(b) additional members with a total vote of 150 apportioned to each State on the basis of that State's representation on the Standing Committees of the 1972 Democratic National Convention, which members shall include

each Committeeman and Committeewoman selected to serve at the close of
the 1972 National Convention who would have served for the 1972–76 term
in the absence of the new provisions governing membership contained in this
Article;

(c) the chairman and two others designated by the Democratic Governors' Conference;

(d) the Democratic leader in the United States Senate and in the United
States House of Representatives and one additional member from each body
designated by a caucus of the Democratic members of each House; and

(e) additional members not to exceed 25 may be added by the foregoing
to provide balanced representation of all Democratic voters.

The rules governing voting on the national committee provided that:

Each member of the National Committee shall be entitled to one vote on
each issue before it, except in voting to fill a vacancy on the national ticket
and except as follows:

(a) the chairman and highest ranking officer of the opposite sex of each
recognized state Democratic party, as authorized under Article II, Section
1(a), shall share one vote to be divided equally when both are present.[9]

Thus, the Democratic state chairmen were finally included as members
of the national committee, but with only one-half vote each.* They determined to press on with their effort to gain full voting status, and their
next attempt was directed at the new Charter Commission created by
the 1972 convention. The Democratic Charter Commission, chaired by
Barbara Mikulski of Maryland, met during 1973 and 1974 and eventually agreed upon a compromise document which again restructured the
Democratic National Committee for the second time in two years.

The charter which was eventually adopted by the 1974 mini-convention in Kansas City provided that:

---

* It might be noted that during the Democratic Mini-Convention, August 8, 1972,
held for the purpose of nominating a new vice-presidential candidate to replace
recently resigned Senator Thomas Eagleton, the state chairmen were not forced to
cast their one-half votes. The Rules of the 1972 Convention prevailed, and Article
VII of those Rules provided: "In the event of the death, resignation or disability
of a nominee of the Party for President or Vice-President, the Democratic National Committee is authorized to fill the vacancy or vacancies by a majority of
the total number of votes provided at the Convention. The full vote of each delegation is to be cast by its duly qualified member or members of the Committee
with each member casting a proportionate share of his delegation's votes." Thus,
each member of the new national committee cast a proportionate share of all the
votes to which that state was entitled at the national convention.

The Democratic National Committee shall consist of:

the Chairperson and the highest ranking officer of the opposite sex of each recognized state Democratic party:

two hundred additional votes apportioned to the states on the same basis as delegates to the National Convention are apportioned, provided that each state has at least two such additional members;

the Chairperson of the Democratic Governors' Conference and two additional Governors selected by the Conference;

the Democratic Leader in the United States Senate and the Democratic Leader in the United States House of Representatives and one additional member of each body appointed by the respective leaders;

the Chairperson of the Democratic National Committee;

the two Executive Vice-Chairpersons of the Democratic National Committee;

the Chairperson of the National Finance Council;

the Treasurer and the Secretary of the Democratic National Committee;

the Chairperson of the Conference of Democratic Mayors and two additional Mayors selected by the Conference;

the President of The Young Democrats of America and two additional members selected by the organization biennially; and

up to twenty-five additional members may be added by the foregoing members of the Democratic National Committee.

As noted in the exchange of letters between ASDC President Robert Vance and National Chairman Robert Strauss in April 1974, the chairmen and ranking members of the opposite sex did eventually receive a full vote on the national committee. The strengthened position of the state chairmen's association was reflected in the charge by one powerful Democrat that the "Democratic National Committee has become an appendage of the State Chairmen's Association."

Also during 1974 the Association of State Democratic Chairmen drafted by-laws to govern the organization, proclaiming the object of the organization as giving

the State Chairman and the Vice Chairman of each state an opportunity to work more closely together and share their ideas, programs and projects to provide an avenue for better communication and coordination between State Democratic Parties and their officers; to work and cooperate with the Democratic National Committee and its officers.[10]

Members were to be chairmen or the highest ranking state party officer of the opposite sex, and members could retain associate member status for a period of five years after their formal terms ended. Associate members might vote on matters pertaining to the affairs of the association but not on election of officers or matters of policy.

The concept of associate members was designed to retain the expertise of outgoing chairmen who would otherwise be lost to the organization. Some individuals who have served as state chairmen, even briefly, have retained an active interest in the affairs of the association. One Democrat was still attending meetings of the association three years after being defeated for reelection. The proposed by-laws were scheduled to be voted on in August 1974.

Financing the Association of State Democratic Chairmen was, at first, precarious. The Treasurer's Report presented to the chairmen in May 1970, after one year of operation, showed contributions of $1,500.00 and expenditures of $1,150.23. The work of the association was carried on in Omaha, since that was the home base of the first president, John Mitchell. In 1971 the association levied $100 annual dues on each state party to help pay expenses. By 1972 the association reported assets of $5,276.99. In 1973–74 the members approved a budget calling for expenditures of $9,000.00. Included as expenses to be borne by the association were office supplies, expenses for conferences and meetings, staff travel, and a WATS line. The administrative assistant's salary, a secretarial salary, telephone service, and postage costs were to be carried by the Democratic National Committee. In order to cover the costs engendered by the expanding activities of the association, a new schedule of dues was approved to reflect "the capacities of the respective state parties." The new dues schedule called for individual states to pay annual membership fees ranging from $100 to $1,000. Should the dues payments be forthcoming on a regular basis, the association would be able to involve itself in several substantive programs which have been under consideration. These include a vastly expanded research program including materials on opposition incumbents, proposed legislation relating to the election process, and other informational services. Furthermore, additional experiments with the checking account debit procedure, such as those under way in four states in 1974, as well as improved capabilities for uses of the computer in state politics, would be possible.

In early 1975 two important publications were printed and distributed to the members of the ASDC. The Party Building Committee of the association, with the assistance of Johnny W. Allem and Associates, compiled a *Party Evaluation Handbook* to determine present effectiveness, degrees of participation, potential for growth, and recommendations for party building. Described as a "working handbook," the 96-page manual was designed to provide a mechanism to evaluate a state party's electoral performance, central committee, headquarters and staff, personnel resources, financial resources, liaison relationships, and public relations. The manual called for establishment of a party-building committee in each state to take advantage of the available talent by following four basic steps: (1) fact-finding research, (2) assessment of research, (3) goal setting, and (4) recommendations for building the party. Party building was defined as the process of providing the strongest possible mechanisms for identifying and achieving common goals. The program included a film strip and script. The total package cost a reported $18,000.

At approximately the same time the association also distributed a *State Party Handbook*. In a letter to state chairmen, President Robert Vance noted that

The idea of a State Party Handbook can be attributed to several growing concerns among state chairmen: 1) the need to improve communication between state parties; 2) the absence of the means by which we might consistently inventory, identify and share each other's program ideas and expertise; and 3) the desire to provide new state chairmen and vice-chairmen immediate assistance in the form of basic information and tools with which to undertake their new responsibilities.

This handbook contained two basic kinds of information: (1) general materials on election laws, party rules tax regulations, and a general bibliography; and (2) a section dealing individually with each state party. It was hard-bound and loose-leaf to facilitate updating.

The general information section included a copy of the national party charter, delegate selection rules, affirmative action models, the membership of the Compliance Review Commission created to supervise and approve state affirmative action initiatives in delegate selection, copies of the federal campaign finance laws, a compilation of state campaign finance laws, a "who's who" list of Washington-based associations and organizations, a bibliography of campaign-related source materials, and other matters of this type.

The second section, outlining specific information fo reach state Democratic party, was based on a twelve-page questionnaire sent to each state chairman in December 1974. In addition to routine information such as names, addresses, and phone numbers of party officials, the section also described the organization and structure of the party, the state's election law, past election results including offices won and lost, sources of party finance, budget information, staffing, and political services rendered to local party organizations.

The first copies of these two publications were distributed at a state chairmen's meeting early in 1975 at the same time that Donald Fowler of South Carolina defeated Robert Vance of Alabama by a vote of 64–40 for the presidency of the association. Some observers believed that Fowler would downgrade the emphasis on the party-building program and distribution of the handbooks because they were perceived to be Vance-conceived projects, and there was fairly widespread suspicion directed by state party officers toward prepackaged programs of this type.

Other projects under consideration by the ASDC included the development of additional political manuals and handbooks designed specifically for state political contests; a series of regular regional conferences of state party officers; a volunteer polling system which would enable state parties to reduce the costs of polling by up to 70 percent according to some professional telephone pollsters; and the development of a campaign resource package including films, slide strips, and workbooks for use in state politics. The potential total cost of all of these projects was estimated at over $125,000, and their implementation would necessarily have to wait for financing. National association staff members were watching with interest local experiments of this kind being carried on in Florida and Minnesota in 1974, to be described in chapter 9.

Conversations with Democratic state chairmen in the early 1970s revealed a strong undercurrent of criticism of the Democratic National Committee. Many state party officers believed that they had been neglected in favor of the congressional and presidential elements in the party. They noted repeatedly that political battles are fought in their bailiwicks, yet they receive no rewards commensurate with their services. During their struggle to organize, state chairmen often reflected their antagonism to the national committee:

I think the state chairmen are the salvation of the party. It is a disgrace that the Democratic party has an $8 million debt and that these Washington prima donnas, selected by individual candidates, have been allowed to do this to us. Most of them don't understand what politics is really like. It is about time they turned the mess over to us and let us clean it up.

I think the whole Democratic National Committee system is idiotic. The national committeemen and women don't do anything and never have. They wouldn't know how to practice politics if you hit them over the head with it.

We have to have some drastic changes, but unless the state chairmen get together and figure out what they want to do, the changes will never be made.

I think it is a disgrace that the Republican party, which we have always said was the party of the rich and the fat cat, voluntarily brought their state chairmen into voting membership years ago. Yet every time we mention it you would think we were trying to legalize prostitution. They better let us in or the Democratic party will cease to function as it has in the past.

In spite of these strongly worded protests against the pre-1970 Democratic national party organization, several chairmen were reluctant to become embroiled in controversy with national party leaders. Some did not believe they could win, and others simply believed that state party organizations did not need strengthening. Typical of the half-dozen chairmen who had reservations over formation of an association was one who said:

I don't feel that the state chairmen's association [then only one year old] is really very important or very useful. It doesn't have any objectives that I think are important. Most of those who are active in the group are full-time, paid chairmen who are trying to feather their own nests and increase their own power. Most of them have paid directors back home running the party for them so they can dabble in national party affairs. I guess I think party politics is for the people in Washington. Out here we never win anything anyway.

The bitterness of the struggle for full recognition was a product of intense loyalties and personal and political ambitions. The chairmen, on the whole, believed that the future of the Democratic party rested in the states—at the grass roots. At the same time, they felt that national party leaders, dominated by presidential aspirants and labor leaders, did not acknowledge their importance or recognize the true nature of the party. They were also, in many cases, deeply disturbed by the fact that national committeemen and women, with full voting power in national party councils, were often of little importance within the state parties from which they were elected. At the very least, the state chairmen believed that they should have equality with national committee members in national party affairs.

Regional Party Organization: Past, Present, and Proposed

In a country so vast, it would have seemed natural for the political parties to develop some form of regional substructure. Yet historically this has never happened. Both parties do hold occasional regional conferences, have shadow organizations within the geographic regions, and support limited field staff, but until recently no party organization chart included anything remotely resembling regional units within the established hierarchy. Regional events have tended to be episodic and discrete. They have seldom extended much beyond the sponsorship of periodic conferences.

Nevertheless, some of the regional party associations have served as unofficial vehicles for state party leaders to improve their power positions vis-à-vis the national party organizations. Nothing of note ever came of these associations until the Republican State Chairmen's Association emerged out of the midwestern-Rocky Mountain group in the early 1950s. Even that was due to the collective strength within the Republican party of the states involved and to the personal power and influence of Ray Bliss.

The Democrats also have a regional conference system, but it has played little part in the affairs of the party. The Democratic regional associations are lacking in uniform strength and have received little encouragement from national party leaders. Regionally, the strongest states in the party have traditionally been those in the South. The national party, however, has exhibited little interest in strengthening that particular segment of the party since it has often not been in step with national party principles. Furthermore, the southern Democrats have not needed the national party, or a regional association, in order to maintain their position of strength within the party structure, particularly in Congress.

There has been little activity directed toward a regional unit in the East, and the efforts of midwestern Democratic leaders to organize a regional association in 1970 fell far short of success. An organizational meeting held in Omaha that year failed to attract national party interest and was attended by only four state chairmen, including its two organizers, Iowa Chairman Clark Rasmussen and Nebraska's John Mitchell. Both of these party leaders, however, were instrumental in helping to establish the original Democratic state chairmen's organization.

The only regional group in the Democratic party that has generated interest and momentum, both within the member states and from the national party, is that in the West. One of the more successful regional meetings in recent years was sponsored by the Western States Democratic Conference in Salt Lake City in 1970. An attractive program included speeches by Senators McGovern, Muskie, and McGee, and other party dignitaries. Public hearings by both the McGovern-Fraser Commission and the O'Hara Commission were incorporated into the program. Workshops and planning sessions were held for party officials and campaign workers, and the Democratic National Committee sent a large contingent of staff members and officers, including newly elected Chairman Lawrence O'Brien, to take part. The four-day conference drew a large attendance from throughout the West and was one of the most successful held by either party in the early 1970s.

The Democratic regional groups might have been more successful and had a greater impact on the party had it not been for the success of the Association of State Democratic Chairmen. The development of that group undercut the need for regional conferences from the state chairmen's point of view. While such meetings have had a major role to play in both parties in bringing leaders together, the fact that the state chairmen were meeting regularly on their own took the edge off the need for regional meetings.

The Republicans have now incorporated their regional associations into the formal party structure. As described earlier in this chapter, four distinct regional associations have been recognized, and their chairmen make up the Republican State Chairmen's Advisory Committee. The chairmen of the Advisory Committee, in turn, is a member of the executive committee of the Republican National Committee. The practical effect of this, however, has been to strengthen the state chairmen, not the regional associations. The latter remains responsible primarily for organizing periodic regional conferences for the exchange of ideas and information and to attract attention to the party. There are no formal powers assigned to them.

In accordance with Rule 29(b) adopted by the 1972 Republican National Convention, Chairman George Bush, on April 16, 1973, announced the appointment of

a committee broadly representative of the Republican Party, including members of the Republican National Committee, to review, study and work with the states and territories relating to the Rules adopted by the 1972 Republican National Convention, and the relationship between the Republican National Committee, the Republican State Committees, and other Republican organizations.[11]

The Rule 29 Committee, under the chairmanship of Wisconsin Congressman William A. Steiger, was instructed to report recommendations by January 1, 1975, and the national committee was instructed to take action to implement the proposed changes within ninety days. Any recommendation, however, which would require a change in the Rules of the Republican party would necessarily have to be acted upon by the 1976 National Convention since the party itself has no constitution, charter, or by-laws. Rules adopted by each convention establish the basic structure of the national committee.

The Rule 29 Committee held its first meeting on September 11, 1973, and voted to hold hearings in conjunction with scheduled regional conferences and to solicit the views of a wide spectrum of party members by mailed questionnaire. By mid-1974 the questionnaires had been returned, and the committee was distributing the preliminary results along with direct quotations from respondents.

In its preliminary report, adopted in Saint Louis on June 16, 1974, the Rule 29 Committee made some recommendations which would institutionalize some aspects of the network of regional party associations. Proposed Rule 25, for instance, recommends that the officers of the Republican National Committee consist of:

(1) A Chairman and a Co-Chairman of the opposite sex who shall be elected by the members of the Republican National Committee and who shall be full time, paid employees.

(2) Eight (8) Vice Chairmen, one (1) man and one (1) woman from each of the four following regions:

The Western State Chairmen's Association

Alaska	Montana
Arizona	Nevada
California	New Mexico
Colorado	Oregon
Guam	Utah
Hawaii	Washington
Idaho	Wyoming

The Midwest State Chairmen's Association

Illinois	Nebraska
Indiana	North Dakota
Iowa	Ohio
Kansas	South Dakota
Michigan	West Virginia
Minnesota	Wisconsin
Missouri	

The Northeastern State Chairmen's Association

Connecticut	New Jersey
Delaware	New York
District of Columbia	Pennsylvania
Maine	Puerto Rico
Maryland	Rhode Island
Massachusetts	Vermont
New Hampshire	Virgin Islands

The Southern State Chairmen's Association

Alabama	North Carolina
Arkansas	Oklahoma
Florida	South Carolina
Georgia	Tennessee
Kentucky	Texas
Louisiana	Virginia
Mississippi	

(3) A Secretary, a Treasurer, and such other Officers as the Committee shall deem necessary, all to be elected by the National Committee.[12]

Adoption of this new structure would, in effect, formalize the regional associations by making their officers an official part of the party's leadership. The eight vice-chairmen of the national committee, under this proposal, would be elected at regional caucuses by the national committee members of the four regions. They would be required to be residents of as well as national committee members from the region from which they are elected. All eight would also serve as members of the newly constituted executive committee of the Republican National Committee, which also includes, among others, the chairman of the Republican State Chairman's Advisory Committee.

The Rule 29 Committee's report was approved by the Republican National Committee in March 1975. It will be referred to the Rules Committee of the RNC, then to the national committee itself, and finally to the 1976 National Convention which could implement the recommendations for the 1980 convention. The only provisions in the report that would apply to the 1976 convention are those dealing with delegate selection guidelines. One recommendation from the committee has already been implemented: a Task Force of State Chairmen was created in 1975 to assist the national chairman in a continuous study of the relationship between the national and state parties. Chaired by New York

State Chairman Richard Rosenbaum and co-chaired by the chairman of the state chairmen's association, John McDonald, the task force has six other chairmen as members.

In the proposed charter for the Democratic party which was approved and jointly recommended by the McGovern-Fraser and O'Hara commissions in March 1972, there was a complicated structure which would have divided the nation into seven regions. Regional conferences were to be held in odd-numbered years with policy recommendations to be submitted for consideration by the national convention and a new National Policy Conference. A formal structure of regional committees was proposed, with party leaders in each region responsible for implementing regional, state, and local education and training programs. Each committee was to be composed of about forty-three members selected in a variety of ways from the states within each region. (See chart 7.1.) The proposal was not acted upon by the national convention because its complexity and the controversy surrounding it convinced Senator McGovern and other party leaders that it would be divisive and required further refinement.

On July 13, 1972, Congressman Fraser introduced a resolution to the convention which (1) created the newly proposed Democratic National Committee and (2) provided for appointment of a new Charter Commission to continue the modernization process. The resolution also required that the work of the new commission be presented to a party conference to be held in 1974 to consider adoption of the new charter.[13]

The proposed charter, which was adopted by the Charter Commission on March 16–17, 1974, contains no reference to regionalism at all. The concept of a regional substructure was dropped, and there was no provision for electing any party officials by region.[14] The proposed charter was adopted at the Democratic Mini-Convention in Kansas City in December 1974.

As a concept, regional party organization might be described as a means through which the political needs of a group of contiguous state parties might be met. Generally, those who support greater regional party efforts restrict themselves to narrow organizational requirements. They recognize the futility of attempting to unify state parties within a region into a philosophical whole. They express their support of regional efforts in terms of cost saving, labor sharing, and convenience.

It is surprising that in a country so large there has been so little interest in the concept of regional party organizations. Party leaders, when questioned about it, cite a number of reasons for the notable lack of in-

Chart 7.1

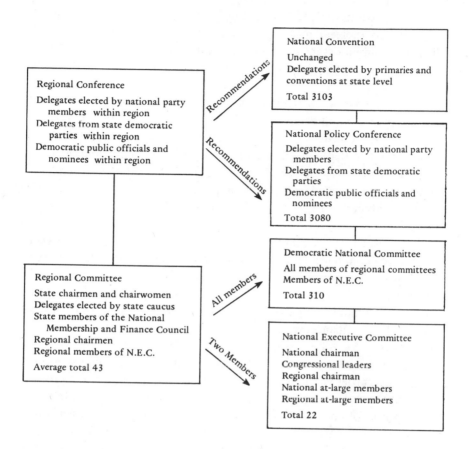

This chart shows the relationship between the regional and national organizations under the proposed Fraser-O'Hara charter.

The regional conference would make recommendations to the National Policy Conference and the National Convention. The entire membership of the regional committees would make up the Democratic National Committee and each region would have two representatives on the National Executive Committee.

terest. The generally weakened condition of the national and state party organizations has, in the past, discouraged experimentation with other artificial party units. There is often great disparity between the states in a given geographical region; California and Idaho, for example, have little in common except their mutual membership in regional affiliations of the western states. Not only are the states different in terms of population, politics, and culture, but the parties themselves present a vast spectrum of party types: competitive and noncompetitive, one-party and two-party, organized and disorganized. One need only look at the differences apparent in midwestern parties to see evidence of that. Finally, there are those who note that political resources are in short supply, and the states and the national parties are little disposed to spread them even more thinly over a regional network. It is probable that all of these factors have contributed to the general lack of interest in regional political organizations.

The recent moves of the Republicans to institutionalize some aspects of their regional party units and of the Democrats to consider, but eventually reject, even more striking experimentation suggest that the paucity of interest may have come to an end. Without engaging in debate over the merits of multistate party organization, it can still be noted that those who seek to enhance regional cooperation generate some compelling arguments.

An established regional party unit, responsible for providing assistance to all state parties within the designated headquarters area, might provide substantial costs savings by enabling the individual state parties to share the expenses of computerized politics, mass fund raising, contract printing, and many other joint ventures. A regional computer, for example, might not only provide substantial savings to those parties already renting equipment but also make the service available to those parties presently unable to afford it. Regional bids for printing contracts could result in substantial savings, assuming that the problem of contract patronage which some state parties might encounter could be overcome. Outside speakers might be scheduled on succeeding days throughout a block of states, thus reducing the costs of travel and the physical wear and tear on the speaker and his hosts. These are but a sampling of the advantages some party officials claim for formalized regional organizations. Neither party has approached the concept in this way. Instead, both have sought to implement limited regional association as a structural convenience. The regional associations were there—so why not incorporate them into the formal party hierarchy? They quite possibly may have better uses.

Lateral Relationships of the State Chairmen

The state chairmen in each party have received vastly different treatment from their national leaders since the Republicans were first recognized in 1952. The GOP chairmen were incorporated into full voting participation on the national committee almost as an afterthought to the first Eisenhower nomination. The feat was accomplished with a minimum of conflict and, in fact, almost no debate. The Democrats, on the other hand, engaged in five years of intense controversy, often including divisive behind-the-scenes infighting, before voting to include the state party leadership as full voting members of the national committee. In spite of the trauma associated with gaining membership, the Democrats went the Republicans one step better by including an equal number of male and female state party leaders, each with equal voting rights. Without taking away from that action, it is doubtful that, given the climate of opinion in the early 1970s, they could have done otherwise. The consciousness of both men and women has been raised since 1952.

Now that the state parties have accomplished their original mission, some believe that they should undertake to disassociate themselves from their respective national committees to the degree that they can. It has been noted by individuals among them that holding meetings in conjunction with the national committees automatically places them in a subordinate role and tends to force greater formality upon their deliberations. Both national committees have repeatedly demonstrated their desire to dominate internal party groups. This has been true of women's federations, organizations of youth, governors, and state chairmen. In their embryonic stage the chairmen's associations had little choice but to accept largess from the national committees. Having gained a toehold, however, some chairmen believe they should strike out for more independence. They might, for instance, assert more authority over their own budgets, raise substantial portions of their own money, and hold independent conferences with controlled agenda.

There has been a good deal of evidence in the past few years that the concept of regional and national associations of state chairmen is a valid one. There are many pressures working against such internal coalitions of interests, but the chairmen in both parties have been reasonably successful in overcoming them. Their mutuality of interests transcends the divisions within their own ranks. Nevertheless, both groups have been able to strengthen their collective position in their respective parties. They have, in effect, accomplished the goal they set out to achieve: belief in themselves. Many state chairmen have now convinced themselves that they have an important role to play in party politics, and they cite as evidence the role that they have carved out for themselves. This may be a self-sustaining prophecy, but it has worked to enhance the power of the state party organizations. And it has provided new respect for them in both local and national political circles.

8 The Organizational Role: Working with the National Parties

I haven't paid much attention to the national committee since the 1960s when they were pouring all that money and staff time into the South. Every time I went in for something I was told there wasn't enough money because it was going to the South. Well, the South gave us Barry Goldwater and Spiro Agnew, and I can't say that either one of them made any great contribution to my party. If the national committee can be that easily led, I don't see that it has much to offer us.

An eastern Republican state chairman

The difference between the Nixon and Ford White Houses is like the difference between night and day. The Nixon people thought the party was a bother. We [the state chairmen] were able, over the years, to embarrass them into inviting us over as a group, but on the whole they wanted nothing to do with either the state or national party. Ford knows that the party is important. I think he will make as much use of the organization as he possibly can.

A southern Republican chairman

My job at the Democratic National Convention in 1972 was to distribute tickets to our delegates and alternates. That is how important the state chairmanship was to me. These new people didn't have anything in mind but to nominate McGovern.

A western Democratic state chairman

Organizational pyramids always show the state chairman positioned midway between the national and local party units. This strategic location, however, does not carry with it the power requisites necessary for him to capitalize on his position. Even though the American parties appear to be structured as hierarchies, they seldom function in a way that meets the technical requirements for hierarchical management. Neither the flow of responsibility nor the exercise of authority moves cleanly through the structure. This leaves most chairmen with the role of middleman but without the power to carry out the responsibilities. The authority that they exercise is often not their own, and their accountability is often to outside forces which are impervious to their commands.

The problem, of course, is our federal system with its divided powers and responsibilities. The parties, having evolved in an unplanned fashion over a period of years, simply were superimposed upon the federal structure. At no time were party leaders furnished with basic power which would permit them to command support. It has always been necessary, therefore, to accomplish goals by persuasion and compromise. Like the government, the parties are federal, each representing only one foundation stone in the national political structure. Yet, unlike the national and state governments, there is no constitution to provide a division of powers and responsibilities. There is no Supreme Court to decide which party can do what to whom or how. The national party leadership is usually a temporary creature of an incumbent president or a defeated presidential candidate. The state parties are often mere collection points for a profusion of precinct, ward, city, and county groups, each representing a separate and distinct part of the political jigsaw puzzle.

Occupying the central pivotal point between these contending factions is the state party chairman. As has been noted before, he may be a "true" party leader exercising power in his own right, or he may be a political agent of an incumbent governor. He may be powerful or impotent. His influence may be a derivative of his political supporters or a consequence of personal qualities which have permitted him to develop leadership capabilities. And, of course, he may be a failure, serving out his term without political muscle, impervious to advice, resisting change, and perpetuating atrophy.

Nevertheless, the chairman is positioned in the party framework to enable him to serve as a conduit. Within that framework, national elements of the party include the national committees and chairmen, members of the Senate and House of Representatives, and, for the party in power, those who work in the White House. Quadrennially, the "national" party is broadened to include national convention delegates, convention organizers, and presidential candidates' entourages.

Local party organizations, those below the state level, include a multitude of natural and artificial districts from which party and governmental officers are chosen. Precincts, towns, wards, cities, counties, and congressional districts, in various combinations, serve as the framework of the party. In most states the chairman does not have the power to order lower party units to carry out his wishes, but he always has the capability of attempting to influence those in the understructure. In election years the chairman's responsibilities expand to include state conventions—nominating and platform.

It should be noted that in some states real political power may not be centered in the formal party structure at all. For years Mayor Richard J. Daley has controlled the Illinois Democratic party through his domination over Cook County. Even Daley lieutenants acknowledge, however, that the Democratic state chairman of Illinois has considerable freedom to control downstate elements in the party—there simply are not many downstate Democrats to control.

Parties in other states are sometimes so dominated by a single politician that the organization works within the shadow of the man. The New York Republicans under Nelson Rockefeller and the Massachusetts Democrats under Edward Kennedy are examples of this phenomenon. In the case of New York, the Republican state party became so dependent on the Rockefeller name and money that it became impossible to separate them. In Massachusetts the Kennedy name has dominated the Democratic party for so long that, even though the family pays little attention to party affairs, the party organization cannot extricate itself from its influence.

In some other states weakened party structures have permitted extra-party groups to play an expanding and dominant role in politics. The historical weaknesses of the parties in California paved the way for the emergence of the California Republican Assembly, the United Republicans of California, and the California Democratic Clubs. In the same vein, the New York Democratic Reform movement has occupied an important place in the recent history of that party.

Whether a political agent, an autonomous in-party leader, or an independent serving without a governor, the chairman occupies the middle rung on the ladder. He is the only party official who has the opportunity to have an impact on both the national and local party organizations. In this chapter and the next the efforts of the chairman to carry out his day-to-day responsibilities, both external and internal, are discussed. The external functions include the chairman's relationship with Washington—members of Congress, presidential aides, and national committee members and staff—as well as his role at the national conventions. Chapter 9 considers the chairman's outreach to party members, candidates, and officeholders within the state and local parties. It is noteworthy that the chairman's support will normally depend upon his internal relationships, but his success may depend upon those who are external to the state party. The role of the state party chairman in his relationships with the Washington governmental and party bureaucracies has expanded greatly in recent years. Consequently, most chairmen are devoting greater amounts of time to national responsibilities.

As shown in table 8.1, the state chairmen were asked to list in rank order the most important party officials, either elected or appointed, in their respective state organizations. Governors were ranked first by most respondents, with the second and third first-rank choices being United States senators, senior and junior respectively. Most of the chairmen who ranked the senators highly did so either because the governorship was controlled by the opposition or because they placed a high premium on federal patronage and members of the Senate occupied key roles in appointment decisions. Other officials, congressmen, and national committee members did not receive high rankings from the chairmen. The failure to rank members of the national committees highly is noteworthy.[1] Intraparty rivalries account for some of the low national committee rankings, but most appear to reflect respondents' views that national committee members are not very important to the workings or the success of the party. Only three chairmen had formerly served as members of the national committees, and only two of those were later elected to that office. Subsequent interviews with those two determined that both considered

Table 8.1   State Party Leaders Ranked First and Second in Importance

	First-rank importance	Second-rank importance
Incumbent governor	34.6%	7.8%
U.S. senator, senior	19.3	12.9
U.S. senator, junior	12.8	16.8
Incumbent state chairman (respondent)	11.5	19.5
Former governor	6.4	6.5
Congressman (individually named)	2.6	5.2
National committeeman	2.6	6.5
National committeewoman	1.3	2.6
Big city mayor	1.3	2.6
Miscellaneous state officials (public and party)	5.1	9.1

their service as chairman of much greater importance than their terms on the national committee.*

It seems likely that the low ranking of national committeemen and women reflects the recent expansion of roles for the state chairman without a commensurate increase in the scope of the committeeman's role. This assertion was supported by a number of national committee members who noted a diminution of their power over federal patronage. It was once common in one-party or modified one-party states for patronage clearance to be channeled through members of the national committee in lieu of an effective state party organization. With the decline in one-party states, the reduction in federal patronage, and the expanded role for state chairmen, there has been a shift in the responsibilities for the two major leadership positions in the state parties. In less than a half-dozen state parties was the elected national committee member (as opposed to the ex officio state chairman member) singled out as the most important national committee figure by leading party officials. In most instances these members were elected from the minority party in one-party states.

In each instance where a congressman was ranked as the most powerful, the party was without the services of either a governor or a U.S. senator. With one exception the congressmen in question showed little interest in state party affairs and made little effort to provide leadership or thrust.

To determine the direction and scope of state-national party interaction, each respondent was asked, "What national elected or party official do you deal with most directly?" Follow-up questions were designed to ascertain the subject matter discussed and the frequency of contact. As shown in table 8.2, U.S. senators and congressmen served as the primary contact between state party leaders and Washington. Two types of problems predominated: (1) federal patronage clearance; and (2) party

---

* In 1959 Bancroft Henderson found that 40 percent of the Republican national committeemen and 31 percent of their Democratic counterparts had formerly served as state chairmen. He concluded that, "in terms of channels of access, the route, if there is one, is through the Chairmanship 'up' to Committeeman." A more likely conclusion today would be that outgoing chairmen view service on the national committee as the only nonelective alternative to dropping out of politics. Bancroft Henderson, "The Comparative Role of the State Chairman and the National Committeeman," in *Formal and Informal Structures in State Political Parties,* Arnold Foundation Monographs (Dallas: Southern Methodist University, 1959), pp. 6, 7.

policy considerations affecting up-coming campaigns. As noted in chapter 5, the U.S. senator(s) often serves as the principal contact point between the state party's patronage committee and the White House. Usually the senator is a member of the party patronage committee, although he normally does not directly take part in deliberations.

A Republican administration was in office during the entire period covered by this study. Consequently, Republican respondents were more likely to list senators, congressmen, and national committee members, since some combination of those officials usually participated in the party's patronage considerations.

In 1964 Cornelius Cotter and Bernard Hennessy found in a survey of state party leaders that national committeemen were rated as important figures in the state parties. Over 90 percent of the committeemen in both parties were included among the top twenty-five leaders in their individual parties. National committeewomen, on the other hand, were found to enjoy very little power and were often described as "unimportant." [2] Considering that the respondents in this study were state chairmen (among whom the Republicans were also members of the national committee), the fact that they rated 20 percent of the national committeemen as primary or secondary national contacts is interesting. It lends weight to the argument that the male members of the national committee *are* of importance in their respective state parties in spite of the fact that they are not elected public officeholders. The failure of the national committeewomen to rank highly as principal contacts suggests that their role may not have changed significantly in the decade since the Cotter and Hennessy study.

Table 8.2   Principal National Party Contacts, Primary and Secondary

	Primary	Secondary	Total
U.S. senator(s)	37.5%	16.7%	54.2%
Congressman	13.7	18.7	32.4
National committeeman	7.5	12.5	20.0
National chairman	7.5	16.7	24.2
White House staff	7.5	4.2	11.7
National committee staff	2.5	10.4	12.9
Cabinet member	1.3	2.1	3.4
Presidential candidate	1.3	6.2	7.5
National committeewoman	0.0	2.1	2.1

If there is a surprise to be found here, it is that the national party chairmen and the national committee staffs rated no higher than they did. It might be assumed that state chairmen would look to the national chairman for assistance and leadership when dealing with national government or party officials. The fact that 24.2 percent of the chairmen and 12.9 percent of the staff persons were singled out as primary or secondary contacts is not particularly impressive. An explanation might be the relatively rapid turnover of national chairmen in the past five years. Both national committees have been led by four chairmen (or women) during that time. This relatively short tenure has not permitted the state leaders to build close relationships with them.

It is not a common occurrence for state chairmen to deal directly with the White House, as illustrated by the few presidential staffers to be singled out as important contacts in Washington. Several of those who were, in fact, had been state chairmen in their home states prior to joining President Nixon. Best known among them was Harry Dent, former chairman of the South Carolina Republican party and a key political advisor and assistant during the early years of the Nixon administration. The restricted contact between state party officials and the president's men is nothing new, but the closed and isolated nature of the Nixon White House brought it into clearer focus. Most state party officials do not come into direct contact with cabinet officers, although a few were referred to a particular member of the president's cabinet by a home-state senator or congressman and usually for substantive policy assistance.

Relationships with Congress

In addition to patronage considerations, chairmen work with their congressional delegation with regard to pending legislation. Most of the examples furnished concerned national election laws which might possibly have an impact at the state level. One chairman noted, for instance:

I have been to Washington several times to discuss with the senator the impact of the elections reform package on the party here in ———. He agrees with me that it is going to hurt us in the pocketbook because of the reporting provisions, but he feels that he cannot go back to the people having voted against election reform. He agreed with me but refused to help the party.

Another chairman was invited by a congressman from his state to testify before a House committee on a committee substitute for a bill that would directly affect the metropolitan areas of his state. He did so but, in retrospect, did not think it proved useful.

There have been many reports over the years of U.S. senators and congressmen seeking to dominate state party affairs by a take-over of the political leadership. One of the earliest treatments of such an episode was Frank Munger's description of the efforts of Indiana senators Homer Capehart and William E. Jenner to impose their will on the Republican party in the Hoosier state. Munger reports that in 1954 a meeting between the two Indiana senators resulted in the resignation of the state chairman, a personal protégé of Governor George Craig. The resignation cleared the way for a Capehart-Jenner man to be selected as a replacement. This signaled a long fight in the Indiana Republican party—a fight with significant national overtones. Craig had been the only candidate for governor of Indiana to support the presidential nomination of General Dwight D. Eisenhower. Jenner and Capehart had been in the forefront of those who supported Ohio's Robert A. Taft. The state chairmanship served as the focal point between the two contending sides, and an intraparty quarrel ensued extending over a number of years.[3]

Such behind-the-scenes maneuvering is not uncommon in politics. Skirmishes between party factions have been particularly prevalent in the out-party or the party that has just lost the governorship, allowing a power vacuum to develop. A recent example was the rumored power play undertaken by Nebraska's Republican Senator Roman Hruska. After the defeat of incumbent Republican Governor Norbert Tiemann and the resignation of his hand-picked state chairwoman, a philosophical contest between the conservative and progressive forces in the party broke into the open. Hruska successfully installed his own choice as state chairman, thus giving the conservatives the victory.[4]

A similar struggle took place in Ohio in 1970 after the Republicans lost the governorship, several state offices, and thousands of patronage jobs in the November elections. The questions being discussed inside the party according to the *Dayton News* were:

Is Senator-Elect Robert A. Taft moving to oust outgoing Governor James A. Rhodes as dominant leader of the Ohio Republicans?

Is Rhodes determined to fight Taft for control of the party and another shot at the governorship when Democrat John J. Gilligan's term ends in 1974?

Will State Republican Chairman John Andrews be dumped as a move to curb Rhodes and reorganize the party?

Will organizational wizard Ray Bliss, a former Republican National Chairman, be key man for Taft behind the scenes? [5]

Nothing came of the move to oust Andrews although the *New York Times* reported some months later that Bliss had indeed been asked to take over the party chairmanship in case there should be a vacancy but that he had refused.[6] Andrews went on to serve out his term, retiring in 1973, and Rhodes was reelected governor in 1974.

Whether or not such efforts are successful is of little consequence. The more important consideration is that a United States senator, operating out of Washington and usually elected through a personal campaign organization, can mount an effort to dominate the state party through choice of a personal representative as state chairman—or, to back up one step, that a senator can exert pressure of sufficient magnitude to force the resignation of a state chairman, thus opening the way for him to thrust for the party leadership.

In each of these instances a U.S. senator sought to influence action within his own state party organization. In 1970 the officially recognized Democratic party of Mississippi attempted to pressure the House leadership into taking action to deny seniority privileges to the five congressmen from that state. As noted before, Mississippi has had two Democratic parties since 1968. The party in question, led by State Chairman Aaron Henry, a nationally recognized black leader, won official recognition from the 1968 Democratic Convention. The old, mostly white, Democratic party still retained state recognition, however, complete with its own state chairman as well as an incumbent governor, John Bell Williams. The Henry group, a mixture of blacks and whites, unsuccessfully challenged the five Mississippi congressmen, including the chairman of the House Rules Committee, on the grounds that they could not retain seniority when they were elected by an unrecognized faction in Mississippi.[7]

Generally speaking, there has been little interplay between the state parties and their elected officials in Washington. The parties, except on patronage matters, have not pressed the congressmen for much, and they, in turn, have concentrated largely on maintaining their own personal organizations, paying little attention to official party groups. Clapp, Huckshorn and Spencer, and Fishel have all noted that state party organizations are relatively unimportant in the campaign plans of congressmen.

However, they now appear to receive more attention than they formerly did.[8]

An area of considerable mutual interest to congressmen and state party leaders is congressional redistricting. Traditionally, districting took place after the decennial census if at all. The succession of federal court cases in the 1960s, however, forced many state legislatures into extraordinary sessions to furnish more equitable districting that might meet the requirements of the courts. Several chairmen noted that contacts with congressmen, nil before the one-man, one-vote decision, multiplied a hundredfold afterward. The prospect of court-ordered redistricting stirred the members to action as nothing had before. Efforts to encourage the state party structure to intercede in the legislative politics of apportionment and districting were common. As one midwestern Democrat described his experience:

> Congressman ———, who represents the ——— District and has been in Congress for a dozen years, never once called me or my predecessor about anything at all until he got scared by the court-ordered redistricting in the late 1960s. The legislative leadership, with a Republican majority in one house, began to leak stories about what they were going to do to him and one other guy, and they really got shook up. He began to call us every day to insist that we do something. Anything. His calls actually became frantic. I told him that I was working the halls and was going to testify but that we didn't have the horses to stop them from doing whatever they decided to do. As you can imagine, that didn't calm him down much. The upshot was that they did chop a big piece off his district, but he went on and won anyway and I haven't heard from him since.

The role of the state chairman in legislative or congressional redistricting is often an adversary's role. This is particularly true of those chairmen who represent parties that do not control the legislature and are at the mercy of the opposition. In an interview in 1971, Earl Davenport, Republican chairman of Washington, complained that the new districts proposed by the Democratic majority in the Washington legislature did not treat the population equitably and would not stand up in court. He argued that a plan proposed by the Republicans had a better chance for judicial approval. As is often the case, the political arguments came down to what area was to be included in which district. Davenport offered to compromise over the choice of counties to be included in two districts if the Democrats would release the Republican-passed House bill from a Senate committee where it had been bottled up. The incident demonstrated the advocate's role that may be assumed by a party chairman in such circumstances.[9]

Congressional districting is one area of judicial review which has important poltical overtones. Court intervention in districting decisions in the late 1960s and early seventies was quite common. District boundaries in forty-four states were subject to challenge under a Supreme Court ruling in April 1969, which held that the states must strive for congressional districts with absolutely equal populations. So sweeping was the ruling that only those six states with an at-large congressman were excluded from its effects.[10] In some states party chairmen were not involved at all and took pains to remain uninvolved. One described the controversy in his state as a "no win" situation.

Other party leaders, however, were heavily involved in the political aspects of districting decisions made by the legislature. In 1972, for instance, a three-judge federal court ruled that the Connecticut districting plan then in effect was unconstitutional and ordered a court-designed plan to go into effect. "Great inequalities in population have developed since the districting plan was drawn after the 1960 census," the court declared, then ruled that the old plan so seriously debased the voting rights of the plaintiffs that it resulted in invidious discrimination. The plan imposed by the court was one put forward by the Democratic state chairman, John Bailey. It was the same plan, for the most part, that had been approved by the Connecticut General Assembly, under Democratic control, and vetoed by Republican Governor Meskill.[11]

Relationships of the In-Party with the White House

Most recent presidents and presidential candidates have treated state party organizations with disdain. Their own campaign organizations within each state have been established parallel to the regular party structure, and little attention has been given to providing meaningful tasks for elected leaders. Some have allowed an excess of zeal to substitute for understanding, as reported by Samuel Lubell in his discussion of President Dwight Eisenhower's relations with the Republican party:

Not until after the 1954 elections . . . did he acquire an all out zeal for revitalizing the Republican organization. Some of those close to him interpreted this as indicating he had decided to run for a second term. Others thought he wanted to build a strong enough organization so the Republicans could win without him.

Whatever the motivation, with characteristic intensity Eisenhower began demanding "a Republican party worker in every precinct in the country." Some veteran politicians tried to explain that no party has ever been able to recruit enough precinct workers to reach down to the last precinct. But the President brushed aside their objections impatiently. After one such session one aide walked out of the President's office muttering, "He thinks if the Army can be organized down to the smallest unit, a political party can be." [12]

Most state party officials would probably be just as happy to be left alone by their president and his aides. On many occasions, having injected themselves into some delicate local situation, they have exacerbated the problem and left the solution to be finally worked out by the state chairman. Under the Nixon administration, encompassing the time frame in which most of this study was carried out, White House intervention in state politics was fairly common. At times these presidential forays were carried out by White House staffers, but there were occasions when a cabinet officer or an official of the Republican National Committee performed the surrogate's function.

Efforts to build party support for presidential programs at the grass roots were largely the responsibility of Vice-President Spiro T. Agnew during the first Nixon term. Agnew, at that time a popular figure in many state and local Republican organizations, served as overseer of the White House Office of Intergovernmental Relations. It was widely believed by state party officials and members of the Washington press corps that Agnew was also responsible for carrying out the "southern strategy" associated with the first Nixon term. These roles brought him into close touch with state and local party leaders; it was at a meeting of the Midwest Republican Regional Conference in Des Moines in 1970 that the vice-president launched his attack on the television media. At election time, however, many incidents emerged to illustrate the methods used by the White House to inject itself into the politics of various states.

Every president has attempted to use the influence of his office to alter election outcomes. Some of them have been quite subtle about it, and others have adopted blunderbuss techniques.* Such incidents have often

* Riker and Bast report that between 1913 and 1960 there were only 37 public presidential interventions in congressional primaries. Since there were about 12,000 nominations during this period, the number of public interventions is infinitesimal. They conclude that "It seems fair to say ... that Presidents have been deeply reluctant to attempt, at least publicly, to control congressional nominations." By specifying that their analysis included "public" endorsements, the authors clearly recognized the possible existence of private interventions. In most instances Nixon

brought the White House into conflict with state political leaders, and the Nixon efforts resulted in sharp exchanges between the two levels of the party.

In 1971, Utah Republicans, in an angry letter to national party leaders, sharply criticized the White House's handling of the 1970 congressional campaign in that state. The letter charged that an administration-recommended campaign management firm had completely misread local voter sentiment and had caused the loss of important contests for the U.S. Senate and the House. Signed by State Chairman Fred T. Wright, the vice-chairwoman, and both national committee members, the letter asserted:

that Civic Service, Inc., the St. Louis political concern that handled Senate races in Maryland and Wyoming as well as Utah, had conducted the Utah contest as "a classical example of 'not knowing the territory.' "

The letter reported that these strategists projected Laurence J. Burton, whom President Nixon had personally persuaded to make the Senate race, "in cowboy shirt, as matching Utah's mountains" and "put Burton on a horse as a cowboy. . . . The vote clearly indicated that the majority of Utahans did not want a heavy, hard-line cowboy as U.S. Senator."

After complaining that the firm also contributed to the defeat of Republican congressional candidate Richard Richards, the letter concluded "that Civic Services, Inc., will not be allowed back in the state on a Republican campaign; nor can they use the Utah G.O.P. as a favorable reference." [13]

On several occasions in 1970 and 1972 Nixon aides reportedly gave support to friendly Democratic senators and were charged with undercutting state Republican candidates who were running against them. The incident that received the most attention was the president's support of Washington Senator Henry M. (Scoop) Jackson in his 1970 reelection bid. As early as June 1970, *Miami Herald-Los Angeles* Times Wire Service reported that "It looks like clear sailing for Sen. Henry M. Jackson in the November elections. And that's the way President Nixon wants it

administration interventions were private, although there were some well-publicized public endorsements including outright public campaigning by administration officials. Furthermore, the Riker and Bast study was published in 1969 and predated the Nixon administration and the interviews upon which this study is largely based. William H. Riker and William Bast, "Presidential Action in Congressional Nominations," in Aaron Wildavsky, ed., *The Presidency* (Boston: Little, Brown and Co., 1969), pp. 250–67.

for the friendly Democrat who generally supports Administration policy in Southeast Asia." Governor Daniel Evans and Republican Chairman C. Montgomery Johnson were reported to be upset over news breaks the White House had given Jackson plus direct intervention by presidential aides who urged state Republican leaders to do nothing in the election that would "embarrass the President, like running someone against Scoop Jackson." At one point during the controversy the state chairman dismissed the entire fourteen-member State Finance Committee because they showed no enthusiasm for raising $50,000 to help finance a Republican campaign against Jackson and were, instead, backing him for reelection.[14]

The controversy continued in Washington through the summer, and in mid-October Chairman Johnson charged that Vice-President Agnew refused to come into the state to assist the state party with fund raising to support its legislative candidates. The consequence of his refusal, according to Johnson, was that "for the first time in memory, the state GOP has no money to give Republican congressional candidates." He attributed the lack of White House support to a desire by the president to reelect Scoop Jackson.[15]

It has long been a common practice of presidents to send key White House aides or cabinet members into selected states to work for support of issues being pressed by the administration. All recent presidents have followed this practice, and Richard Nixon was no exception. There were numerous reports during the first Nixon term of such excursions into state party domains.

In 1971 Herbert Klein, the president's director of communications, took part in an all-day meeting in Wilkes Barre, Pennsylvania, attended by Republican county chairmen from thirteen northeastern counties as well as the state party leadership. The session was one of seven arranged by state GOP headquarters and held throughout the state. The principal purpose of the meetings was to develop rapport between the national, state, and local party leaders. During the sessions various issues were discussed and explained by Klein such as revenue sharing, governmental reorganization, and the Nixon welfare plan.

Vice-President Agnew also made a series of issue-oriented excursions into several states during 1971. In June, Agnew visited South Carolina to address the state legislature in support of the administration's revenue-sharing proposals. Although his visit was billed in the press as "nonpolitical," the South Carolina Republicans had been engaged in a feud with the White House over appointment of a Democrat to the federal bench. The state party leadership was excluded from participating in the planning for the Agnew visit, and the state chairman was not able to attend the speech because "he had not been issued credentials." He also was not invited to see the vice-president off at the airport until the last minute, several days after other party officials received such invitations.[16]

These incidents were considered by many party leaders as clear-cut attempts by the president and his advisors to impose the will of *the* party leader on those further down the hierarchy. Such efforts are seldom popular with state party leaders but, if carried out with some finesse, are often accepted by them in order to avoid public conflict within the party. The fact that so many incidents of this kind reached the news media during the first Nixon administration suggests that the minimum tolerance level had been reached.

Presidents have, on occasion, attempted to directly intervene in state elections either to purge recalcitrant senators or representatives or to aid in the election of candidates from the opposition party. The classic textbook example was the effort of President Franklin Roosevelt to purge conservative southern Democratic senators Walter George, Millard Tydings, and "Cotton Ed" Smith in 1936. Although he lost the most publicized of his personal efforts, the work of his lieutenants paid off in the defeat of John O'Connor, a Tammany congressman who was chairman of the Rules Committee in the House and had used his power to frustrate Roosevelt's New Deal measures.[17]

Other presidents made similar, but much less obvious, efforts to thwart the reelection chances of officeholders within their own parties. In 1970 Richard Nixon sent Spiro Agnew to aid in the defeat of Republican Senator Charles Goodell of New York by giving well-publicized support to Conservative party candidate, and eventual winner, James Buckley. The Nixon strategy used in assisting Democrat Henry Jackson's bid for reelection to the Senate from Washington was repeated in 1972 in Mississippi. The *New York Times* reported a month before the election that

The Nixon Administration has taken quiet steps to try to insure the reelection of Mississippi's venerable Democratic Senator, James O. Eastland, despite its hopes for a Republican Congress.

Word has been passed "from the highest White House level," . . . that nothing is to be done to help Gil Carmichael, the Meridian businessman who is Mr. Eastland's Republican opponent.[18]

The administration reached the decision to support Eastland, chairman of the Senate Judiciary Committee, after he gave staunch support to the administration in its battles over the nominations of Clement F. Haynsworth, Jr., and G. Harrold Carswell to the Supreme Court. When Vice-President Agnew arrived in Jackson, Mississippi, he told one Republican leader, according to the press, that the administration could do nothing to "help defeat someone who has been so helpful to us in the past." He proceeded to elaborately endorse three GOP congressional candidates while conspicuously failing to mention Carmichael.[19]

Out-party chairmen sometimes face similar problems. Early in the 1972 preprimary campaigns, Washington Democratic Chairman Neale V. Chaney found himself in the middle of a dispute between contenders for the Democratic presidential nomination. The Western States Democratic Conference was scheduled to meet in Seattle, chosen because the chairman of the conference was long-time Democratic power Luke Graham, the Democratic national committeeman from Washington. Chaney decided to use the affair as a money raiser for the 1972 campaign and invited all of the party's presidential prospects to attend. He reasoned that this would kill two birds with one stone—collect a good deal of money from party faithful interested in a preliminary look at the candidates, and permit a friendly forum for Washington's own Henry Jackson. A good showing by Jackson might possibly have kept the others from coming into the state on an individual basis, and Chaney wanted to reap the publicity that would come with such visits. Chaney talked with as many candidates as he could and got tentative promises from representatives of Senator George McGovern and Senator Edmund Muskie, who was, at that time, considered to be the front runner. The scenario began to fall apart when Muskie people realized that his presence might give too much status to the other lesser candidates, at which point he began to show signs of withdrawing. By the time Chaney received an affirmative answer from Hubert Humphrey and a positive answer from McGovern, the Muskie forces had pulled out and Jackson had retreated until he could decide whether or not to make the race at all.[20]

This episode seems to illustrate the view of one state chairman who said, "Unless you represent a major state, your dealings with presidential candidates and campaigns are pretty much at the whim of the candidate. It's hard to maintain control over powerful outside forces even when they want to come into your own state." The same could be said of incumbent presidents. If an incumbent president wishes to involve himself in a state party, there is little the local officials can do without considerable risk. The president is the national party leader. He normally does have the support of most of the state party leaders. Even so, there is some quid pro quo involved between the two levels of the party hierarchy. The president must normally rely on state officials to handle arrangements, ticket sales, or crowd generation. Presidents do not travel unobtrusively. Their moves are watched and followed. Their failure to draw crowds— or worse, their suffering indignities from the crowd—is noted and widely commented. They do need the state party organization. At the same time, however, the state party, in normal times, needs the president. There have been recent occasions, both Johnson and Nixon being examples, where a president could not move freely due to personal unpopularity with specific groups. Most presidents, however, have taken their leadership of the party for granted and have assumed support in the state parties. In most cases they have been correct.

The State Parties and the National Committees

The relationship between the two national committees and their respective state organizations is a complex one. One national chairman may enjoy more respect than another, and that fact alone may add prestige and power to his national committee. Ray Bliss, Republican national chairman between 1965 and 1969, commanded such widespread respect that he added stature to the committee just by being there. As described by two political scientists who worked closely with him:

In assessing a new party leader, one must go beyond the political conditions that led to his election. His personality, style of leadership, and background are all important to an understanding of the leadership role he plays. Bliss is a quiet, almost shy, man who does not enjoy public speaking or the spotlight of publicity. He is an intense perfectionist, capable of extended periods of concentration and attention to detail. His standards and expectations for himself and his staff are high, and he insists that the programs initiated by his office be fully and carefully executed. His consuming interest is politics. He is totally immersed in political life, and this has left him little time for outside interests or hobbies. Bliss places a high priority on personal integrity and honesty in politics. He considers himself a straight shooter who levels with political associates and does not promise things he cannot deliver. As a political professional and an expert in organization, he attaches great importance to party loyalty. He also exercises great care to protect the organization of which he is a part from real or potential opponents—without or within the party. He knows that a miscalculation or mistake on the part of a major party leader can have reverberations throughout the party structure. Consequently, he exercises great care in making decisions.[21]

Almost 25 percent of the state chairmen listed the national chairman as a prime or secondary contact in Washington (see table 8.2). An additional 13 percent indicated national committee staff persons as their principal national contacts. For the party in power the national chairman and his staff often serve as the lightning rods for internal party criticisms emerging out of White House decision making. National Chairman Robert Dole, after the 1970 congressional elections, was besieged by irate state party officials complaining about heavy-handed campaigning on the part of President Nixon's assistants as well as White House intervention in the politics of individual states. On at least one occasion Chairman Dole arranged for presidential advisor Harry Dent, a former South Carolina state chairman, to meet with Republican state chairmen in a Washington hotel to explain and defend campaign strategy.

At the January 1971 meeting of the Republican National Committee at which Senator Dole was ratified as President Nixon's choice for national chairman, the state chairmen held a series of meetings by regional groups. They generated considerable criticism of the White House for what Mississippi Chairman Clarke Reed called its "lack of political direction." These meetings illustrated the pressures facing any president in attempting to deal with the many factions within his party. While the northeastern Republican chairmen were encouraging the president to give more consideration to urban programs and minority groups, the southern chairmen were worrying that Nixon might be promising too many new health and welfare programs and risking a big budget deficit. Many of these complaints are registered through the national chairman, and he in turn is expected to carry them to the White House.

Contacts with staffers at the national committees usually involve more mundane political matters such as speech scheduling, fund raising, and campaign strategy. During a campaign calls to long-time Republican staff advisor A. B. Hermann average between thirty and fifty per day from state and local party officials. Hermann offers advice, redirects callers to specific divisions within the RNC, and serves as a conduit to the national chairman. During the tenure of Lawrence O'Brien as chairman of the DNC, Deputy Chairman Stanley L. Greigg, a former member of Congress, served in much the same capacity.

As we have noted, most of the Republican state chairmen were included as members of the Republican National Committee in 1952 and the remainder were given full membership in 1968. The Democratic state chairmen were included, along with vice-chairmen, under the revised structure of the Democratic National Committee adopted by the 1974 mini-convention in Kansas City as discussed in chapter 7. The chairmen themselves have reacted to membership on the national committees quite favorably. For one thing, it opened new avenues for them to gather ideas and exchange information. As noted by one: "I get a great many ideas from the meetings and they are often ideas that I can use back home." Another stated that his national committee membership was one of the most valuable experiences of his chairmanship because of the party resources that became available to him.

The largest number of chairmen viewed their national committee membership as a source of enhanced power and prestige within their own states. A sampling of opinions illustrates the point:

Local people think that you are more powerful by being on the national committee, and in fact, you probably are. The positions of national committeeman and woman are positions of prestige—the chairmanship is a position of power.

Membership of the chairmen on the DNC has always been favored by me. We know what is going on—the national committee members in most states do not. I would like to be a member.

Membership on the Republican National Committee has enhanced my power a great deal. I have been on it because we have controlled the governorship ever since I became chairman. I think it has been very helpful in my relationship with others. They usually react as though it has made me a more important leader.

Some national chairmen in both parties have served previously as state chairmen. The last two Democrats to do so were J. Howard McGrath and John Bailey, who retained his state chairmanship during the years he served in Washington. With the exception of Ray Bliss, one must go back to B. Carroll Reece (1946–48) and C. Wesley Roberts (1953), former chairmen of Tennessee and Kansas respectively, before encountering a national Republican leader who had served an apprenticeship as state party leader. As recently as 1972, on the other hand, two Democratic state chairmen were among the major candidates for national chairman, although neither won the office.

The State Chairmen and the National Convention

During the last two years of every quadrennium, the planning for the two national party conventions brings state party leaders into close contact with national committee staff personnel. Although every convention differs in substantial ways, both parties have well-established procedures for selecting convention sites, dispensing tickets, arranging hotel space, and maintaining security. Unexpected problems may develop, as happened at the Democratic convention in 1968, or substantial changes in rules and procedures may cause dislocation within the party, as happened in the 1972 convention that nominated George McGovern. However, long experience has taught the parties how to run national conventions with few disruptions in the transaction of their principal business. This is particularly true of the Republicans, due in large part to the experience of Convention Director Jo Good, who has organized every convention since 1956. As convention planning escalates, the mail and telephone and personal contacts between national committee members, party staff persons, and state chairmen mount.

The role of the state chairmen in the national conventions has not always been an important one. As we shall see later, the numbers of chairmen who were delegates have not changed much in the past several conventions, but the impact of their attendance may have. In the past the role of the chairmen in the conventions has been a personal one, depending in part on the individual's relationships with national party leaders and presidential candidates and on whether or not he was in a position to influence the nomination.*

Only 25 percent of the chairmen interviewed had never attended a national convention, most because they were not in office at the time.

---

* Among elected officeholders in 1968 and 1972, governors had the highest representation at the two national conventions with U.S. senators and congressmen having fewer of their numbers attending. As noted below, representation of all elected officeholders declined in 1972.

Office	1968 Conventions		1972 Conventions	
	R	D	R	D
Governor	24 (26) 92.3%	22 (24) 91.7%	16 (20) 80.0%	19 (30) 63.3%
Senator	21 (36) 58.3	41 (64) 64.1	22 (45) 48.9	18 (55) 32.1
Representative	58 (186) 31.2	91 (247) 36.8	78 (177) 44.1	30 (255) 11.8

Note: Number in parentheses represent total offices held.

Table 8.3   Number of National Conventions Attended by State Chairmen Prior to 1972

Number of conventions	Percentage attending (N80)
One	39.2
Two	21.5
Three	3.8
Four	3.8
Five	3.8
Six	1.3
Seven or more	1.3
None	25.3

NOTE: Column totals to more than 100 percent due to rounding.

As noted in table 8.3, the majority (39.2 percent) had attended one convention while 21.5 percent had attended two. The number of conventions attended decreased rapidly from that point, although one chairman had attended six conventions and another seven or more.

Since these figures represented an N of only eighty respondents, it was desirable to determine the actual participation rate of all chairmen who were in office at the time of the last several conventions. Delegate lists were available for both parties extending back through 1960.[22] A comparison of the delegate lists with the official rosters of state chairmen in office at the times of the conventions provided the data contained in table 8.4.

Only two state Republican parties sent their chairmen as delegates to all four of the conventions, while three more chairmen attended three.

Table 8.4   Participatory Roles of Democratic and Republican State Chairmen in the National Conventions, 1960–72

Chairman's role	1960		1964		1968		1972	
	D	R	D	R	D	R	D	R
Delegate	27	37	38	38	40	37	28	32
Alternate delegate	4	3	2	0	0	3	2	0
Did not attend or attended in unofficial capacity	19	10	10	12	10	10	20	18

In the Democratic party, only one state elected the chairman as a delegate all four times (he actually was a delegate to a total of seven conventions), but four of them attended three times.

In some states it has become traditional for party leaders to voluntarily forfeit their "right" to be a delegate in favor of nonofficeholders. The purpose is to reward those who work in the party cadre but who do not hold an official position. In others the state or district conventions chose not to elect the chairman of the party as a delegate, and in still others the party leaders lost their bids for delegate status in a preference primary. For instance, in three of the four states which sent their chairmen as delegates to three of the four conventions, the delegates were elected in presidential preference primaries. One of several who failed to be elected was Caroline Wilkins, Democratic state chairwoman of Oregon, who ran on an uncommitted delegate slate and lost out in the McGovern domination of the Oregon primary.

Table 8.4 shows that the number of state chairmen attending conventions as a delegate or an alternate has not changed much since 1960. It might be noted that after peaking at forty in 1968 the number of Democratic chairmen elected as delegates dropped to thirty in 1972, probably a result of the McGovern-Fraser guidelines for delegate selection. Those guidelines made it much more difficult for party leaders to control the selection of delegates and generally brought to an end the practice of "reserving" convention places for those in positions of leadership. Quorums were set, proxy voting was eliminated, the participatory base was expanded, and presidential primaries multiplied; all changes were designed to reduce the influence of party officials in delegate selection. Since thirty state chairmen were selected as delegates, the impact of the guidelines was obviously mixed. A number of Democratic chairmen reported that they were thwarted in their efforts to gain a seat for themselves, while others suggested that such an effort would have been futile and so was not undertaken.

Even so, it was the state chairmen who were primarily responsible for seeing that the new delegate selection guidelines were carried out. Florida Democratic Chairman Jon Moyle appointed a twenty-three-member committee to study delegate selection.[23] In July 1971, Moyle announced new proposals to "democratize" the selection process; proposals were hammered out during a two-day bargaining session held in the state capital.[24] The new proposals were subjected to a series of hearings, distributed to all state committeemen and women and county chairmen, and were then the subject of public hearings in all twelve congressional districts before being adopted and implemented.

Kansas Democratic Chairman Norbert Dreiling presided over one of three parties which had not complied with the guidelines in any way by early 1972. He explained that "everyone came back from Chicago [in 1968] screaming at one another, and I didn't feel this was the atmosphere in which we could reason together." He later led the state party in adoption of the rules changes necessitated by the guidelines.[25] Connecticut's John Bailey was forced to go to court when he ordered fifty town committees to abolish a long-established self-endorsement process in delegate selection and was challenged by a competitor for state party leadership.[26] These were but a few of the problems faced by the Democratic chairmen between 1970 and 1972. Some were less than enthusiastic about the changes, but all eventually gained temporary approval of their delegations in time for the convention.

The Democrats were not the only ones who were troubled in attempting to accommodate reform. Ohio Republican Chairman John Andrews encountered difficulty in implementing the nonbinding recommendations of the DO Committee of the Republican National Committee. The DO recommendations called for half of the convention delegates to be women and for young people from eighteen to twenty-five to be represented in proportion to their share of the population. A major problem for Andrews was Ohio Republican tradition. In the Ninth Congressional District it had been customary for one delegate to be the county chairman and the other a representative from the local party finance committee; the two alternate slots were reserved for a woman and a local officeholder or candidate. In the neighboring Fifth District, party leaders from one-half of its ten counties traditionally selected two delegates and alternates in one election year, the other half in the next, four years later.[27]

The role of the chairman at the convention is enhanced when he or she is elected as delegation chairman. Of the twenty-eight chairmen who were certified as delegates to the 1972 Democratic National Convention, only about a half-dozen served as chairmen of their respective delegations. Of the thirty-two elected to the Republican Convention, ten served as delegation leaders. Most of them represented parties which were out of power, but some were selected to avoid choosing a leader from one of the numerous presidential factions within each delegation. An effort to be elected delegation chairman by Joseph F. Crangle, New York Democratic chairman, failed during the convention, and Crangle had to settle for one of four co-chairmen's positions. This compromise plan was offered to patch a growing rift between supporters of Senator McGovern and the New York Democratic leadership, most of whom were defeated in the McGovern sweep of the presidential primary in that state.[28]

Crangle was not the only leader actively seeking the delegation chairmanship. Bronx Borough President Robert Abrams, with the covert backing of the McGovern forces, sought to be elected chairman, but once the important New York delegation became bitterly embroiled in controversy, the compromise plan was adopted and implemented with both Crangle and Abrams included.

Twenty-eight percent of the chairmen responded affirmatively when asked, "Were you consulted personally by any of the presidential candidates at your 1968 national conventions?" Most were Republicans, and the consultations were initiated by the candidates, who included Richard Nixon, Nelson Rockefeller, and Ronald Reagan. Usually the candidate was seeking information concerning the prospective voting behavior of particular delegations. Efforts to ascertain the potential voting patterns of a particular delegation are quite common.

Some chairmen do not hesitate to show public support of some particular candidate for president. Republican Chairman L. E. Thomas of Florida announced in mid-1971 that he would quit before he would support Representative Paul McCloskey should he win the Republican nomination. He noted that he would not seek to keep McCloskey off the ballot but said that the party would give the California Republican no assistance whatsoever.[29]

Thomas later came under attack from the right wing of the Republican party in Florida for his open preconvention support of President Nixon. A state committeewoman from Miami charged in early 1972 that Thomas was trying to speak for the entire party without giving those who supported other candidates a chance to be heard. Her concern was that Congressman John Ashbrook of Ohio, a staunch conservative, would be denied facilities at state headquarters. Thomas responded that all legitimate Republican candidates were entitled to distribute their literature through the state headquarters in Tallahassee. She noted that there was a long-standing tradition of noninvolvement on the part of the chairman and the headquarters that was being violated.[30]

Maryland Republicans, acting through the state executive committee, endorsed the Nixon-Agnew ticket a year before the national convention in order "to head off support for GOP candidates challenging the President." Chairman Alexander Lankler noted that the "committee is usually reluctant to take sides in a primary, but these are not normal times."[31]

The role of the state chairmen at the national conventions has been a mixed one. Some, especially those from larger states who have been elected as delegation leaders, have occupied positions which enabled them to bargain and barter. Others have been little more than errand boys. One chairman noted that his duties at the convention were limited to distributing tickets to the daily sessions and seeing that communications to delegates were delivered. He admitted that he volunteered for the job and did not want a position of more responsibility because the convention would be divisive and any position he might take would work to his disadvantage. Other chairmen, however, relished the give and take of convention battle. Those from large states, with many delegates, were sought out by presidential candidates and their representatives. They not only felt important, they were important.

Some state chairmen undertake to carve out a place for themselves or their states in the preliminaries of a presidential year. Early in 1968 three key southern Republican chairmen concluded that, given the right combination of events, they might exercise an unusual influence in the presidential nomination of that year. State chairmen Clarke Reed of Mississippi, Harry Dent of South Carolina, and William Murfin of Florida, old friends and political allies, decided to seek bargaining power for the South by forcing the presidential candidates to work for their support and, at the proper time, by lending the weight of their combined influence to achieve the nomination for a particular candidate. The three, later joined by the remaining members of the Southern Republican State Chairmen's Association, all privately pledged their support to Richard Nixon but considered it essential that the candidacy of Ronald Reagan be kept alive to be used as a lever with the Nixon people. Repeated meetings of the southern party leaders with the managers of the three candidates, Reagan, Nixon, and Rockefeller, kept the surface indications alive that the group remained uncommitted. All three candidates, at one point in May, addressed all thirteen of the southern chairmen, but none of them emerged with an endorsement. By the time the convention came around, the coalition had begun to come unstrung, especially in the Florida and Texas delegations. Ultimately, however, they were held for Nixon, to whom private pledges had been addressed by Reed, Dent, and Murfin early in the year. The result was a strong belief on the part of Nixon and his aides that the southern efforts had been crucial to their success and the widespread rumor that, in return, they held a veto power over Nixon's vice-presidential choice.[32] After the election Murfin moved into an important post in the Small Business Administration, an agency of great importance to the South; Dent moved into the White House as a presidential aide; and Reed emerged as a recognized party leader within the Republican national organization.

It is unlikely that any group except the southerners could unite in behalf of a particular goal of this kind. The major reason for their success was the developing influence of the Southern State Chairmen's Association as a force within the party. No other regional association wielded the power of this particular one, and individual leaders had tenuous holds on power either because of personal commitments to particular candidates or because lack of substantive issue agreement precluded formation of coalitions.

State Parties in the National Political System

Traditionally, control of the national party organization has been shared by the White House, Congress, the national committees, and the national conventions. In general they have collectively demonstrated little sustained interest in building a unified and strengthened national party structure. Each has attempted to use the party to its own purpose. Rivalry has often prevented joint effort. Nearly all of their efforts have ignored the state and local parties unless some specified need, such as patronage clearance, intruded.

At the same time, state parties have resisted pressures from Washington; party leaders have often expressed fear of domination and have consequently not always been cooperative. As a consequence, no one has successfully advanced a sustained program to develop the potential of state parties, and few efforts have been made to effectively bridge the gaps between the levels of the hierarchy. Many state chairmen, as well as national party leaders, believe that their inclusion as voting members of the national committees may be a first step in overcoming some of these problems. Overcoming problems will not by itself strengthen party systems, but greater participation in national politics by state party officials and greater awareness of state problems by national party officials do offer an avenue through which to approach real and lasting change.

If the state chairman is a middleman in the party system, he has responsibilities to both the national and local units. In this chapter we have discussed his relationship with national party leaders; in chapter 9 we shall turn to the relationship between the state and local party organizations.

9 Servicing the State and Local Parties

> Our party would not be able to survive
> without our headquarters. We have a large
> staff and have been operating since the late
> 1940s. The county parties have come to
> depend upon us, and we have tried to make
> them dependent on us. They now look to us
> for leadership.
> *A midwestern Republican chairman*

> My headquarters is in my kitchen. When I
> took over we were so far in debt that I
> closed the office, disconnected the phone,
> and fired the secretary. I am trying to re-
> duce the debt so that we can reopen an
> office. Right now I even type my own letters.
> *A western Democratic chairman*

> Our county people won't give us the time of
> day. They have gotten along without the
> state party for so long that they don't even
> realize how bad some of them are. We're
> working on it . . . but I don't expect miracles.
> *A southern Democratic governor*

State political parties, as we know them today, emerged from the conflict and trauma of the Civil War. For the most part they remained somewhat stable until after World War II when a number of hitherto one-party or modified one-party states nurtured competitive second parties. The earliest manifestation of the changes that were to come developed in the South as Republican presidential candidates received increasingly impressive voter support during the 1940s and fifties. The Republican National Committee's "Operation Dixie" during the 1960s, spurred by the Goldwater presidential candidacy, contributed to a climate of opinion which opened parts of the South to a competitive party system.

The most newsworthy successes were the Republican gains in southern governors, senators, and congressmen. In 1966 both Florida and Arkansas elected their first GOP governors since the post-Civil War period. They were joined in later years by Republican chief executives in Tennessee, Virginia, and North and South Carolina. Also during this period the Republican parties of Florida, North and South Carolina, Tennessee, Texas, and Virginia elected United States senators, and every one of the southern states had elected at least one Republican congressman by 1974. Furthermore, by 1973 Republicans had elected a total of 336 members of the twelve southern state legislatures.[1]

Only slightly less impressive were Democratic successes in formerly staunch Republican states. Such traditional GOP strongholds as Maine, Vermont, New Hampshire, Kansas, Nebraska, and Iowa all elected Democratic governors, and several sent Democratic senators to Washington. The obvious result of these breeches of customary party lines was more competition between the parties.

The spread of two-party politics came about for a variety of reasons, including the continuing migration of people between the North and South and the East and West. The most politically significant aspect of this population movement was the parallel migration of northern whites and southern blacks. The latter have moved north in search of jobs and have carried their post-New Deal Democratic allegiance with them into traditional Republican areas. Simultaneously, the ripening of the southern economy and a more moderate racial posture have attracted large numbers of northerners, about half of whom were Republicans, to the once "solid" Democratic South. The result has been to increase the vote potential of the opposition party in each region, while in the South it also provided the Republicans with a new source of articulate, educated, and invigorating political talent.

The spectacular growth of the West also resulted chiefly from in-migration by easterners. The results have been less noticeable in the short run, but there is already evidence that the long-run effect will be a more competitive political system. In any event, postwar interstate migration of peoples has had the healthy effect of increasing competition and providing real targets for political activists.

Greater political competition also came about because the complexion of the electorate changed. In 1972 the voting-age population of the United States was the largest in the history of the nation. For the first time young people between the ages of eighteen and twenty-one were eligible to vote for president in every state, with the result that over 19 million more people were eligible to vote in 1972 than in 1968. In some traditionally Republican states this increase in the voting population had the effect of increasing competition, since most of the newly enfranchised voters were registered as Democratic. Most of them (52 percent) voted for Richard Nixon for president, but many split their tickets to vote for Democratic candidates further down the ballot. It could be argued, therefore, that in selected states with a predominantly Republican electorate the increase in youthful Democratic registrations might have brought about greater competition between the parties.[2]

Therefore, even though the number of competitive two-party states has increased since 1945, it is not entirely clear why that has come about. The two reasons cited here provide part of the answer, but there certainly are other factors which have played a part. One, with which this chapter deals, is the substantially increased emphasis that state party leaders have placed on buttressing their organizational capabilities. The last two chapters have considered the relationship of the state party organizations with each other, especially through the national state chairmen's organizations, and their relationship to the national parties. In each instance—first, through the organization of the chairmen's associations, and second, through acceptance as voting members of the national committees—state party leaders were able to fortify their positions. They gained both stature and strength.

There are many other factors which help to condition the effectiveness of the parties. The impact of laws and internal rules on party operations was discussed in chapter 1. Along with local tradition, they are used to give direction to party affairs.

The in-party/out-party distinction usually determines whether or not the party organization will have an impact on policy making. The governorship is widely recognized as the key factor in achieving successful policy implementation. Even with a recalcitrant or opposition legislature a strong governor can exercise his or her will. Possession of the governorship can loosen contributors' purse strings to provide money for campaigning, headquarters management, or program innovation. Considering the rapidly emerging needs of changing political systems, money becomes an increasingly important factor in achieving electoral success. An incumbent governor is an important ace in the hole to financial solicitors. And that, in turn, often affects policy outputs.

One of the oldest chestnuts in undergraduate American government classes holds that federalism, as one of its advantages, permits each state government to serve as a laboratory for experimentation in governmental techniques. Should a substantive or procedural innovation prove to be worthwhile in one state, it can then be adopted with small risk by others. There is little doubt that such is sometimes the case. It would appear, too, that if the "laboratory" analogy applies to governmental structures and policy making, it would apply equally well to the political party structures and initiatives.

There are four intraparty responsibilities which most state chairmen have some obligation to perform. The first is to maintain a working relationship with the state central committee, but, as was noted in chapter 4, this usually is determined by the manner in which the chairman was originally chosen. The way in which he discharges his duties will be closely tied to the method by which he was selected in the first place— by the governor or gubernatorial candidate, or independently by the state committee.

The second obligation is to maintain a working relationship with county, city, and other local grass-roots party units. Only in this way can a chairman hope to build a strong foundation for the state party superstructure. Furthermore, a cohesive party depends upon mediation and arbitration—a role which, in some states, the chairman alone is able to perform.

A third and relatively new undertaking for most state parties has been to serve as a source of substantive and political assistance to elected officeholders, particularly those who are members of the state legislature. This casts the chairman in the role of lobbyist. As such he finds that he is responsible for selling the programmatic goals of the elected party leaders and, in recent years, urging the party's position with regard to election law changes.

Finally, a fourth responsibility is to manage the party headquarters. Parties, like all large organizations, require an administrative structure in order to accomplish the goals assigned to them. There are funds to raise, people to hire, books to keep, plans to make, and political functions to perform. They require space and staff. The rapid growth of two-party politics accompanied by technocratic innovation has brought the management function to the forefront. The state chairman is responsible for seeing that it is carried out.

Obviously, not all political parties perform all political functions equally well. Indeed, some do not accept responsibility for performing them at all. Nevertheless, the number of permanent party headquarters has multiplied rapidly, and that fact alone signals the willingness of some party leaders to invest necessary resources in order to carry out the internal responsibilities of the party.

Working with the Central Committee

As noted in chapter 4, the working relationship between the state chairman and his party's central committee will vary according to role classification. It is usually of little consequence for a chairman serving his governor as a Political Agent to maintain much more than a perfunctory relationship with the state committee. Ordinarily the committee's *pro forma* endorsement of the governor's choice for chairman carries with it recognition by all that he will run the party as an agent of the chief executive.

Political Agents usually go through the motions of keeping the central committee informed or asking for ratification of some action already determined upon. Members of these committees are normally willing to go along with this arrangement because, as one Democrat put it, "after all, he got elected governor and [the chairman] managed his successful campaign. Who are we to argue with that?"

In some states the committee does not possess the power to act against the chairman even if it wanted to. In others the formal power is there, usually in the by-laws, but it is politically unwise for the committee to attempt to use it. The better course often seems to be to get along by going along.

In-Party Independents are much more likely to give attention to their state committee. They not only consult the members more often but they seek more votes as committee endorsement of their policies. Although majority support is usually certain, the mere fact that a vote is sought at all testifies to the more obsequious relationship of the In-Party Independent. He is well aware that the environment in which he operates is more dangerous and that he might be replaced by either the governor or the state committee.

The Out-Party Independent has the most dependent relationship with the state committee. There is no governor or other recognized party leader to becloud the lines of authority and responsibility. The committee is the closest thing available to a representative party body and, technically, has responsibility for the election of the chairman. The relationship between the chairman and the committee is much more complex than that faced by either of the other two types of chairmen. The chairman himself operates with more freedom and exercises more personal power as party leader. The committee members, however, are more cognizant of their position as the principal elected body representing the party. They are well aware that they elected the chairman without dictation. They talk convincingly of their supervisory role whether or not they actually have one. In some parties this greater sense of importance stems from adroit politicking by the chairman. He seeks the committee's support by appearing to ask its permission. As one committeeman put it: "I voted for him and his margin was pretty thin. He has really gone out of his way to show us that he knows we are boss. He consults us on everything before he actually goes ahead and does it."

Thus, the attitude of the chairman toward the state committee is dependent in large measure on the manner in which he was elected and whether or not his party controls the governorship. Aside from these considerations, the day-to-day relationship of the chairmen to their committees is a composite. Some consult regularly while others seldom do. Generally, neither the chairmen nor the committeemen and women expect their formal relationship to consume much of their time.

Patterns of State-Local Party Relationships

The great grass-roots party organization in the United States begins with the precinct, the smallest voting unit used by the states. The party hierarchy above that level, however, is shaped to a large extent by the urban-rural configuration of the political system. Committeemen and women in urban areas are usually elected from wards composed of groups of precincts. They, in turn, may be a part of a complex political machine or a loosely knit mass devoid of any centralizing force.

Rural party organizations center around the county unit in most states. A few in New England are based on townships, while some midwestern parties use the congressional district as a local party unit. Ultimately, however, it is the county that serves almost universally as the principal unit of local party government. In fact, the 3,050 counties in America constitute one of the most stable elements in the political structure. Some of them may be ineffective—even atrophied—but they have existed almost everywhere in some form for decades. The number of counties has not changed appreciably for years, withstanding the pressures of centralization and consolidation that reduced the numbers of other local government units. The stability of the county system has been a mixed blessing to the political parties. Stability has often translated into a deadly lack of dynamism in government, and that, in turn, has caused the party systems in those areas to atrophy.

Research involving grass-roots party officials is sparse. Much of it is impressionistic or descriptive of isolated, usually machine-style, organizations. Most of the metaphors used to describe the role of local party officials in the total party system rely heavily upon images of orderliness and precision—pyramids or concentric circles. They assume clear lines of authority and responsibility, clearly defined patterns of organization, and neatly structured divisions of power. The American parties, however, seldom match these assumptions. The lines are not that clean, the patterns are not that clear, and the structure is not that stable.

Instead, we have vast numbers of local party units that are dormant, precinct leaders who are elected independently of the party and owe no allegiance to it, and a confusing amalgam of party officials with separate goals and distinct personal followings. Now, that is not to say that there are no textbook party organizations anywhere. But they merely provide an added dimension to the problem of describing the American party system.

The party structure consists of a loosely formed hierarchy representing the various layers of the federal system of government. The decentralization of governmental authority associated with the national, state, and local levels is paralleled in the party system. Many of the problems associated with describing the party apparatus are really those associated with the complexities of the federal division of powers.

I have noted before that the state party organizations have emerged from their languor since World War II. The general impact has been a strengthening one, although some formerly strong parties have suffered disastrous reverses in recent years. In any dynamic system, however, there is constant change, and gains in some states may be accompanied by losses in others. If this is true of 100 state parties, it is true many times over for many thousands of local parties. It is the relationship between these two levels with which this chapter deals.

It is not an easy matter to categorize local party systems. Some are structured and militant, while others are disorganized and impotent. They range from cadre to mass membership parties, and they change from year to year as the fortunes of the national and state parties ebb and flow. The success of local party units may depend upon whether the parent state party is in or out of the governor's office—or that particular measure of success may have no impact whatever on the counties or wards.

Table 9.1 shows five patterns of state-local leadership relations. In the smallest of the categories (6.3 percent), the chairman was by-passed and had no role at all to play with the local party units. In these few states the governor, for various reasons, deliberately excluded the state chairman from his personal dealings with county or city leaders. A governor might be out of harmony with the chairman, by-passing him in order to establish direct control over local political affairs. In most such instances the chairmen were In-Party Independents elected prior to or in spite of the governor. In one case a governor established a personal network of local relationships because the state chairman failed to do so despite repeated urging.

The parties to such arrangements displayed different motives for operating outside party channels. In one western state, interviews were conducted on the same day with the governor, the state chairman, and a county chairwoman. According to the governor,

> I built a separate party structure within the governor's office to deal with the county chairmen. I deliberately chose weak state chairmen because I want to keep direct control over the local party. It seems to me that for the next three years I am the party. So I ought to be able to run the local party to my own satisfaction. My state chairman runs the office whenever he is in town and answers the mail.

The chairwoman of the county in which the state capital is located described her relationship with the governor and the state chairman:

> I get along very well with ———— as state chairman. But he lives 300 miles away and only comes to town every couple of weeks. If I really want something I call ———— in the governor's office. ———— runs the governor's

Table 9.1   Patterns of State-Local Party Relations

Relationship	Percentage (N80)
Governor by-passes state party to deal directly with local party units	6.3
State chairman deals with local party units in behalf of governor	25.0
In-party or out-party independent state chairman deals with local party units on own authority	32.5
Local units operate autonomously, independent of state party control	22.5
Local units are inactive for most part	13.7

NOTE: These classifications of normal state-local relationships were arrived at by a panel of three judges who read each series of responses and agreed upon a categorical allocation by majority vote.

political operation. They give me what I want because they can't afford not to. I have too much of the party's money behind me and I have too much influence. Since [the governor] doesn't want a strong state party because he doesn't want any threats, he works with about a half-dozen of us county people. It's been great for us so far.

The state chairman furnished his side of the relationship:

Yes, it is true that [the governor] by-passes me often. He does it primarily on patronage matters—both jobs and state contracts. He leaves the routine day-to-day operations to me, though, and he gives me special projects such as voter registration and state fund raising. I also organize the state conventions and help with recruitment. I was supposed to get our operation computerized, but [the county chairwoman for the capital] opened a county office and got [the major industry in town] to loan her computer time and stole my thunder. I just stay out of her business and hope that she stays out of mine.

Here, then, are three noncontradictory but differing accounts of the same web of relationships. They represent a not uncommon phenomenon in American state politics.

The second pattern of state-local party relations is not only more prevalent but also more traditional. As shown in table 9.1, 25 percent of the state chairmen deal directly with the city and county party officials in behalf of an incumbent governor. Most of these chairmen were Political Agents, although a few were In-Party Independents. Regardless of the level of organizational sophistication, the chairman has virtually all local party matters channeled through him and, in turn, transmits the political desires of the governor to the local leaders. This normally means that the state works with those county chairmen who are more important to the party's success. The state chairman noted:

County chairmen are important. But only certain county chairmen are important. Many either don't know what they are doing or are old-timers who hold on to their own little fiefdoms.

I have concentrated my attention on building support in those counties that support the governor and me. I ignore the other fifty.

Other state chairmen attempt to provide equality of treatment for county or ward leaders. The problems encountered are those generated by the great variety of local party systems. Some are rural and some are urban; some are active and some are not; some have strong activist leadership while others are controlled by individuals who maintain themselves in office for personal gratification. One midwesterner stated it this way:

My relationships with the county chairmen are generally good because I was a county chairman for so long. Our rural problems in ———— are organizational. It is very hard to maintain a rural organization. We control many of the counties and are seldom threatened, and that has allowed a lot of our party organizations to petrify.

Our city problems, on the other hand, are financial. It takes a lot of money to make a city organization go; yet that is the very place we do less well and money is harder to come by. It's a never-ending struggle to keep our local parties going, but we have to if the governor is to get the kind of local support he needs in dealing with the legislature.

The third group, and the largest of the five (32.5 percent), were those state chairmen who deal with local party organizations as independently elected leaders. They include both in- and out-party independents, each exercising the authority of the state party. The In-Party Independents have been given authority by the governor to run the party as they see fit. The Out-Party Independent *is,* usually, the real party leader. In either case the chairman recognizes himself as *the* party leader and uses the authority that gives him to seek cooperation on the local level. These chairmen have more freedom of action than do others, but collectively they may not have as much influence as the Political Agents who operate in behalf of a governor.

Out-Party Independents often try to invoke the authority of the state executive committee to strengthen their hand in local party relationships. In-Party Independents can invoke the prestige of the governor even though they operate relatively free of his control. Such subtle distinctions are sometimes not apparent except from the inside. Here too, though, the state chairman normally concentrates on selected counties. One Democrat from the Midwest stated:

We do not currently have the governorship. The Republicans won it unexpectedly two years ago. I was elected by the executive committee at that time, and I have its strong support.

My relation with the county parties is generally good. It is especially good with the active county leaders. You can easily spot those counties where the leadership is old and dead. The chairmen don't do anything. Where we have active chairmen, though, it is quite noticeable by seeing how many offices they win and how strong their bank account is. You can pick the good counties out because they are identified with good people.

As has been noted throughout this book, some local party organizations operate independently, either because they are ignored by the state leadership or because they have the power to insist on autonomy. Some of the 22.5 percent included in this group are independent only because they resist outside leadership as a threat to their personal tranquillity. They have done nothing in the past, plan little more for the future, and do not wish to have attention focused on their lack of initiative. In other instances the local leaders are strong and active but operate independently because the state party leadership is too weak to care. This is often true in highly politicized rural counties with long histories of independence from state control. It is also true of some tightly knit urban organizations. Sometimes they are modern-day versions of the machine politics of an earlier age.

Urban county chairmen can be individuals of eminent power. In New York the county leader has been a figure of power and prestige for decades. Although the era may be passing, the five county (borough) leaders of New York City and the leaders of some upstate counties have enjoyed control over recruitment, nominations, fund raising, and patronage within their own bailiwicks. They attempt to provide old-fashioned constituent services and to collect payment in voter support.

In 1970 the *New York Times* described the voter-related activities of James V. Mangano, one of forty-six Brooklyn Democratic leaders, whose political services are performed in exchange for votes. In one week, Mr. Mangano arranged for an Army private to be brought home from Vietnam to visit his ailing mother, secured school crossing guards for a parochial school, managed an inter-departmental transfer of an employee in a private business, and was successful in getting a retarded child admitted to a specialized school. Mr. Mangano acknowledged his hope that constituent satisfaction would be translated into voter support for Democrats.[3]

Mangano is one of the elected leaders in Brooklyn who serve Meade Esposito, the long-time leader of that borough's Democrats. Some, like Mangano and Erie County leader Joseph Crangle (Democratic state chairman from 1972 to 1975), hold patronage jobs with the state or county. Others, like Esposito, do not. Both New York City and the state of New York were under Republican control during this period, but there were still rewards for Democrats to distribute. In addition to many patronage positions for leaders, the Democratic state controller invests $4 billion in retirement funds and $58 million is deposited in banks. Some New York county organizations derive power from their ability to fill vacancies on city councils, nominate judicial candidates and their law secretaries, arrange for judicial patronage (trusteeships, receiverships, guardianships, and so on), and to nominate candidates for the state legislature. Because of high stakes and strongly personal competition among the leadership, there is considerable infighting throughout the local parties of New York State.

The New York Democratic county organization is a modern version of a nineteenth-century machine. The county organizations are far from invincible, as shown by the nearly unanimous failure of their endorsees for top state offices in the 1974 primary. But they have enough successes to permit them to continue their independence of the state Democratic party.

Although Mayor Richard Daley's control over the Cook County Democratic party had begun to crack by 1974, for twenty years it represented the kind of local party independence of the state party organization of which we have been speaking. In fact, at times it appeared that the Illinois Democratic party was little more than an appendage of the Daley machine, although there was a division of power between Daley, who presided over Cook County, and the state Democratic chairman, who was permitted to preside over downstate counties.

In the nation's rural counties the role of the organization is usually intimately tied to courthouse politics. Rural party leaders can personalize politics to a greater extent than their urban colleagues. Rewards and punishments have a greater impact upon the party. An active county party leader keeps in close touch with the party's officeholders as well as with local party leaders. The tasks required of him are endless. Many, however, do not perceive an active role for themselves. They do not choose to exercise the power which they have, or they do not have the resourcefulness to do so. One of the most striking phenomena in American politics is the widespread dormancy prevalent at the grass-roots level.

Of the state chairmen included in this study, 13.7 percent reported their local party organizations to be inactive. Their debility results from a number of factors. Some of them represent the minority party in a one-party state, where the lack of political reward kills political stimulus.

An illustration was reported from a rural Georgia county Republican party:

William C. Peterson, Chairman of the Treutlen County Republican Committee, was presented an award . . . for attaining his GOP fund-raising goal. . . .

Amazed that Peterson could maintain a Republican organization in a rural county traditionally controlled by Democratic machine politics, a reporter asked Peterson about GOP strength in Treutlen.

"There are four of us around Soperton who will admit to being Republicans—me and my wife, and another fellow and his wife" Peterson smiles, but he adds that there may be a little more GOP strength than that. "In the last election 24 people . . . voted Republican." [4]

There are many Treutlen counties in America—counties which have been so one-party dominated that the organization of an opposition party was impossible.

Other counties are dominated by an old-line party machine which the state chairman views as Neanderthal and nonproductive. One southern Democratic chairman noted that "The county chairmen aren't of the slightest importance to me. I pay no attention to them at all. In fact, I would be glad to drive them all out of the party and into the Republican party so we could start fresh. They are all Wallaceites."

Another small group of respondents reported that their local organizations were lacking in strength or interest because the party's gubernatorial and other statewide candidates, almost all of whom are successful, simply ignore the party in favor of personal campaign organizations. Once elected, they continued to ignore the formal party leaders in favor of those personal supporters who aided them in their campaigns. Without regular use, the local party organizations fall into a lethargy not easily shaken.

Working with Local Parties

Many state party officials speak with considerable conviction about their efforts to strengthen local party organizations. The recent emphasis in some states on professionalization has permitted the state chairmen to offer greater assistance and expanded services to the city and county groups in an effort to make them more viable instruments of party politics. The opportunities for experimentation have expanded and the resources available have improved. Most chairmen acknowledge their interest in assisting local parties but are frustrated in their efforts to do so. As shown in table 9.2, 28.5 percent of the chairmen reported no assistance whatsoever to the city and county organizations. Sometimes this was because the state party was too weak to offer assistance; and sometimes the local units were offered aid but rejected it, often because of personal jealousies, internal rivalries, or policy disagreements between the state and local parties.

A study of local officials in five communities conducted in 1963 found that most of them concentrated their attention on campaign-related activities such as contacting voters, raising money, or participating in voter registration drives. The second most frequently mentioned activity was party organizational work, which included participation in meetings, recruitment of workers, and assisting with organizational activites. Other activities were oriented toward ideological matters and nominations.[5]

Table 9.2   State Party Aid to Local Party Units

Type of assistance provided	Responses of state chairmen in percentages*
Patronage clearance	30.2
Research assistance (voting records, speech materials, informational services, etc.)	28.4
Fund-raising programs	20.8
Get-out-the-vote drives	19.1
Organizational development (training sessions, mediation between factions, worker recruitment, etc.)	15.7
Legal information (delegate selection procedures, financial disclosure laws, campaign finance reporting, etc.)	11.2
Voter registration drives	10.3
Candidate recruitment for local contests	8.3
Staff services through field aides	5.2
None (weak state or local party organizations; assistance offered but rejected; etc.)	28.5

* Column does not total to 100 percent due to multiple responses. Since respondents were all state chairmen, it is possible that these responses might be exaggerated since some chairmen might view the availability of these services as a measure of their own success. Efforts to spot-check the accuracy of the responses with local party officials did not raise any serious questions as to their accuracy, however, and it is believed that they are a fair reflection of the services offered.

The state chairmen do not view their relations with local party officials in so compartmentalized a fashion. The distinctions are blurred and ill defined. They do not perceive that organizational functions differ markedly from the campaign-related activities of fund raising, contacting voters, or getting people to register. Both organizational and campaign activities are directed at the most evident measurement of success—the number of offices won or lost. Electoral success provides a visible, although not altogether realistic, measure of party effectiveness. Most local party people, therefore, insist upon maintaining direct control over local campaigns insofar as candidates will let them. Consequently, state party people enter into local campaigns only when asked. Briefly, let us review the activities associated with each form of state party assistance, as shown in table 9.2.

Patronage clearance   The role of the state party in patronage decisions was discussed in chapter 5. More state chairman (30.0 percent) reported this kind of assistance than any other single type. Clearance, as noted earlier, is a two-way street. The local party, on the one hand, can suggest local supporters as nominees for positions, in which case the state party leadership must decide whether to approve the nomination. More often than not, though, the nomination is made by people outside the local jurisdiction. This triggers a process of clearance designed to protect the local party's territorial rights. Clearance of patronage appointees, according to many politicians, is both a blessing and a curse. It is normally necessary, however, to protect the tranquillity of the infrastructure of the party.

Research assistance   Over one-fourth of the state organizations attempt to provide research assistance to local party groups. Many local organizations are not equipped in either money or manpower resources to undertake the kind of staffing and record keeping necessary to maintain a research operation. In recent years there has been a vast expansion in the number of state party organizations capable of providing this kind of assistance. Obviously, the caliber of the product varies greatly, but 28.4 percent of the respondents could cite some effort to provide campaign or organizational data to local candidates, managers, or headquarters personnel.

The better research divisions have undertaken to maintain computerized legislative voting records, especially those of the opposition party members. Some have expanded this service to include members of their own party, although this is often controversial inasmuch as it provides primary opponents ammunition to use against incumbent legislators. The most traditional research products are informational materials for use in speeches, advertisements, and campaign literature. There is an enormous flow of such materials from the two national committees as well as the campaign headquarters of presidential candidates, but there are few sources for local and state races. Consequently, some state party leaders are beginning to initiate efforts to disseminate such materials insofar as their headquarters or campaign budgets will permit, but compared to national party research efforts, or those of pressure groups and private enterprise, state political research is in its infancy.

Fund raising   Most of the 20.8 percent who made an effort to assist local party units in meeting their funding needs did so (1) by providing name speakers for local fund-raising dinners or (2) by providing pre-printed mailing labels or envelopes for a finance drive. Some attempted to assist with headquarters expertise in money-raising techniques, but this was generally in the large states with sizable numbers of party staff experts.

Get-out-the-vote drives   State headquarters personnel are becoming more interested than they once were in drives to get out the vote on election day. Democrats in many areas have serious turnout problems among those voters who have provided traditional support for their party. At the same time they have benefited from the get-out-the-vote drives of private groups such as organized labor. Republican party officials express less interest in get-out-the-vote drives than do their Democratic counterparts. This is partly because Republican voters are more likely to go to the polls on their own without outside urging. Some GOP state leaders also said that it was more difficult to persuade Republican workers to take part in such drives. In spite of the continuing decline in voter participation, only 19.1 percent of the chairmen indicated that get-out-the-vote drives were a part of the services they offered to local parties.

Organizational development   In a sense, state party assistance in the development of local organizations is a catchall for a variety of activities associated with party politics. The kinds of activities cited by the 15.7 percent who acknowledged their involvement included conducting training sessions for candidates and/or workers, recruiting workers, mediating factional disputes, and locating potential local leaders in order to revitalize a moribund party. Most of those included in this category had undertaken (often for the first time) to develop formal campaign schools for managers, candidates, and/or workers. The quality of these programs varied greatly, but their growth in popularity suggests a new area of growth potential for state parties. (An example is described in a case study later in this chapter.) Some of those who offered training sessions also worked to bring new volunteer workers into the party through programs outlined and implemented by state party personnel. A few were called into wards or counties to act as mediators between warring factions. Most state chairmen resist being drawn into factional disputes because they fear alienating key people in one or both factions. When open warfare breaks out, however, it is often necessary to become involved in order to protect the party's name or to save the local organization.

Legal information   With the advent of financial disclosure laws, detailed campaign finance controls, and complicated delegate selection procedures, state chairmen have been more and more beset by demands for legal assistance on the part of local party officials. Most of the 11.2 percent who noted this kind of assistance to local officials provided generalized legal aid rather than particularized legal advice. The chairmen usually resisted efforts to demand specific "advisory opinions" but relied instead on prepared descriptions aimed at providing generalized assistance in completing official forms or performing particular functions. At times, however, the need for legal advice became more demanding as lawsuits were threatened and local party chiefs asked for counsel.

Voter registration drives   Much emphasis has been put on efforts to increase the number of registered voters in recent years. Most of it, however, has been generated by private groups. The parties have never maintained consistent interest in increasing the potential vote. Periodically one or the other of the national parties organizes a registration drive, but they are almost always underfunded and understaffed and usually fade in the aftermath of an election. More successful efforts have been those of the League of Women Voters and other citizen groups which concentrate upon regular, nonpartisan registration drives. The undisputed champion at voter registration, however, is the AFL-CIO through its political education arm COPE. Theodore H. White reported that in 1968 organized labor registered 4.6 million voters prior to the presidential election. Almost one-half million were registered in Pennsylvania alone while 690,000 were signed up in Michigan. White estimated that labor spent nearly $10 million on registration, almost all designed to benefit the Democratic party.[6]

Only 10.3 percent of the state party organizations engaged in any type of registration activity at all. Generally, the state headquarters provided encouragement and back-up support to local party efforts. This normally took the form of training sessions for registration workers, negotiations with local election officials to gain proper certification or deputization for party registrars, or funding support.

Candidate recruitment   It was noted in chapter 5 that 73.8 percent of the state chairmen engaged in some form of candidate recruitment. These efforts were usually directed at state offices down to and including the legislature. Recruitment activities for city and county offices have traditionally been left to local party organizations, and most of them have been unwilling to call upon the state party for assistance in the delicate process of persuading potential candidates to run. Some have expressed jealous resentment of outside interference. Others have undertaken to organize recruitment activities themselves and have been quite successful at it. Only 8.3 percent of the state chairmen reported any role in local recruitment efforts, and those who did usually had been called in to assist in filling the ticket of a minority party in a noncompetitive system. It is difficult for local chairmen to persuade local citizens to run in hopeless contests, and in these few instances the city or county chairman appealed to the state party chairman for help in getting reluctant potential candidates to run. Sometimes a personal call from the state chairman to the individual being sought would suffice, but on some occasions the governor himself was enlisted in the effort.

Staff services   Most state parties cannot afford to furnish field men or women to local organizations. The 5.2 percent who do normally involve them in campaigns only. Field men can bring an expertise to the mechanical aspects of campaigning that would otherwise be unavailable. They can assist with public relations, opinion polling, telephone banks, and other modern campaign techniques. They serve another function, however, in that they provide a means through which the state headquarters people can be kept informed of local campaign progress.

State chairmen make little distinction between pure campaign assistance and ongoing organizational aid. Most profess to believe that the campaign is but an extension of the organization—that is, you cannot have one without the other.

Strengthening Local Parties:
A Case Study of the Florida Democrats

Prior to the growth of the Republican party in the state, Florida Democrats have never been forced to worry about formal party organization. Campaigns were traditionally run by personal organizations, and the party did not even have a state headquarters until 1966. With the election of Republican Governor Claude Kirk in 1966 and Senator Edward Gurney in 1968, however, the party organizations in the state began to develop at a rapid rate.

After being selected as state chairman by newly elected Governor Reubin Askew in 1970, Jon Moyle began to search for ways to strengthen the Democratic party at the county level. He and his staff, working with a Washington, D.C., political consultant firm, developed an experimental program called the Servicenter program, which was designed to:

build the kind of party structure in Florida that:

(a) brings into the party as many people as possible who share broad Democratic ideals and goals,

(b) uses these party workers as the basis for responsiveness between voters and their government, and

(c) equips these workers with the tools of campaign success so that mandates for action can be sought and won from the voters at large.[7]

The three basic aims of the Servicenter program within these broad goals were to:

1. Provide resource development such as computerized printouts targeting contributions, research, or issues, and voting record information on Republican incumbents in the legislature

2. Establish a delivery program to explain to county party workers and leaders how to use the materials once they are made available

3. Establish a training program to prepare volunteers to use the services which are provided

None of these programs is new to politics. They have all been provided by state parties to county parties before. But in Florida Democratic leadership was concerned that the raw materials were of little use to local parties if the county volunteers did not understand what it was they were supposed to do. The real mission of the Servicenter program was to provide a corps of workers in each target county who would know how to read a printout, run a sophisticated voter profile program, or successfully inaugurate a fund-raising project.

An initial survey of Florida Democrats suggested that a potential for effective local campaign assistance did exist. When asked if they would be willing to work ten to fifteen hours for their party during the campaign period, 39 percent replied in the affirmative; 38 percent said that they would be willing to contribute from $5 to $25 to the Democratic state party for use in the campaign; and 25 percent agreed to both. These positive responses, plus the soaring costs of election campaigning, added a new dimension to the importance of volunteer resources in politics. The Servicenter project was basically a system of tapping those resources in such a way that they would make a positive contribution to Democratic electoral successes. A by-product, it was hoped, would be a continuing interest in party affairs by the newly recruited and trained volunteers.

The Servicenter project was carried out through a series of forty-seven county training sessions that exposed 1,100 volunteers to the program. Sessions had been planned for fifty of Florida's sixty-seven counties in hopes of reaching 1,500 volunteers, but a few programs did not materialize. Each county session was limited to thirty volunteers. The sessions, run by the executive director of the state Democratic party and his aides, began with an overview of politics and the potential for group action. They extended over two days on successive weekends from January through June 1974. Each series concluded with a wrap-up session designed to put the training into the perspective of practical politics.

The sessions were built around a series of handbooks produced and copyrighted by Allem/Hamilton, a Washington-based consultant firm with old ties to the Florida Democratic party. One, entitled *Getting Democrats to Work,* described the process by which volunteer workers are recruited. Another 27-page handbook explained the process of *Getting Democrats to Give,* while still another provided detailed motivations for *Getting Democrats to Vote.* Following the introductory overview, a typical two-day training session carried the class step by step through work plans to recruit volunteers, raise funds, target resources, and bring out the vote.

The Servicenter program cost the state committee approximately $55,000, or about $50 per volunteer. While the immediate goal was a massive get-out-the-vote drive on election day, one long-range goal was to permanently establish an actual and ongoing cadre of volunteers who would continue to lend their energies and their talents to the Democratic party at the county level. John French, executive director of the state Democratic party, put it succinctly when he said: "Motivated people are a dime a dozen. People who can use their skills are rare."

As is often the case, the results of the first Servicenter effort in 1974 were mixed. State party leaders were disappointed that many of the volunteers trained in the county sessions defected to work for individual candidates. This, of course, had a salutary effect on those who benefited from their help but did not provide direct assistance to the ticket as a whole. Some leaders expressed disappointment that the effort to broaden the base of the party was not successful. Entrenched county leaders were not anxious to participate in a program which they expected would undercut their authority. A substantial number of new Democratic officeholders, however, may owe their allegiance to the state party and not to the old county leaders.

The major thrust of the Servicenter effort, of course, was designed to get out the vote. In practice, this involved three techniques:

1. A telephone canvas of three major counties during which 70,000 contacts were made urging voters to go to the polls and vote Democratic

2. A door-to-door literature distribution, originally intended to gather information on voter motivation but thwarted by a shortage of volunteers committed to the state party

3. A "sweep" canvas intended to include large numbers of neighborhood door-to-door contacts to remind people of the approaching election

As described by party leaders after the 1974 election, the Servicenter program produced the following results:

1. Over $130,000 contributed directly to opposed candidates

2. Distribution of over 100,000 plastic bags filled with campaign literature and used in targeted precincts

3. Over 1,800 radio spots broadcast throughout Florida urging citizens to vote

4. Thousands of telephone contacts with voters, including 70,000 in Miami, Jacksonville, and Tampa alone

5. Personal visits by volunteers to 180,000 households in 550 precincts

6. Mail-o-grams (computer-printed telegram look-alikes) urging support of Democratic candidates sent to 153,000 homes in targeted precincts.

7. Analysis of precinct-by-precinct results in the 24 most populous counties to identify Democratic support areas

8. Precinct lists by street address provided for those counties with computerized voter registration lists

9. Republican voting records distributed to nonincumbent Democratic candidates

10. Lists of names and addresses of over 2 million of the state's 3.5 million registered Democrats compiled for storage in the computer files

Many of the benefits of the program are permanent. Nevertheless, the new state chairwoman in early 1975 was forced to terminate many of the Servicenter programs because of costs. Ann Cramer announced shortly after taking office that the state party was nearly $9,000 in debt and could not afford to continue the program.

There is so much variation in the level of performance of party organizations at the city and county levels that generalized comment is virtually impossible. There has been little empirical research to show the degree to which local organizations do their jobs, and there is none whatever that measures the levels of improvement in their performance over time. Much of the available research is noncomparable and provides little guidance on the growth in the role of local parties. Some scholars have viewed local organizational activity from local perspectives; others have relied upon state party officials for information regarding local operations. Some have striven for empirical accuracy, while others have been content with impressionistic descriptive accounts of selected local organizations. Both have made contributions to knowledge but not nearly on the scale that the study of state legislatures, national party organizations, Congress, or the judiciary has.

The fact is that organization implies party discipline, and discipline implies authority. Yet discipline and authority are no easier to measure than they were in 1900. They are elusive qualities which refuse to lend themselves readily to empirical research. Consequently, what we do know about local party organizational activity remains fragmented and lacking in substance.

The State Chairman and Legislative Liaison

There are four points at which the average state legislator may be touched by his political party. The first three—recruitment, nomination, and election—have been discussed in earlier chapters. All of them occur on or before election day. The fourth, however, relates to the lawmaker in his legislative role. A majority of the state party organizations now maintain some degree of regular liaison with legislators elected under their party's banner. These contacts take three forms: (1) efforts by the party to persuade legislators to support substantive policy legislation; (2) efforts to gain support for election law changes; and (3) services provided to members by the state headquarters.

Efforts to generate legislative support for substantive policy proposals emerge more often in parties which control the governorship. It is important to the success of the governor's program and the adoption of the party's platform that legislators be supportive. It is sometimes important to the legislator because some party leaders have sufficient power to inhibit the ambitions of those who wish to move up. Consequently, it is commonplace for Political Agents to work the legislative lobbies in behalf of administration bills. Many of these efforts in the early 1970s dealt with tax packages which usually became divisive issues between the parties. One Republican chairman described his lobbyist role in this way:

> The governor proposed an income tax, even though we all thought it was suicidal. I ended up in the role of villain because the burden of selling it to our group fell on me and ————, the governor's chief political staffer. We spent three weeks doing nothing else. We threatened. We begged. We bought. But we still couldn't get a majority. We just barely got a majority of our own group in the House.

Other issues, such as mass transit, land use regulation, and social welfare, were also lobbied by state chairmen. Inherently controversial issues, such as abortion reform and the Equal Rights Amendment, were usually avoided as divisive. Because those issues, as well as other moral or ethical questions, cut across party lines and tend to require highly personal judgments, most party leaders are content to leave them to individual decision.

A second area of contact between the chairmen and the legislators concerned proposed changes in election laws and laws affecting party organization. After the 1968 national conventions, both parties undertook to revise the rules and/or the structure of their organizations. The recommendations which emerged from the McGovern-Fraser Commission of the Democratic party and the Delegates and Organization (DO) Committee of the Republican party required extensive revisions of law in many states. Between 1968 and 1972 state legislators were called upon to bring the state laws governing the parties into line with national party requirements. These changes dealt with delegate selection, equal rights to participation, and mechanical revisions to prohibit proxy voting, fee requirements as a prerequisite for serving as a delegate, or other less significant matters. Although many changes were accomplished by routine amendment of party by-laws, almost every state legislature was involved in one way or another. After 1972 the Watergate scandals prompted a considerable public outcry for election reform, and by 1974 these public pressures had resulted in widespread changes. Several states adopted laws establishing election commissions with varying degrees of enforcement power. Others set new limits on campaign spending and attempted to regulate "dirty tricks," while still others moved to financial disclosure of personal income as a means of restoring public confidence in the electoral system. New systems of voter registration were considered, and legislation permitting greater experimentation in the use of voting machines was adopted. The states proved to be real laboratories of experimentation, as originally envisioned by the founding fathers.[8]

Each of these proposed bills affected the political parties in the state. In some instances the party leaders were called upon to provide ideas and drafts to the legislators. In other states the bills emerged in the session without prior consultation with party officials. One Republican chairman in a state with a Democratic legislature described his surprise when

I got to the office one morning and discovered in the newspaper that the leadership of both parties had jointly introduced a series of bills which we could not support. The Democrats in the House were just as upset as we were but didn't want to offend the governor. We were eventually able to get some restrictive amendments adopted, but most of the package passed. . . . I would have to admit that the results so far have not been nearly as bad as I thought they would be.

An unusual cooperative venture in Michigan found the Republican and Democratic parties joining together to recommend a package of revision bills and constitutional amendments covering the method of selection of judges and other state officers, party registration, election recounts, use of voting machines, and the recruitment and training of poll workers. Other areas were discussed by a joint committee representing both parties, but agreement could be reached only on those listed. The most far-reaching proposal provided for the adoption of a party registration system which, if adopted, would remove Michigan from the group of fourteen states which did not use voter registration in 1973. The initiative for this cooperative venture came from the Republican State Committee, and the result was the creation of a permanent, ten-member, bipartisan committee to consider further election reforms.[9]

State chairmen often found themselves in the role of lobbyist regarding proposed bills which would affect the parties or the political system in general. The adoption of Florida's new election laws in 1973 was a case in point. Both the Democratic state chairman, Jon Moyle, and the Republican state chairman, L. T. (Tommy) Thomas, were active in seeking passage of the legislation, although both sought amendments to the original bills that were introduced by a House Elections Committee. One result was the establishment of the Florida Elections Commission, the selection of which closely involved the two party chairmen. Under the law, each chairman nominates fifteen party members to the governor. From this list of thirty nominees, Governor Reubin Askew appointed three Democrats and three Republicans who took office after confirmation by the Florida Senate. The six commissioners then nominated three persons to the governor, one of whom was appointed as the seventh commissioner and chairman. New appointments are to be made in the same manner. This was the first direct legal involvement of the state party chairmen in the process of appointing state election officials.

As table 9.3 shows, over half of the chairmen (56.25 percent) reported a close relationship with many members of their legislature. An additional 11.25 percent had a limited relationship with some members, but these usually included no more than one or two contacts per session. A mere 5 percent dealt exclusively with the leadership, and 27.5 percent had no relationship at all. The latter group of respondents represented states with one-party legislative domination or a tradition of noninvolvement in legislative affairs.

Also included are a couple of respondents who reported a single, rare legislature effort:

We play a very small role with the legislature. We leave them alone and they get elected on their own. We assume they are going to support the party, and for the most part they do. Only one time in five years have I actually had to talk with legislators on an issue and that was a veterans' issue the governor had staked his reputation on. I actually went over there and lobbied members. That is extremely rare. We just ignore them.

Finally, the growth of headquarters services to party leaders and members may be one of the most significant aspects of this study. Over half of the state parties now provide some form of service to their state legislative delegation. As shown in table 9.4, these services range from research assistance and public relations aid to fund raising, legal advice,

Table 9.3   Nature of relationship Between State Chairman and Legislators

Relationship	Percentage (N80)
Close (with most party legislators)	56.25
Limited (with some members)	11.25
Limited to leadership only	5.00
Nonexistent	27.50

speech writing, and campaign help. Only 35 percent of the respondent chairmen reported that they provided no headquarters services to their legislators at all. Sometimes this resulted from lack of initiative or lack of resources in the party headquarters, but that was not always the case. One chairman of a small state's Republican party explained: "The state legislators of _____ want to be on their own. We don't offer them much—never have. Up until now we didn't have anything to offer them. So the candidates and the members don't expect anything."

More chairmen (32 percent) reported providing legal aid than any other type of assistance. This was due in large part to the nationwide rash of legislation which was required to meet citizen demands for financial disclosure, more democratic delegate selection, and limitations on campaign finance. There is certainly some effort to answer legal questions at all times, but the period of these interviews coincided with great levels of activity in all these areas and, without doubt, greatly escalated the headquarters' responses to requests for legal aid. This might be called a legislative service of a lawmaking nature.

The legislative appetite for research services has become more voracious with every passing year. Back-up for bill drafting and spot research for speeches and debates consume an enormous amount of time and energy where they are available within the legislative establishment. Most of these needs are met through the legislative reference service and bill-drafting agencies set up by some of the legislatures themselves. In those

Table 9.4   Services Performed by State Party for Legislators

Service	Percentage (N80)
Research (bill drafting, spot research, etc.)	17.50
Public relations (new releases, radio-TV spots, etc.)	12.25
Fund-raising (dinners, speakers, mailings, etc.)	27.50
Legal assistance (delegate selection, financial disclosure, campaign finance, etc.)	32.00
Campaign assistance (speakers, field men, caravans, printing, etc.)	27.50
None	35.00
NA/DK	5.00

NOTE: Column totals to more than 100 percent due to multiple responses.

states which do not provide these services, however, members sometimes turn to the headquarters of their political party for assistance. Even so, except for some of the larger and better-financed headquarters, most parties have not been able to undertake the level of research operations necessary to perform this job. Only 17.5 percent of the chairmen claimed to provide some level of research service to members of the state legislature.

Three other services provided by state party headquarters were primarily campaign oriented. Fund-raising assistance was provided by 27.5 percent and encompassed mailings, WATS lines, selection of speakers, and other services to help make local fund-raising dinners successful. Another 27.5 percent provided general assistance to legislative campaigns, usually in the form of printing, speakers, staff field men, or sponsorship of candidate caravans traveling through the district. Finally, 12.25 percent furnished legislators with public relations services. Almost always confined to the period of the session or the campaign, such assistance included TV and radio spots, news releases, or canned weekly columns.

It is clear that many party agencies are limited in the resources available to aid legislators. Some provide one or two services only; others are well staffed and funded and offer a wide variety of assistance. One sophisticated Republican headquarters operation was geared almost exclusively to the legislators and was described by the chairman as follows:

Our main thrust is toward the legislature. The state headquarters is primarily a service organization: we avoid ideological disputes; we never get into a primary contest unless we have recruited the candidate and owe him an obligation. Our platform committee consists mostly of legislators. The platform is a legislative election device. I engage in candidate recruitment. Forty-five percent of the legislators were first-termers in 1968. Recruitment was very important. The state headquarters compiled election statistics and legislative statistics for our candidates. Each cabinet officer prepared a position paper for the use of candidates. Two weeks after the primaries, we held a two-day seminar on issues and organizations. A master campaign speech which dealt with problems of the state was drafted, and we established a party line. During the campaign, state headquarters was coordinator of campaigns. We provided money for the candidates. Three formulas were used. The safe districts got as little as possible. Districts that were Democratic got as much as possible, to help the Republican candidate for the best possible campaign. Marginal districts, which were one-third of the total, got most of the money. Contests cost varying amounts depending on the media cost. We won two-thirds of them, however.

We have what amounts to a twenty-four-month legislative campaign. We go at it all the time. We don't believe that a legislative campaign can simply gear up and go for a month or so before the election. It has to be done on a full-time basis.

As chairman I try to moderate the differences between party leaders. We furnish a weekly column for the weekly newspapers in the smaller counties to which the legislator can add his name. The columns are carried in the newspaper usually with a picture of the legislator as well as his by-line. We maintain a full-time photographer, we have a weekly radio program for fifty radio stations, and all the time we are emphasizing the legislature.

It is noteworthy that seven state chairmen were members of their respective legislatures at the time of these interviews, but the dual role appeared to have little relationship to the level of services performed for legislators.

State legislators are probably subject to greater sanctions and control from state parties than congressmen are from national party agencies. Most attempts to empirically measure levels of control have been unsatisfactory. Nevertheless, even though proof is lacking, the impression remains that the services provided by the party to the legislators are likely to have an impact upon the loyalty of the members to the party and/or its leaders.

The Party Headquarters: A Reflection of Professional Growth

The state headquarters should be the nerve center of the political party. It should be the focal point for recruitment, patronage clearance, campaign strategy, public opinion analysis, research, fund raising, data processing, public relations, the newsletter, and relations with other party groups. The fact is, however, that many state party leaders did not recognize the value of a headquarters operation until recently.

Even though less than 10 of the 100 state parties currently operate without a state headquarters, over 50 percent were developed since 1960.* The exact number of party headquarters must remain indefinite

---

* A personal note might serve to illustrate this point. While a staff member of the Republican National Committee in 1962–63, I made campaign or organizational trips to eighteen state Republican parties. Of the eighteen state parties visited,

at any given time. There is some fluidity in that a party occasionally is unable to continue operating a headquarters because of temporary financial setbacks. Furthermore, there is a definitional problem in that a few chairmen call their personal place of business the headquarters. Generally, the operating definition used here requires that office space be rented or leased outside the state chairman's home or place of employment. That necessarily describes a building open to the public from which state party affairs are conducted.

There appear to have been three forces at work in the past twenty years which led to the rapid escalation of the number of permanent state headquarters. The first was the rapid growth of two-party competition in many states. This, of course, accounted for the large numbers of new party headquarters in the South. As the fledgling Republican parties grew in the southern states, they opened headquarters to provide greater visibility and a base for party building. This, in turn, was often responsible for the opening of southern Democratic headquarters, which had not been needed in the past to maintain that party's monopoly.

Second, a need for state headquarters grew out of the trend toward party professionalism which usually carried with it increased demands for service from constituent groups. Any state party's determination to assist local parties in fund raising, mailing, public relations, or campaigns required permanent staff as well as centralized contact points. At the same time, county and city demands on state headquarters accelerated as the national party's guidelines on delegate selection were put into effect or as legislation on campaign finance and other election reforms became effective.

Finally, the creation of the national state chairmen's organizations brought party leaders together. These meetings enabled them to compare notes and discover what others were doing. When those without headquarters were exposed to those with, they were forced to conclude that there were advantages to be reaped from this symbol of permanence and respectability.

All but one of the existing headquarters operate the year around. Fifty-two percent lease space, while 31 percent rent, and 10 percent own their headquarters building. Most headquarters (57 percent) are located in a downtown business building in the state capital; 15 percent maintain

---

seven did not have a permanent state headquarters. Now, twelve years later, all but one of those eighteen state parties maintain a permanently staffed Republican headquarters. I visited thirty state headquarters during the course of this study.

a separate building; 9 percent a storefront; and 4 percent a hotel suite. Party headquarters range in size from two to fifteen rooms with the average being about four or five.

There is a general consensus among party leaders that the headquarters should be permanently located, and 75 percent of them are. Ten percent, however, are moved to the home town of each newly elected chairman. This has the obvious advantage of being convenient to the chairman but the considerable disadvantage of inconvenience to other party officers, legislators, and elected state officials. The remaining 15 percent were so new that no decision had yet been made as to permanence of location.

Headquarters staff ranged from a single secretary-receptionist to as many as thirty, including division heads and specialists. The median staff size was five people during nonelection periods and ten during campaign periods.

The annual costs of operating a full-time, permanent state headquarters depend on whether it is an election year or not. Off-year operating budgets were reported from under $25,000 to almost $1,500,000. The median expenditure was about $100,000. Election-year operating budgets escalate rapidly. Taking into account the 27 percent who reported that operating expenditures remained the same in election and nonelection years, the median expenditure in election years rose to about $225,000, and one chairman reported operating costs of over $2,000,000.*

Party fortunes often determine the level at which state party headquarters can function. In one western state the Democratic party headquarters operated out of one and one-half rooms on the ground floor of a hotel. The half-time secretary said that no one ever visited and that she spent most of her time answering correspondence for the chairman who dictated letters over the phone from his home. The state party performed no services, and the headquarters served as little more than a mailing address.

When Joseph F. Crangle took over as New York Democratic chairman, he found a $300,000 debt and the headquarters suite of seven rooms staffed by a switchboard operator and a part-time research clerk.

---

* These figures must be viewed with some caution, as respondents were unable to clearly differentiate between "headquarters" and "campaign" expenses in all cases. This is clear from the fact that 21 percent could furnish no figures for election-year operating expenditures at all. Most of them contended that many of the services they performed for candidates during a campaign are always available but are not used except in election periods.

He promptly organized a $25-per-year sustaining program to try to get the headquarters back in operation and later moved to less extensive quarters.[10]

In spite of financial travail, most chairmen contend that maintaining a full-time headquarters is the first priority for their parties. It not only permits the party to provide services to its officeholders and members but has an immeasurable symbolic meaning. The existence of a head-quarters, no matter how poorly funded or meagerly staffed, is a symbol of vitality. It serves to inform the faithful that the party is functioning and that there really is a party banner to rally around.

Improving Relations between State and Local Parties

By its very nature American politics generates natural tensions between elected officials and party leaders. They represent different constituencies, both compete for money and workers, and neither can demand loyalty or cooperation from the other. One of the many phenomena of the past two decades of party history has been the intensified efforts of state party leaders to bring the two groups more closely together.

These efforts have required the skills of a political impressario. Obviously, not all chairmen and women have qualified, nor have some who did been successful. The focal point of these labors has been the state party headquarters. Without the growth and expansion of headquarters operations, it would not have been possible to do many of the things that have been done. Headquarters serves as a symbol of permanence and stability. It provides a base from which to direct party-building efforts. It permits the party to offer the advantages of technocratic political services if necessary resources are available for support.

Nevertheless, the gap between elected officials and party officers cannot be bridged by a new or expanded headquarters alone. There must also be concentrated effort on both sides to bring about greater degrees of cooperation and mutual loyalty within the party. These goals cannot be accomplished unless the chairman, with the support of his state committee, can persuade city and county party leaders and legislators that it is worth their while to work with the state party. Most of the expanded services described in this and prior chapters serve tangentially to accomplish that goal. Ultimately, the survival of the party system may depend on greater cooperation; and that in turn may depend on the ability of the party organization to prove its usefulness to the elected leadership.

10   The Evolving Party System
in the States

State political parties began as loose
aggregations of people who shared beliefs or who wished to cooperate in
a quest for control of the government. Parties were essentially private
organizations, outside the purview of constitutions and laws. That was
the nature of parties until after the Civil War. In many states parties were
strong and effective, performing all the duties normally assigned to them
by definition. In still others, the parties never reached maturity at all and,
in some cases, are only now stirring with life.

The first half of this century was not a good period for party development. Political scandals, bribery, "boss rule," and big-city machines
caused many people to demand that party organizations be brought
within the law. During that period the party organizations watched as
their power and influence waned and their effectiveness eroded. There
were a number of reasons for their difficulties.

The Decline of Party Organization and Influence

The most easily identified reason for the decline was the emergence of the Progressive Era which extended roughly from the Spanish-American War to the years immediately following World War I. The American political parties were the prime institutional casualties of the Progressive movement led by Robert LaFollette of Wisconsin. The Progressives' advocacy of institutional innovation may have strengthened democracy, by their definition, but it undercut party government and political organizations at almost every turn.

Foremost among the changes brought about by the Progressives were reforms which transferred electoral power to the public, resulting in non-partisan local elections, popular nomination through the direct primary, direct election of U.S. senators, presidential preference primaries, and the power to legislate directly through the initiative and referendum. Party influence in government was weakened by the development of professionally trained, nonpolitical city and county managers as well as the introduction of civil service reforms and the merit system. Public disappointment with official performance might result in the recall of the unfaithful officeholder. Strict controls on lobbying would reduce corporate and other outside selfish influences. Furthermore, the effective use of these new and expanded institutions of democracy depended upon reform of the governmental machinery. Because of that, the reform movement encompassed changes in administrative structures including strengthened chief executive officers, improved budget systems controlled by the executive, and widespread consolidation of offices and functions at the state and local levels. The principal targets of the movement were state and local governments; the chief victims of Progressivism were the political parties.

The loss of organizational control over candidate selection permitted, indeed encouraged, candidates to self-declare and, having done so, to go their own way. This, in turn, ultimately led to the technocratic management of personal campaigns, the stock-in-trade of the private political industry. Without control over nominations, the parties watched as their hesitant and tentative hold over issue positions further eroded. Candidates needed to pay no heed to traditional party positions. Often, in fact, they ran against the party, attacking "bossism" and the "evils" associated with organizational politics. In effect they borrowed the party's banner under which to run for office but did not pay the homage which might be a quid pro quo for the use of the party's name.

Due to the rise of personal politics, few party organizations today are able to field a "team" of candidates. Earlier campaigns built around party "slates" have given way to individual efforts by candidates to enlist support from among separate voter groups—support which often cuts across political identifications. These efforts to enlist segments of the electorate—blacks, women, laborers, farmers, and others—have gone forward in many areas without the participation of party officials. In short, modern candidates have become less dependent upon the parties and now, as often as not, seek election by mobilizing their own personal resources.

Party organizations and leaders must share the blame for this state of affairs. Parties have suffered from neglect from their own officials, government officers, presidents, congressmen, and voters. It is not possible to totally isolate and quarantine state and local party systems from the influences of national politics. The Washington-based party units—national committees and congressional campaign committees—have concentrated their resources and their attention on presidential and congressional campaigns. By doing so they have lent their support to the most personal of all campaigns. Elections to presidential and congressional offices are almost universally controlled by personal political organizations working in behalf of a single candidate. The national party groups do not run these campaigns, they merely act as service factorums for them.[1] National party neglect has been based on an unofficial "trickledown" theory of politics—one that holds that what is good for the national parties will ultimately benefit those at the state and local levels. But, for the most part, this has not proven to be the case, due to the weakening of the traditional roles that parties play.

As noted earlier, one important goal of the Progressives was to reduce the complexities and frustrations of government by reorganization and consolidation of agencies and strengthened executives. Although these efforts were successful in some places, the growth of governmental responsibilities brought expanded bureaucracies and even greater frustrations for the citizen-voter. It is paradoxical that this particular failure of Progressive initiative has contributed to the erosion of the party role. Truncated terms, restrictions on the powers of elected officials, shared responsibilities, and the failures of state governmental organizations to consolidate and redistribute responsibilities have confused the electorate and compounded the party's problems of candidate recruitment and unified campaigning. It is likely that reform of state and local governmental agencies would enhance the chances for the parties to serve effectively as a catalyst between the officeholders and the electorate. To bring this about would require changes in state law of considerable magnitude.

Constitutions often mandate the number of officers to be elected at all levels of state and local government. To change them would require engaging in the full amendment process. Statutory law covers local government like a blanket in many areas of the nation. Legislative majorities to change laws governing localities and city or county officials are often hard to come by. Ironically, the political parties themselves are often in the forefront of efforts to maintain the status quo. Party leaders fear an erosion of their powers, a reduction of the number of offices they have to fill, and additional encumbrances imposed by the state on their local operations. It is most difficult to convince many party leaders that they are working against their own best interests.

Finally, an important cause of the decline of state and local party organizations has been the erosion of public trust in government and politics generally. The percentage of eligible voters who vote in presidential elections has steadily declined from 63.1 percent in 1960 to 55.4 percent in 1972. In off-year congressional elections, the decline has been from 46.3 percent in 1962 to 43.8 percent in 1974.[2] In 1972, an election study conducted by the United States Bureau of the Census and based upon extensive national voter surveys found that 27 percent of those who were eligible did not vote. Their reasons ranged from apathy to skepticism toward government and hostility toward politicians.[3] In mid-1975 pollster Louis Harris found that only 14 percent of the American people expressed confidence in the local governments of the nation, a drop from 43 percent in 1965. Furthermore, Harris pointed out that only 13 percent had confidence in the national government. So deep does public cynicism run that more people expressed confidence in garbage collectors (51 percent) than in any other group in the public sector.[4] The rapid increase in ticket splitting and the growth of registered and self-proclaimed Independents both constitute further evidence of mass dissatisfaction with government and political parties. Many reasons are cited for the escalation in public disaffection: some citizens believe that they are neglected by the government and used by the political parties; others are of the opinion that it matters little who wins an election, nothing of importance will happen to change the life style of most people. This general disenchantment extends from the national to the local levels of government and politics.

It is a curious phenomenon that the movement to strengthen state party organizations discussed in this book emerged during the same time frame that produced the mass cynicism about government and erosion of public support for the political parties. As David Broder of the *Washington Post* has noted: "The reason we have suffered governmental stalemate is that we have not used the one instrument available to us for disciplining government to meet our needs. That instrument is the political party." [5] Widespread recognition of this view is one reason for the renewed efforts in some states to improve the workings of the political parties. Others have responded through the emergence of a national urge for self-protection. Party leaders in some areas have managed to reverse the antiparty trends of past decades by assuming greater leadership roles and by seeking to refocus public attention and loyalty toward the party as opposed to individual candidates. In most instances outside the South these leaders have sought to avoid engaging in party building within an ideological framework. Recent experiences with presidential candidates who were outside the moderate mold convinced many state chairmen that they must continue to build support from the middle. Many have concluded that party building and organizational improvements are not dependent upon the development of ideologically directed parties. Therefore, even though there has been a decline in voter commitment and candidate dependence, a renewed and strengthened state party organization led by imaginative leaders could evolve the technological aspects of campaigning and in so doing gradually provide the means through which voters and candidates might be attracted back into the party fold.

The variety of party systems along with rapid changes in leadership have always made it difficult to assess intraparty relationships in the United States. Those who have studied state parties over extended periods of time have often noted the rapidity with which an organization can decline under unimaginative or less than industrious leadership. At the same time, however, a new and dynamic leader can revitalize a party and make it viable as a political instrument in a relatively short period of time. The quality of leadership is of great importance to party success. Not only is it crucial to the proper functioning of the organization within the state itself, but it provides the more perceptive national leaders with a middleman with whom they can deal on an equal basis with some expectation of results. Those changes which need to be made may only demand aggressive and decisive leadership. Unless a state chairman is willing to sample the dangers of politics he may never discern its mysteries.

In early 1974 an important member of the staff of the Republican National Committee, a veteran of many years of service, asked me to list those state chairmen whom I considered to be the "best" in the Republican party. He obviously agreed with the first three names that I mentioned, but upon hearing the fourth he asked for my justification. I explained that the chairman in question had turned the party around, gotten it out of debt, served as an effective spokesman against a popular opposition governor, and had begun to rebuild the grass-roots structure of the party. I noted that these activities, if continued, should have a major payoff in the future.

His response startled me. He said, "Has he won anything? He can't be effective unless he wins elections!" I disagreed with that view, but at the same time I understood the reasons for it. Many professional politicians measure "effectiveness" by the number of election "wins." The end product of politics for them is always victories and offices. According to this view there is no other measure worth considering.

That position, it seems to me, is short-sighted, and its application can result in an unfair evaluation of party leadership. It is possible to be an effective and successful state party leader without winning offices. Several chairmen in both parties have impressed impartial observers as well as their associates with their success in organizational politics but at the same time have been unable to translate that organizational rebirth into electoral victories. This is obviously always going to be the case in a minority party in a one-party system. It is also true in some parties that have begun a long and tortuous rebuilding process after suffering setbacks at the polls. In short, it is not possible to measure political success in organizational politics by citing the number of wins the party has. Party effectiveness must be measured by promise as well as practice. Success may also be measured against the in-out status of the party at some particular time. A party represented by a popular and powerful governor may have the edge on one that is out of power. At the same time, it should be noted that some parties with incumbent governors are the poorer for it. This may be because the incumbent is uninterested in party affairs and allows the organization to drift, or it may be due to his having become unpopular, tarnishing the party's reputation through his own behavior, however reasonable, in office.

In short, it is not possible to measure each party by the same yardstick. Party history, public attitudes, and the quality of leadership all work to shape the image of a party. A distinction can be drawn between the "public" party and the "organizational" party. The public party is the electoral party; the one that captures offices and organizes government. The organizational party is a more private group composed of the cadre who carry out both the short- and the long-range affairs of the political mechanism itself. It is the latter to which most of this book has been devoted.

The Growth and Renewal of State Party Organizations

After a decade of organizational growth and development, state parties are in a position to claim a major leadership role in the national party system. There is little to suggest that either the national or congressional campaign committees will broaden their focus to include state and local parties and campaigns. Because of the decentralized and fractionalized nature of the party system, it would be difficult for them to do so even if they so choose. The state parties, however, have an opportunity to capture for themselves a new and vital role which could shape American politics for many years to come. Indeed, they have many advantages which might be exploited.

In a federal system with a decentralized party structure the state and local units are by far the most numerous. That fact not only permits greater experimentation but also allows for easier control over party affairs. State and local units of the parties tend to be homogeneous and less likely to have those elements built in which breed divisiveness. In many states unified action requires less compromise. With stronger leadership and a better sense of direction many state parties could develop into serious and competitive political operations.

The state parties also have more political prizes to award. The elected and appointed officials necessary to run 50 states and 3,000 counties provide the glue with which a party can weld itself together. As noted before, there is good reason to work toward reducing the number of elected officeholders in order to reduce the confusion and complexities of government and the alienation of the electorate. Such a reduction, however, would probably enhance the role of the parties in most areas since fewer but more powerful offices would make the party's recruitment, nomination, and election job that much more important. For the average citizen interested in government and politics, the opportunities for reward are far greater at the state and local levels.

State parties are small enough to adapt to new techniques of campaigning without being captured by the mechanics of the new politics. The experience of the Democratic-Farmer-Labor (DFL) party in Minnesota has demonstrated that parties at the state level can play a central role in modern campaigning by assuming the leadership in making the new technology available to party candidates.[6] Fifteen years ago the

Minnesota Republicans were experimenting with statewide campaigns employing some early developments in new campaign styles as they existed at that time. In many states the party organizations could create an important and indispensable role for themselves acting as directorate and clearinghouse for state and local candidates wishing to undertake opinion polling, professional advertising, automatic computer processing of voter data, and other forms of electoral analysis.

Finally, the states provide a greater opportunity for the out-party to serve a useful function. The number and diversity of the offices elected virtually guarantee in most places that the minority party will hold some positions at either the state or local levels. This is a base upon which a minority party organization can build. In fact, the out-party chairman may have a better chance to build effectively than the in-party chairman. It would not be unreasonable to hypothesize that the out-party chairman has more opportunities and more means of taking advantage of them than does the chairman of the party in power.

Clearly, imaginative and strong leaders who are dedicated to the whole party can effect major change. There are too many examples to prove the case for it to be in question. Just as surely, the job will be easier in some states than in others. Stronger state and local party organizations will not necessarily develop simultaneously throughout the United States. Some are much further down the road than others, and some have far more resources at their command to bring about attainment of that ultimate goal.

To conclude a work of this kind with a list of recommendations for party building might be considered presumptuous in view of the great diversity which exists between state parties. Nevertheless, so many state party chairmen are experimenting with new organizational innovations and new methods of campaigning that it might be worth reviewing some of those which seem to hold general promise for sizable numbers of state parties. It was clear from the interviews that provided the base for this study as well as from the discussions held at the 1974 Harvard Bi-partisan Conference of State Party Chairmen that many party leaders are cognizant of the opportunities that now face their organizations. It is equally certain that any list of recommendations will fall far short of unanimous endorsement from the men and women who hold offices in their parties. It is most doubtful that they would all agree with any single recommendation due to the great diversity inherent in the state parties and the variety of their experiences. The following recommendations, although by no means an exhaustive list, might nonetheless serve to chart party development and stimulate thought.

Lengthening the State Chairman's Term in Office

One of the most serious problems facing state parties is the abbreviated average tenure of most chairmen. There is no other position in politics quite like the state party chairmanship, regardless of its individual manifestation. There is no effective way to train for the position, and external forces are always working to reshape it. Consequently, it is imperative that the party leader's term be long enough to permit him to "learn the ropes" and still have enough time to implement his own programs and lead the party through at least one campaign. Innovation in politics is slow and uncertain at best. A chairman needs time to develop his plans and to chart his course of action. He needs even more time to implement and evaluate his programs. Tenure averaging less than three years does not provide enough time for any of these things.

How can a state party improve the chairman's chances for success by increasing the time he has to serve? For one thing, state committees or conventions should question the candidates for party office as to their ability to spend the necessary time and energy on the office. They should institute more formal screening processes in order to make certain that the chairman candidate's ability to commit himself is known to those who make the choice. This kind of public discussion will not guarantee that the person selected will fill out his term, but it will place additional pressure on him to do so.

I have become convinced that it is advantageous for a state chairman to be full time and paid. Only in this way can a party be certain that it will receive the full attention of the party leader. Part-time chairmen who continue to run businesses or practice law or whatever usually cannot hope to spend sufficient time carrying out party responsibilities. If state parties are to undertake expanded roles, then they will need full-time managers. Some will argue that as long as there is a paid executive director the chairman can afford to maintain part-time status, but it is my observation that this is usually not the case. Executive directors are not chairmen. They often do not have long-standing contacts or experience in the party. They are looked upon by many as staff, and most feel that they cannot act independently. Most state parties, if they are to become professionalized, must have a full-time, paid chairman *and* an executive director. Political parties are just about the only important institutions that try to get by on part-time volunteer help. Many observers believe that is a major cause of the parties' decline in public esteem.

To move in the direction of full-time, paid chairmen is very important if the parties are to undertake greater responsibilities. Expanded fundraising programs, computerization, and public opinion polling are all examples of party activities over which the chairman should maintain personal control. To do so, he must be available and in command. None of these responsibilities can be carried out through an intermediary, and most of them are present problems that cannot await a part-time leader's convenience.

Finally, I would recommend that the parties that have not done so work to disentangle themselves from a system that imposes a Political Agent on them. There are those who will maintain that such a recommendation could only emerge from a supreme naiveté. I would disagree. At least two parties have done just that. In one case, the party cadre made a conscious decision to separate the chairmanship from the gubernatorial office. Although the move originated in a pervasive mood of dissatisfaction with an incumbent governor, it has been continued for several years, and succeeding governors who sought to impose their own personal choice on the party have been politely rebuffed. The result has been widespread feeling on the part of its followers that the party belongs to all; that it is not just a part of the governor's personal entourage.

The second state party to separate itself from its own governor did so by the simple expedient of moving the election of state chairmen to a four-year term beginning at the halfway point of the governor's term. Consequently, the chairmanship is not vacant when the governor assumes office. I am fully cognizant of the implications of such a reform; but numerous parties operate in that way now, as evidenced by most of the In-Party Independent chairmen. If fulfilled, this change would result in party systems being segregated from a particular elected official and would go far to create a system dedicated to the whole party rather than to one of its parts.

The implementation of these reforms would create a whole new atmosphere in party politics. Longer terms for independent, paid, full-time chairmen might make the electing bodies more aware of the importance of selecting as leaders men and women who could devote their time and energy to the party and who could undertake internal reform and greater professionalization to the betterment of the political system.

Professional Staff and Technical Advisors

The problems of staffing in politics are monumental. At every level of the party hierarchy, staff positions remain unfilled for lack of experienced or qualified personnel. Sometimes they are filled by men and women who have experience in running campaigns or organizing parties but are in private political employment and cannot afford to risk permanent association with the party. The result is that many technical positions demanding experience and expertise are filled by those who are too young and inexperienced or are too old and tired. One remedy, as is so often the case, is to improve the financial position of the party. Even when that occurs, though, there are relatively few persons who possess the qualifications and experience to undertake party assignments on a professional basis. In 1969 Robert C. Spencer and I recommended that each party, through the coordinated efforts of its national, congressional, senatorial, and state committees,

establish a Political Academy in Washington through which formal training sessions could be combined with on-the-job internships for selected "classes" chosen from throughout the nation. These classes might be composed of 50 or 100 interns, each chosen by the state central committees and/or the national party organizations, with salaries (or fellowships) provided by a fund pool collected from all party sources. The class might last for a year or longer with some specified number of months devoted to attending actual training sessions in Washington, with instruction provided by professionals in politics, elected officials, administration officials (in the case of the party in power or former officials for the party out of power), outstanding state and local political organizers, spokesmen for interest groups, and others who may have a contribution to make. At the end of the formal training sessions the trainees might be assigned to political offices in Washington or across the nation, in order to get some number of months of on-the-job training. At the end of the entire training period the trainee would be returned to the sponsoring state or placed in an employment pool from which the staff needs of the expanded state or regional headquarters could be met.[7]

As we noted at that time, the proposal is not a radical one; both parties have for years run campaign schools during election years. These schools, however, amount to little more than two- or three-day crash courses for candidates, managers, and fund raisers. Our proposal would expand this program into an ongoing training session in an educational setting. Instead of short, ad hoc training sessions at campaign time, this proposal would provide long-range, in-depth training to prospective or inexperienced party officials on a regularly scheduled, formal basis. The program would, over the years, build a reservoir of political talent to help meet staff deficiencies in the state and national party organizations.

Expertise is an increasingly important commodity in organizational and campaign planning. Technical advisors are difficult to enlist. Several state parties have discovered that the complexity and complications of modern election law, particularly with regard to campaign finance and financial disclosure, require regular legal assistance. Parties have met this need in a variety of ways. Some have hired attornies who prepare general statements describing what constitutes compliance; these are then distributed to candidates and campaign officers. Others have relied on advice from attornies who have volunteered their services on a limited and sporadic basis. Whatever the method, state party leaders should be encouraged to procure regular legal advice in one way or another.

In some states the chairman might find it advantageous to create an advisory group composed of former state chairmen. One chairman enlisted the aid of nine former chairmen who agreed to serve in such an advisory group, and he found it to be a worthwhile means of recapturing some of the experience and expertise of those who had served the party in past years. Former chairmen, like defeated presidential candidates, normally do not have a place in the system. If an incumbent chairman is willing to listen to advice, he might consider setting up such an advisory committee.

Shared Technology

Control over organizational and campaign technology should be captured by the political parties. As the trend to new politics is not going to be reversed, it would appear that parties, if they are to have a significant role in the electoral process, will need to direct their energies to mastering the new political techniques. This, however, requires large infusions of money and other resources as well as staff experts employed on a regular basis. Many state parties are unable to afford these services. Increasingly, as that fact has become apparent, nonparty groups with more bountiful resources have moved in to take over campaigns. Labor and other groups have the money and the staff to promote the technological aspects of politics and campaigning. They have already gained considerable experience in the uses of field men, mass fund raising, computerized voter identification, polling, and professional uses of television.

Because of the cost, lack of expertise, or lack of interest on the part of the leadership, most state parties have done relatively little to involve themselves in these activities. Unions and business and professional groups have undertaken to fill the vacuum and have gained stature at the expense of the parties in some areas. The other principal group to explore technological campaigning has been the candidates themselves. As it became apparent that the political parties did not recognize the need to move into those areas or did not have the resources to do so, candidates hired outside private firms of specialists to handle their campaigns. It is clear that one effect of this has been to further separate candidates from their parties.

The movement to private consultants and the increasingly critical role played by private firms should be a cause for alarm on the part of the political parties. At the same time it need not be a source of dismay. The parties already have the framework for cooperative ventures in technocracy. The regional party associations provide the means for the political parties in the states to cooperate in funding and staffing regional party centers with centralized computer facilities, jointly supported technical staff persons, and a shared bank of experts and consultants. Should the proposed political academy ever be inaugurated, the regional party centers would serve as excellent training grounds for the interns coming out of that program. Should the academy fail to materialize, the regional party centers might serve as training experiences in themselves.

The parties in the states, probably with national party support, would need to prorate costs on some fair basis. Plans would have to be formulated so that output would be fairly distributed and one or more parties in large and powerful states could not dominate the available resources. Other safeguards would need to be agreed upon before most state organizations would choose to consider cooperating. Some parties, fearing innovation or loss of autonomy, would probably choose not to take part. But unless some effort is made to retain control of the party functions and some accommodation is made to the new and costly political techniques, the state party organizations may place themselves in serious peril. They have demonstrated in the past few years that they can strengthen themselves organizationally. They need now to work to recapture control over the technical functions of campaigning and political organization.

Improving the Public Understanding of Political Parties

The low public esteem for political parties and politicians as reflected in public opinion polls is of serious concern for a representative democracy. Many factors have contributed to the decline in public respect including, most recently, the controversy surrounding the Vietnamese War, the legal difficulties involving former Vice-President Spiro Agnew, and Watergate and its attendant scandals.

It is important to the future health and vitality of the parties that their leadership counter the negative impact of these various forces. One recommendation that seems appropriate is that state parties should cooperate with public school and college teachers to explain the importance of the educational impact on these agents of representative democracy. Generations of students and teachers have been influenced by secondary school social studies training that instilled in millions of students the belief that politics is dirty and politicians untrustworthy; that a vote for the man instead of the party symbolized citizen purity. Much of this attitude emerged, from the best of motives, out of the Progressive movement. Many forces have honed this public distrust since that time, and there still remains a strong "good government" strain running through many high school classes in social studies.

The political parties should sponsor bipartisan conferences on politics, politicians, and political organizations, arrange for classroom speakers or assembly debates, provide local internships in political offices, and seek to begin to break down the barrier of distrust between young people and the parties.

National Party Attitudes toward State Parties

Both national parties generally tend to take the state and local parties for granted. The Republican National Committee admitted the state chairmen to membership at an early date but has never seen fit to encourage them to have an office in the new Republican headquarters building in Washington. The Republican chairmen consequently have no continuing voice in party affairs except as represented through the Republican State Chairmen's Advisory Committee headquartered in whatever city or town is the home of its chairman.

The Democratic chairmen had to engage in a bitter and divisive fight with their national committee leadership even to get membership. Once granted, however, the DNC did provide an office and staff for national coordination of the association's affairs. Even so, the relationship between the two groups continues to be tenuous.

Rivalry between the national and state parties is understandable and, indeed, inevitable. Establishment of a permanent Washington-based office for the Republican chairmen and additional support for the Democratic office should be encouraged. If the state party organizations are really integral parts of the national party system, they should be nourished and encouraged. There is just as much justification for the national party to support a state chairmen's headquarters as there is for the governors, women, youth, or other groups to have party assistance in maintaining Washington offices. In planning national party strategies, it is not conceivable that the elected state party leaders should be ignored. With a well-manned Washington office, it is less likely that they would be.

A Review of State Law and Party By-Laws

The political turmoil from 1968 onward, particularly in the Democratic party, focused attention on the need for revisions in the statutory law concerning political parties. The work of the various reform commissions concentrated on revising the rules of delegate selection and the organization of the national conventions. From this same movement emerged the reconstituted Democratic National Committee. For the most part, however, few states undertook complete revision of their statutory law or party rules unless required to by nationally imposed standards.

State parties should undertake such a review and seek revisions of those laws which frustrate the effective operations of the party. Laws specifying duties for state chairmen might be reviewed to see if they actually inhibit party growth. New laws governing party fund raising, such as those permitting a tax check-off or providing for party receipt of filing fees, should be reviewed to protect the rights of the organizations. Laws providing for administration of election and campaign enforcement should be of particular interest to the parties.

Party by-laws revision is usually within the prerogatives of the organization itself. Usually by-laws would need to be changed if any revision of the chairman's term or time of election should be undertaken. Obviously, given the great variation in party law, some parties would be striving to expand and others simply to clarify their rights and responsibilities.

If change is desired the state chairmen should work closely with the legislative leadership to attain desired goals. As reported in chapter 9, bipartisan efforts have been undertaken in some states to lend the weight of both party organizations to the revision process.

Reflections on State Party Leaders

It would serve little purpose to review the whole panoply of state party organizations and leadership as discussed in these pages. The thesis advanced here is that effective parties are dependent upon strong party organizations. Furthermore, it is argued that recent years have brought an important strengthening of state organizational structures. There are some who will believe this an overoptimistic evaluation. If one bases his judgment of party "effectiveness" on the level of party "responsibility," I would agree. But it is my contention that parties, in order to recapture and carry out their traditional functions, must build strength in their organizational foundations. That, in turn, demands stronger party leadership. Strong and vigorous leaders can capture for political organizations many of those functions now being performed by private businesses. That is not to say that a chairman can expect power to flow to him by virtue of the office he holds. Power is more a consequence of how the person holding the office conducts himself—his tenacity, his imagination, and his willingness and ability to undertake and carry out new programs. Power should be a handmaiden of success, and that, in turn, should be measured by organizational accomplishment as well as electoral victory.

The professional technological revolution in political campaigning opens up new vistas to party leaders. Far from being a death knell for parties, as some have suggested, it could just as well be a genesis. The impressive organizational reinvigoration that has taken place in some states, the new strength of state chairmen at the national party level, and the climate of change that currently prevails all provide a fertile field for renewed party growth.

The challenge was well illustrated to me during a visit to a local party headquarters in midtown Manhattan. Only one other office door shared that particular hallway with the party. Juxtaposed with the party headquarters was a door bearing the inscription, "Blood, Sweat and Tears, Inc." That might serve as both a challenge and a motto for those who seek to strengthen state party organizations.

Appendix

The author is indebted to David M. Davis, a graduate student in political science at Florida Atlantic University, who undertook the content analysis of state election laws and party by-laws outlined in chapter 1. Davis' master's thesis, "Legal Powers of State Chairmen: A Content Analysis of Party By-Laws and State Election Laws," was completed in 1971 under direction of the author. The eleven parties without by-laws at that time were the Democrats in Illinois, Kansas, Louisiana, Missouri, Ohio, Rhode Island, Texas, and Utah, and the Republicans of Illinois, Kansas, and Utah. Some of these state parties have since adopted by-laws in response to changes brought about by the party reforms of 1971–72.

The first step in the research process was to analyze a sample of ten party by-laws. From this sample, 77 items were classified under fourteen general headings. Each of these items pertained to a particular power or duty of one or more state chairmen. Next, the remaining seventy-nine by-laws and the fifty sets of state election laws were analyzed in a similar manner, generating more than 1,000 additional items. These items were also classified under the original fourteen groups of items, three of which were later combined with other groups.

Recording of the approximately 1,100 items was accomplished by using data input coding sheets, and tabulation of the items determined the number of times each item appeared in the eighty-nine by-laws and fifty state election laws. The frequency varied from a minimum of one occurrence to a maximum of sixty-six occurrences of the most frequently recurring item.

The approximately 1,100 items resulted in between one and sixty-five pieces of data for each of the 100 party chairmen. Following the computer tabulation, many items which were either identical or very similar were combined. The combinations were made in two different phases, both of which included three types of items: (1) those items which were identical; (2) those items which were subjectively judged to be nearly identical; and (3) those items which were similar and lent themselves to combination.

Combinations such as these reduced the total number of items from 1,100 to 249. The 249 items were submitted to a select group of state chairmen from a representative sample of state party organizations. Nine state party chairmen completed the evaluation of the 249 items. For each of the items, the judges awarded ratings of from minus five (for "negative" powers) to plus five (for the most important powers). These 249 judges' means were then awarded to the parties having the evaluated powers and duties.

This procedure was followed for all items contained in the by-laws and state election laws of the 100 parties, and each party's ratings were summed, resulting in a total score for each party.

In addition to the total party scores, other material is presented and analyzed throughout the Davis study, including comparisons among groups of parties with different aspects of degrees of a certain variable. The main techniques used were means and tests of significance. The minimum level of t test acceptance is the .05 level, although many of the mean differences are significant at the .01 level or below.

Notes

Preface

1. Bernard C. Hennessy, "On the Study of Party Organization," in William J. Crotty, *Approaches to the Study of Party Organization* (Boston: Allyn and Bacon, 1968), pp. 20–21.

Chapter 1

1. David M. Olson, "Attributes of State Political Parties: An Exploration of Theory and Data," in James A. Riedel, *New Perspectives in State and Local Politics* (Waltham, Mass.: Xerox College Publishing, 1971), p. 126.
2. James MacGregor Burns, *The Deadlock of Democracy: Four-Party Politics in America* (Englewood Cliffs, N.J.: Prentice-Hall, 1963), p. 237.
3. V. O. Key, Jr., *American State Politics: An Introduction* (New York: Alfred A. Knopf, 1956), p. 271.
4. Noble E. Cunningham, Jr., *The Jeffersonian Republicans* (Chapel Hill: University of North Carolina Press, 1957), p. 33. See also Richard P. McCormick, *The Second American Party System: Party Formation in the Jacksonian Era* (Chapel Hill: University of North Carolina Press, 1966), p. 22.

5. Claude Bowers, *Jefferson and Hamilton* (Boston: Houghton-Mifflin Co., 1925), p. 143.
6. Wilfred E. Binkley, *American Political Parties: Their Natural History,* 4th ed. (New York: Alfred A. Knopf, 1963), p. 78.
7. Cunningham, p. 65.
8. Stephen G. Kurtz, *The Presidency of John Adams* (Philadelphia: University of Pennsylvania Press, 1957), pp. 151–52; David H. Fischer, *The Revolution of American Conservatism* (New York: Harper and Row, 1965), p. 53.
9. Telephone interview with Professor Richard McCormick, Department of History, Rutgers University, August 7, 1972.
10. Cunningham, p. 151.
11. This letter was originally printed in the *Virginia Argus* on March 25, 1800, and is reprinted in Cunningham, p. 153.
12. Binkley, p. 108.
13. Arthur C. Millspaugh, *Party Organization and Machinery in Michigan since 1890* (Baltimore: Johns Hopkins University Press, 1917), p. 127.
14. *Democratic Newsletter* 5, no. 5 (May 21, 1971): 1 and 3, published every other Friday by the Ohio Democratic Party, Columbus, Ohio.
15. *Republican Report* 5, no. 4 (August 1969): 1 and 3, published every month by the Washington State Republican Central Committee, Olympia, Wash. The Washington Republican chairman ranked second in the nation in the formal powers assigned to him even before the changes were made.
16. *The Spokesman* 10, no. 3 (September 1973): 4, published monthly by the Wyoming Democratic Central Committee, Casper, Wyo.
17. *Miami Herald,* November 21, 1970, p. S–A.

Chapter 2

1. Donald R. Matthews, *The Social Background of Political Decision Makers* (New York: Random House, 1954), p. 2.
2. Representative of these efforts are the following: Donald R. Matthews, *U.S. Senators and Their World* (Chapel Hill: University of North Carolina Press, 1960), chap. 2; Frank J. Sorauf, *Party and Representation: Legislative Politics in Pennsylvania* (New York: Atherton Press, 1963), chap. 5; John C. Wahlke, Heinz Eulau, William Buchanan, and LeRoy Ferguson, *The Legislative System: Explorations in Legislative Behavior* (New York: John Wiley and Sons, 1962), app. 5; James Barber, *The Lawmakers* (New Haven: Yale University Press, 1965); Robert A. Dahl, *Who Governs? Democracy and Power in an American City* (New Haven: Yale University Press, 1961), chap. 20; Kenneth Prewitt, *The Recruitment of Political Leaders* (Indianapolis: Bobbs-Merrill Co., 1970); Robert J. Huckshorn and Robert C. Spencer, *The Politics of Defeat: Campaigning for Congress* (Amherst: University of Massachusetts Press, 1971), chap. 2; Jeff Fishel, *Party and Opposition* (New York: David McKay Co., 1973), chap. 2. In addition, many excellent articles in professional journals have contributed to the mass of this research.
3. Cornelius P. Cotter and Bernard C. Hennessy, *Politics without Power: The National Party Committees* (New York: Atherton Press, 1964), chap. 3.
4. Heinz Eulau and Kenneth Prewitt, *Labyrinths of Democracy: Adaptations, Linkages, Representation, and Policies of Urban Politics* (Indianapolis: Bobbs-Merrill Co., 1973), pp. 626–28.
5. Dwaine Marvick and Charles Nixon, "Recruitment Contrasts on Rival Cam-

paign Groups," in *Political Decision-Makers,* ed. Dwaine Marvick (Glencoe, Ill.: Free Press, 1961), pp. 206–7.

6. Joseph A. Schlesinger, *How They Became Governor* (East Lansing: Governmental Research Bureau, Michigan State University, 1957), chap. 1.

7. Henri Peyre, "Excellence and Leadership: Has Western Europe Any Lessons for Us?" in Stephen R. Graubard and Gerald Holton, eds., *Excellence and Leadership in a Democracy* (New York: Columbia University Press, 1962), p. 1.

8. James D. Barber, *Political Leadership in American Government* (Boston: Little, Brown and Co., 1964), p. 5.

9. Austin Ranney and Willmoore Kendall, *Democracy and the American Party System* (New York: Harcourt, Brace and Co., 1956), p. 244. As noted by Ranney and Kendall, the three meanings of *leadership* follow closely the formulation by Maphens Smith in Alvin W. Gouldner, ed., *Studies in Leadership* (New York: Harper and Brothers, 1950), p. 15.

10. Ordway Tead, *The Art of Leadership* (New York: McGraw-Hill, 1935), chap. 6.

11. Robert Agranoff and Edward F. Cooke, "Political Profile of State Party Chairmen" (paper delivered before the Midwest Conference of Political Scientists, University of Wisconsin, Madison, Wisc., May 1, 1964).

12. Charles W. Wiggins and William L. Turk, "State Party Chairmen: A Profile," *Western Political Quarterly,* June 1970, pp. 321–32.

13. The Democratic median age would be even younger were it not for the inclusion of one Democratic state chairman who was eighty-five years old at the time he was interviewed.

14. Wiggins and Turk, p. 322.

15. Agranoff and Cooke, p. 14.

16. Wiggins and Turk, pp. 322–23.

17. Agranoff and Cooke, p. 14.

18. Wiggins and Turk, p. 322.

19. For an extended discussion of this rivalry, see Cotter and Hennessy, pp. 149–54.

20. See Huckshorn and Spencer, p. 176.

21. Ibid., pp. 32–33.

22. Matthews found that between 1947 and 1957 more than two-thirds of the members of the U.S. Senate were born in rural areas or small towns. Donald R. Matthews, "United States Senators: A Collective Portrait," *International Social Science Journal* 13 (1961): 622. Wahlke et al found that less than half the members of the California, Ohio, and Tennessee legislatures grew up in cities and about one-quarter of them were raised on farms. Wahlke et al., p. 489.

23. Avery Leiserson, *Parties and Politics: An Institutional and Behavioral Approach* (New York: Alfred A. Knopf, 1958), p. 199. Leiserson does note that most of the information about state party leadership at that time was from thirty to sixty years old.

24. As of the end of 1974, six incumbent or newly elected state governors had previously served as their parties' state chairmen: Robert Ray (R), Iowa; Marvin Mandel (D), Maryland; James Holshouser (R), North Carolina; Patrick Lucey (D), Wisconsin; Stanley Hathaway (R), Wyoming; and Jerry Apodaca (D), New Mexico. Hathaway was appointed by President Gerald Ford to be secretary of the interior in early 1975 but resigned shortly after assuming office.

25. David G. Pfeiffer, "The Measurement of Inter-party Competition and Systemic Stability," *American Political Science Review* 61 (June 1967): 457–67.
26. Ranney and Kendall, p. 244.
27. Tead, chap. 6.

Chapter 3

1. David M. Davis, "Legal Powers of State Chairmen: A Content Analysis of Party By-Laws and State Election Laws" (Master's thesis, Florida Atlantic University, 1971), p. 83. This study is discussed in chapter 1.
2. *Sacramento Bee,* January 30, 1971, p. 1.
3. *Savannah News,* January 10, 1971, p. C1.
4. The 1961 figures are taken from a confidential memorandum based upon data collected and compiled by the Republican National Committee and entitled *Finances and Staffs of Republican State Committees, 1961* and one prepared by the Democratic National Committee in 1962 entitled *Democratic State Party Organization: Staffing and Programming.* The 1974 data were a part of the interviews used in this study.
5. *Free Press* (Burlington, Vt.), June 9, 1971, p. 2.
6. *St. Paul Pioneer Press,* February 22, 1971, p. 13.
7. The Republican National Committee under Chairman Ray Bliss carried out this survey in late 1968. Responses were received from thirty-six of the fifty state chairmen, and the information furnished included headquarters operations; salary data for chairmen, executive directors, and other officers; finance and budgetary programs; and voter registration figures. The length of my interviews prevented me from asking respondents for such detailed information. No data were available for the Democrats beyond the 1961 survey described earlier.
8. *Pierre* (S. Dak.) *Journal,* June 15, 1971, p. 2.
9. *Washington Post,* November 11, 1969, p. 7.
10. Malcolm E. Jewell and Everett W. Cunningham, *Kentucky Politics* (Lexington: University of Kentucky Press, 1968), pp. 131–32. The discussion of bifactionalism is contained in V. O. Key, Jr., *Southern Politics* (New York: Alfred S. Knopf, 1949), chap. 14.
11. Jewell and Cunningham, p. 131.
12. Ibid., p. 132.
13. John H. Fenton, *Politics in the Border States* (New Orleans: Hauser Press, 1957), p. 39.
14. *Louisville Courier Journal,* June 20, 1971, p. B3.
15. Ibid., June 10, 1971, p. 1.
16. Neal R. Peirce, *The Megastates of America* (New York: W. W. Norton and Co., 1972), p. 465.
17. *Orlando Sentinel,* September 22, 1970, p. 2.
18. *Miami Herald,* November 25, 1970, p. 6–D.
19. Ibid., December 4, 1970, p. 36–D.
20. *Orlando Sentinel,* January 10, 1971, p. 1.
21. *Miami Herald,* January 10, 1971, p. 1.
22. John S. Saloma III and Frederick H. Sontag, *Parties: The Real Opportunity for Effective Politics* (New York: Alfred A. Knopf, 1972), p. 156.

Chapter 4

1. Some of the more useful classifications are: Austin Ranney and Willmoore Kendall, *Democracy and the American Party System* (New York: Harcourt, Brace and Co., 1956), chap. 7; Joseph A. Schlesinger, "A Two-Dimensional Scheme for Classifying the States According to Degree of Inter-Party Competition," *American Political Science Review* 49 (December 1955): 1120; Coleman B. Ransone, Jr., *The Office of Governor in the United States* (University, Ala.: University of Alabama Press, 1956), chaps. 2–4; V. O. Key, Jr., *American State Politics: An Introduction* (New York: Alfred A. Knopf, 1956), pp. 98–99; Richard Hofferbert, "Classification of American Party Systems," *Journal of Politics* 26 (August 1964): 550–67; Richard E. Dawson and James A. Robinson, "Inter-party Competition, Economic Variables, and Welfare Politics in the American States," *Journal of Politics* 25 (May 1963): 265–89; Robert T. Golembiewski, "A Taxonomic Approach to State Political Party Strength," *Western Political Quarterly* 11 (1958): 494–513; and Austin Ranney, "Parties in State Politics," chap. 3 in *Politics in the American States*, ed. Herbert Jacobs and Kenneth N. Vines (Boston: Little, Brown and Co., 1971).
2. Cornelius P. Cotter and Bernard C. Hennessy, *Politics without Power: The National Party Committees* (New York: Atherton Press, 1964), chap. 5.
3. Chester Bowles, *Promises to Keep: My Years in Public Life 1941–1969* (New York: Harper and Row, 1971), p. 218. The material on John Bailey throughout this book is based upon extensive interviews with Bailey in Washington and Hartford, the Bowles autobiography, and Duane Lockhard's *New England State Politics* (Princeton: Princeton University Press, 1959), chap. 9.
4. Ransone, p. 94. At the time Ransome was writing, this was probably a correct statement. Subsequent efforts to strengthen the state party organizations in many states may have softened it somewhat, although without comparable data from earlier years it is impossible to measure party growth objectively.
5. *New York Times*, April 28, 1970.
6. *Columbus Citizen-Journal*, January 11, 1971, p. 1.
7. *Lincoln Star*, March 6, 1971, editorial.
8. *Miami Herald*, November 21, 1970, p. 5–A.
9. *Montgomery Alabama Journal*, February 3, 1970, p. 4.
10. *New York Times*, October 21, 1971, p. 30.
11. *Chicago Tribune*, November 27, 1970. A later effort by Governor Whitcomb to force John Snyder from office is described below, chap. 7.
12. *New York Times*, January 25, 1971, p. 16; also the *San Diego Union*, January 25, 1971, p. 1.
13. *Manchester* (N.H.) *Union Leader*, October 1, 1970, editorial.

Chapter 5

1. Arthur C. Millspaugh, *Party Organization and Machinery in Michigan since 1890* (Baltimore: Johns Hopkins University Press, 1917), pp. 16–17.
2. James MacGregor Burns, *The Deadlock of Democracy: Four-Party Politics in America* (Englewood Cliffs, N.J.: Prentice-Hall, 1963), p. 239. Burns pursues his argument regarding the impotence of modern parties in his *Uncommon Sense* (New York: Harper and Row, 1972), chap. 8.
3. Lester G. Seligman, "Political Recruitment and Party Structure: A Case Study," *American Political Science Review* 55 (March 1961): 77.

4. E. E. Schattschneider, *Party Government* (New York: Rinehart, 1942), p. 101; emphasis in the original.
5. V. O. Key, Jr., *American State Politics: An Introduction* (New York: Alfred A. Knopf, 1956), p. 271.
6. Robert H. Salisbury, "The Urban Party Organization Member," *Public Opinion Quarterly* 29 (Winter 1965–66): 558.
7. *San Antonio Light,* September 15, 1970.
8. Robert C. Ingalls, *Corvallis* (Ore.) *Gazette-Times,* August 3, 1970, p. A4.

Chapter 6

1. Stanley Kelley, Jr., *Professional Public Relations and Political Power* (Baltimore: Johns Hopkins University Press, 1956).
2. "Professional Managers, Consultants Play Major Roles in 1970 Political Races," *National Journal* 2 (September 26, 1970): 2084–85. These totals were not furnished by *NJ* but are a count of each category from the information furnished about each campaign.
3. For a good brief history of public opinion measurement, see Bernard C. Hennessy, *Public Opinion,* 2nd ed. (Belmont, Calif.: Wadsworth Publishing Co., 1970), pp. 84–92.
4. Walter DeVries, "Information Systems and Political Consulting" (seminar on "Information Systems, Computers and Campaigns," American Association of Political Consultants, New York City, March 20–21, 1971), p. 3.
5. Ray C. Bliss, letter to Republican senators, dated May 8, 1967. It should be noted that the RNC had inaugurated the use of electronic informational retrieval systems as early as 1963.
6. Information furnished by the Research Division, Republican National Committee. It might be noted that not all of the innovations of the machine age are products of the computer revolution. As late as 1968 the Republican National Committee was furnishing state party headquarters with copies of a manual describing the necessity of maintaining a mimeograph machine and extolling the virtues of microfilm as a convenient method of storage.
7. *"The Chairman's Report to the Republican National Committee, 1968,"* Republican National Committee, Ray C. Bliss, Chairman, January 16–17, 1969, pp. 12–13.
8. For a good, brief discussion of the move to data processing by the national committees, see Robert Agranoff, *The New Style in Election Campaigns* (Boston: Holbrook Press, 1972), chap. 5.
9. Jonathan Cottin and Charles Culhane, "COPE's Political Craftsmen Build Smooth Organization," *National Journal* 2, no. 37 (September 12, 1970): 1963–73.
10. John S. Saloma III and Frederick H. Sontag, *Parties: The Real Opportunity for Effective Citizen Politics* (New York: Alfred A. Knopf, 1972), pp. 293–97. These authors have an excellent and extended treatment of the use of political consultants in modern politics (see chap. 9).
11. *Pittsburgh Post Gazette,* May 12, 1971, p. 9.
12. *Albuquerque Tribune,* December 5, 1970, p. 6.
13. *Springfield* (Mass.) *Union,* March 1, 1971.
14. *New York Times,* November 15, 1972, p. 29–C.
15. Neil Staebler and Douglas Ross, "The Management of State Political Parties,"

in *Practical Politics in the United States,* Cornelius P. Cotter, ed. (Boston: Allyn and Bacon, 1969), p. 68.

16. *Colorado Democrat* (Denver, Colo.), November 15, 1969, p. 1. Succeeding issues of this party newspaper describe the progress toward meeting these budgetary goals.

17. *Illinois Republican Trunk Line* (Springfield, Ill.), April 1972, p. 1.

18. *The Democratic Party of Oregon* (Corvallis, Ore.), October 1972, p. 7. By late 1973 the cost of being a contributing member had risen to $15 per person or $25 per family.

19. *New York Times,* July 2, 1974, p. 23.

20. *U.S. News and World Report,* August 20, 1973, pp. 31–34.

21. *Congressional Quarterly Weekly Report* 32, no. 27 (July 6, 1974): 1742.

22. *ELECTIONews* (Washington, D.C.), June 1973, p. 5.

23. The case, *Harper* v. *Vance* (Civil Action 72–197, n.d., Ala.), is reported in *ELECTIONews,* March 1973, p. 5.

24. Donald H. Stewart, *The Opposition Press of the Federalist Period* (Albany: State University of New York Press, 1969), p. 605.

25. John C. Miller, *Alexander Hamilton* (New York: Harper and Row, 1959), p. 343.

26. Thomas Fleming, *The Man from Monticello* (New York: William Morrow and Co., 1969), pp. 183–84.

27. Stewart, p. 610.

28. *Pennsylvania Democrat* 1, no. 1 (March 1969): 1.

29. A critical problem with any research utilizing content analysis is that of reliability. The degree of reliability can be checked in two different ways. Either the subject matter can be checked by a different researcher, in this case one who is willing to read through all the newspapers used, or it can be replicated by the same coder at a different time without reference to the earlier results. For this analysis the latter method was used. The content category designations applied on the first reading were affirmed by the second.

30. Angus Campbell, Philip E. Converse, Warren E. Miller, and Donald E. Stokes, *The American Voter* (New York: John Wiley and Sons, 1960); Bernard R. Berelson, Paul F. Lazarsfeld, and William N. McPhee, *Voting* (Chicago: University of Chicago Press, 1954); William H. Flanigan, *Political Behavior of the American Electorate* (Boston: Allyn and Bacon, 1968). Dan Nimmo argues that "election campaigns are essential features of democratic politics and that the advent of new technologies adapted to modern political campaigns is working changes in the character of democratic elections," in *The Political Persuaders* (Englewood Cliffs, N.J.: Prentice-Hall, 1970, p. 5.

31. John W. Kingdon, *Candidates for Office* (New York: Random House, 1966), pp. 22–41. Also, Robert J. Huckshorn and Robert C. Spencer, *The Politics of Defeat: Campaigning for Congress* (Amherst: University of Massachusetts Press, 1971), chap. 8.

32. An excellent selection of materials on new campaign methods is contained in Agranoff's *New Style in Election Campaigns.* A detailed analysis of some of the systems adopted can be found in Robert L. Chartrand, *Computers and Political Campaigning* (New York: Spartan Books, 1972). With the exception of a few recent studies such as these, political campaigning and its impact on election outcomes have been largely ignored by political scientists and others interested in the art (science) of politics.

33. Agranoff, p. 98.

Chapter 7

1. Interview with Jo Good, Convention Director, Republican National Committee, April 18, 1974, Washington, D.C. The minutes of the meeting no longer exist.
2. Resolution to the Republican National Committee, adopted by the Republican state chairmen, meeting ad hoc in Chicago, Illinois, March 13, 1949.
3. *Proceedings, 25th Republican National Committee* (1952), pp. 282–85.
4. *Washington Evening Star,* March 17, 1965, p. 4.
5. Memorandum to All Democratic State Chairmen and Vice Chairmen from Robert Vance, State Chairman of Alabama and President of the National Association of State Democratic Chairmen, dated April 2, 1974. Letter from Robert S. Strauss, Chairman, Democratic National Committee, to Robert S. Vance, dated April 4, 1974.
6. Minutes, May 12–14 meeting, Association of Democratic State Chairmen, Hollywood-by-the-Sea, Fla., p. 3. The author attended each of these meetings.
7. *Official Proceedings of the Democratic National Convention, 1972,* Democratic National Committee, Washington, D.C., pp. 406–23.
8. Ibid.
9. *Rules of the Democratic National Committee,* codified by General Counsel Joseph A. Califano, Jr., August 6, 1972, pp. 3, 5.
10. Association of State Democratic Chairmen, Proposed By-laws, 1974 (mimeographed).
11. Letter from Rule 29 Committee chairman, Congressman William A. Steiger, accompanying a detailed questionnaire sent to Republican activists across the nation in early 1974.
12. Rule 29 Committee, Republican National Committee, Preliminary Report of Subcommittee No. 3, adopted in St. Louis, Mo., June 16, 1974.
13. *Official Proceedings of the Democratic National Convention, 1972,* pp. 406–7.
14. "The Democratic Party of the United States of America, Proposed Charter," unofficial draft as adopted by the Charter Commission on March 16–17, 1974 (mimeographed).

Chapter 8

1. It should be noted that Democratic respondents, in making this ranking, were evaluating the pre-1972 Democratic National Committee composed of one man and one woman from each state and territory.
2. Cornelius P. Cotter and Bernard C. Hennessy, *Politics without Power: The National Party Committees* (New York: Atherton Press, 1964), pp. 57–59.
3. Frank J. Munger, "Two-Party Politics in the State of Indiana" (Ph.D. diss., Harvard University, December 1955), pp. 70–71.
4. *Lincoln Journal,* "A Tough Assignment" (editorial), April 26, 1971.
5. *Dayton News,* November 30, 1970, p. 1.
6. *New York Times,* May 22, 1971, p. 1.
7. Ibid., November 25, 1970, p. 16–C.
8. Charles L. Clapp, *The Congressman: His Work as He Sees It* (Washington: Brookings Institution, 1963), pp. 352–53; Robert J. Huckshorn and Robert C. Spencer, *The Politics of Defeat: Campaigning for Congress* (Amherst: University of Massachusetts Press, 1971); Jeff Fishel, *Party and Opposition* (New York: David McKay Co., 1973), chap. 5.
9. *Tri-City Herald* (Pasco, Wash., May 7, 1971, p. 1.

10. *1969 Congressional Almanac,* p. 1199.
11. *New York Times,* July 24, 1972, p. 15.
12. Samuel Lubell, *The Revolt of the Moderates* (New York: Harper and Brothers, 1956, pp. 31–32.
13. *New York Times,* March 7, 1971, p. 30.
14. *Miami Herald,* June 23, 1970, p. 4.
15. *Washington Post,* October 16, 1970, p. A8.
16. *Columbia* (S.C.) *Record,* June 3, 1971, p. 1A.
17. James McGregor Burns, *The Deadlock of Democracy: Four-Party Politics in America* (Englewood Cliffs, N.J.: Prentice-Hall, 1963), pp. 165–66.
18. *New York Times,* September 29, 1972, p. 46.
19. Ibid., p. 46.
20. *Aberdeen* (Wash.) *World,* August 14, 1971, p. 4.
21. John F. Bibby and Robert J. Huckshorn, "Out-Party Strategy: Republican National Committee Rebuilding Politics, 1964–66," in Bernard Cosman and Robert J. Huckshorn, ed., *Republican Politics: The 1964 Campaign and Its Aftermath for the Party* (New York: Frederick A. Praeger, 1968), pp. 213–14. Bliss was the only national chairman to be singled out as ideal by both Republican and Democratic state chairmen.
22. These lists were furnished through the cooperation of Jo Good, National Convention Coordinator, Republican National Committee, and Sheila Hixson, Assistant to the Secretary, Democratic National Committee. Since the 1960 Democratic delegate lists were unavailable from the DNC, they were procured through the cooperation of the John F. Kennedy Library, Waltham, Mass.
23. *Palm Beach Post,* February 24, 1971, p. E–4.
24. *Palm Beach Post-Times,* July 18, 1971, p. B–7.
25. *Wichita Beacon,* January 18, 1972, p. 1.
26. *New York Times,* January 2, 1972, p. 54.
27. *Toledo Blade,* August 13, 1971, p. 1.
28. *New York Times,* July 10, 1972, p. 23.
29. *Tampa Tribune,* May 17, 1971, p. 30.
30. *Miami Herald,* February 11, 1972, p. 7.
31. *Palm Beach Post,* June 15, 1971, editorial.
32. Lewis Chester, Godfrey Hodgson, and Bruce Page, *An American Melodrama: The Presidential Campaign of 1968* (New York: Viking Press, 1968), pp. 439–69. This account was confirmed in most details through interviews with ●)me of the participants.

Chapter 9

1. Alabama, Arkansas, Florida, Georgia, Kentucky, Louisiana, Mississippi, North Carolina, South Carolina, Tennessee, Texas, and Virginia. All of these figures are based upon records provided by the Republican National Committee.
2. David G. Pfeiffer notes that all of the measures of interparty competition can be criticized as being either too crude for complex analysis, too limited in the number of cases from which to generalize, technically inadequate to the task of analyzing the data, or simply misleading and unusable. "Inter-Party Competition and Systemic Stability," *American Political Science Review* 61 (June 1967: 457–67.
3. *New York Times,* June 1, 1970, p. 1.

4. *Atlanta Constitution*, April 16, 1971, p. 10.
5. Lewis Bowman and G. R. Boynton, "Activities and Role Definitions of Grassroots Party Officials," *Journal of Politics* 28 (February 1966): 121–43. The distinction between campaign-related and organizational-related is the authors'. Other research includes P. R. Gluck, "Incentives and the Maintenance of Political Styles in Different Locales," *Western Political Quarterly* 25, no. 4 (December 1972): 753–60; Dennis S. Ippolita, "Political Perspectives of Suburban Party Leaders," *Social Science Quarterly* 49, no. 4 (March 1969): 800–815; Lewis Bowman, Dennis S. Ippolita, and W. Donaldson, "Incentives for the Maintenance of Grassroots Political Activism," *Midwest Journal of Political Science* 13, no. 1 (1969): 126; Dennis S. Ippolita and Lewis Bowman, "Goals and Activities of Party Officials in a Suburban Community," *Western Political Quarterly* 22, no. 3 (September 1969): 572; and Marvin A. Harder and Thomas Ungs, "Notes toward a Functional Analysis of Local Party Organization" (paper presented to the Midwest Conference of Political Scientists, Chicago, Ill., May 2–4, 1963).
6. Theodore H. White, *The Making of the President, 1968* (New York: Atheneum, 1969), pp. 426–27.
7. "A Party for the People," a planning document describing a program of Democratic party building at the county level, using support services of the Florida Democratic party, published by the Florida Democratic Party, Tallahassee, Fla., Jon C. Moyle, chairman. The material in this case study is based on extensive interviews with Jon C. Moyle; John French, executive director, Democratic state party; and Graham (Rusty) Matthews, administrative assistant to the executive director of the Association of State Democratic Chairmen.
8. All of these changes in election law are documented in successive (January 1973 to present) issues of *ELECTIONews: A Newsletter for Elections Officials,* Institute of Election Administration, American University, Washington, D.C.
9. Interviews with William McLaughlin, chairman, Republican State Central Committee of Michigan, and Neil Staebler, former chairman of the Democratic State Central Committee of Michigan. These interviews took place during the Bipartisan Conference of State Party Chairmen held at Harvard University, January 10–12, 1974, and sponsored by the Institute of Politics, John F. Kennedy School of Government. Further details of the arrangement and copies of the joint committee's report were furnished by Mr. McLaughlin in a letter dated February 26, 1974.
10. *New York Times,* January 8, 1972, p. 15.

Chapter 10

1. Robert J. Huckshorn and Robert C. Spencer, *The Politics of Defeat: Campaigning for Congress* (Amherst: University of Massachusetts Press, 1971). See also Jeff Fishel, *Party and Opposition* (New York: David McKay Co., 1973).
2. Bureau of the Census, U.S. Department of Commerce, *Voting and Registration in the Election of November 1972,* Current Population Reports, series p–20, no. 253 (Washington, D.C.: Government Printing Office, 1973).
3. Ibid., p. 6.

4. *New York Times,* July 8, 1975, p. 19.
5. David S. Broder, *The Party's Over: The Failure of Politics in America* (New York: Harper and Row, Harper Colophon edition, 1972), p. xx.
6. See Robert Agranoff, "The Role of Political Parties in the New Campaigns," in *The New Style in Election Campaigns* (Boston: Holbrook Press, 1972), pp. 96–116.
7. Huckshorn and Spencer, p. 238.

Index

...man

...sachusetts Institute of Technology

Comprehensive and thorough, this original work provides a systematic and comparative description of the physiological mechanisms underlying the behavior of animals from simple invertebrates to human beings. Espousing a biologically oriented view of psychology, the author develops a detailed exposition that takes in fundamental biological processes, the structure and function of the brain and the nervous system, and a functional model of behavior. Thus *Organic Foundations of Animal Behavior* serves to bring psychology out of its isolation from the rest of the life sciences, and furnishes an integrated system of biological psychology.

The book offers a critical review of the leading models of behavior, ranging from simple mechanism and vitalism through classical and operant conditioning to a dynamic feedback system. It includes, moreover, a wealth of illustrations, ample references for further study, and a full bibliography.